The years between 1790 and 1830 saw over a hundred and fifty
million people brought under British imperial control, and one of
the most momentous outbursts of British literary and artistic production, announcing a new world of social and individual traumas
and possibilities. This book traces the emergence of new forms of
imperialism and capitalism as part of the culture of modernization
in the late eighteenth and early nineteenth century, and looks at the
ways in which they were identified with and contested in romanticism. Saree Makdisi argues that this process has to be understood
in global terms, beyond the British and European viewpoint, and
that developments in India, Africa, and the Arab world (up to and
including our own time) enable us to understand more fully the
texts and contexts of British romanticism. New and original readings of texts by Wordsworth, Blake, Byron, Shelley, and Scott
emerge in the course of this searching analysis of the origins of the
cultural process of globalization.

CAMBRIDGE STUDIES IN ROMANTICISM

This series aims to foster the best new work in one of the most challenging fields within English literary studies. From the early 1780s to the early 1830s a formidable array of talented men and women took to literary composition, not just in poetry, which some of them famously transformed, but in many modes of writing. The expansion of publishing created new opportunities for writers, and the political stakes of what they wrote were raised again by what Wordsworth called those "great national events" that were "almost daily taking place": the French Revolution, the Napoleonic and American wars, urbanization, industrialization, religous revival, an expanded empire abroad and the reform movement at home. This was an enormous ambition, even when it pretended otherwise. The relations between science, philosophy, religion and literature were reworked in texts such as *Frankenstein* and *Biographia Literaria*; gender relations in *A Vindication of the Rights of Women* and *Don Juan*; journalism by Cobbett and Hazlitt; poetic form, content and style by the Lake School and the Cockney School. Outside Shakespeare studies, probably no body of writing has produced such a wealth of response or done so much to shape the responses of those notions of "literature" and of literary history, especially national literary history, on which modern scholarship in English has been founded.

The categories produced by Romanticism have also been challenged by recent historicist arguments. The task of the series is to engage both with a challenging corpus of Romantic writings and with the changing field of criticism they have helped to shape. As with other literary series published by Cambridge, this one will represent the work of both younger and more established scholars, on either side of the Atlantic and elsewhere.

For a complete list of titles published see end of book

CAMBRIDGE STUDIES IN ROMANTICISM 27

ROMANTIC IMPERIALISM

William Blake, *Michael binding Satan*, c. 1805. The Fogg Art Museum,
Cambridge, Massachusetts.

ROMANTIC IMPERIALISM

Universal Empire and the Culture of Modernity

SAREE MAKDISI

University of Chicago

CAMBRIDGE
UNIVERSITY PRESS

PUBLISHED BY THE PRESS SYNDICATE OF THE UNIVERSITY OF CAMBRIDGE
The Pitt Building, Trumpington Street, Cambridge CB2 1RP, United Kingdom

CAMBRIDGE UNIVERSITY PRESS
The Edinburgh Building, Cambridge CB2 2RU, United Kingdom
40 West 20th Street, New York, NY 10011–4211, USA
10 Stamford Road, Oakleigh, Melbourne 3166, Australia

© Saree Makdisi 1998

First published 1998

Printed in Great Britain at the University Press, Cambridge

Typeset in Baskerville 11 / 12½ pt [VN]

A catalogue record for this book is available from the British Library

Library of Congress cataloguing in publication data

Makdisi, Saree.
Romantic imperialism: universal empire and the culture of modernity / Saree Makdisi.
p.   cm.—(Cambridge Studies in Romanticism; 27)
Includes bibliographical references and index.
ISBN 0 521 58438 8 (hardback) – ISBN 0 521 58604–6 (paperback)
1. English literature — 19th century – History and criticism.   2. Imperialism in literature.
3. Great Britain – Colonies – History – 19th century.   4. Great Britain – Colonies – History
18th entury.   5. Literature and society – Great Britain.   6. Modernism (Literature) –
Great Britain.   7. Romanticism – Great Britain.   8. Colonies in literature.   I. Title.   II. Series.
PR468.I49M35 1998
820.9'007–dc21   97-20599 CIP

ISBN 0 521 58438 8 hardback
ISBN 0 521 586046 paperback

For my parents

Contents

Contents

Preface and acknowledgments

Where today are the Pequot? Where are the Narragansett, the
Mohican, the Pokanoket, and many other powerful tribes of
our people? They have vanished before the avarice and the
oppression of the White Man, as snow before a summer sun.
> Tecumseh, in Dee Brown, *Bury my Heart at Wounded Knee*

All Love is lost Terror succeeds & Hatred instead of Love
And stern demands of Right & Duty instead of Liberty.
> William Blake, *The Four Zoas*

In the years between 1790 and 1830, over one hundred and fifty million
people were brought under British imperial control. During those same
years, one of the most momentous outbursts of British literary and
artistic production took place in romanticism, announcing the arrival of
a whole new age, a new world of social and individual traumas and
possibilities. The starting point of the research project that resulted in
this book was an intuitive assumption that these events were somehow
related to each other; what I realized by the end was that an adequate
understanding of either event requires an understanding of both – at
one and the same time – if it is not to be seriously flawed.

Romanticism cannot be understood properly without reference to
modern imperialism and modern capitalism: perhaps this seems clear
enough. Modern imperialism and modern capitalism cannot be properly understood without reference to romanticism: this may not seem
quite so clear at all. In this book, I will argue both these points at once.
To understand British romanticism as more than merely a random
collection of literary texts – as a specific cultural formation – requires us
to locate it as an event within the historical map of modern imperialism
and modern capitalism. Moreover, to understand modern imperialism
and modern capitalism as more than merely socio-economic practices –
as cultural processes – requires us to locate those practices on the

literary-historical map precisely where we have customarily found romanticism. What I want to propose is that the dynamics between these
discourses and practices constituted an overall *cultural revolution* called
modernization, which is most adequately grasped at the multiple horizons where the economic and the literary, the poetic and the imperial,
the social and the philosophical converge.

While the primary reference point of this book will be British romanticism, I believe that modern capitalism and modern imperialism – and
modernization itself – must ultimately be understood as global processes, and not (for all their Eurocentrism) as specifically British or
European phenomena. Much, therefore, of what I will propose here as
an account of British romanticism should help us to understand the
transformative processes of imperialism and capitalism in places and
times far removed from late eighteenth- and early nineteenth-century
Britain. However, one of the central and underlying hypotheses of this
book is that those other developments – in India, Africa, the Arab world,
and elsewhere, up to and including our own time – should *also* enable us
to understand more fully what was happening in romantic Britain. They
should do so not only in that they would force us to broaden our
perspective away from a dangerously myopic concern with Britain, or
even with Europe, and their literatures, but precisely because modernization has always been, and continues to be, a worldly and a global
process, in which the so-called margins and peripheries have always
played a central role.

When all is said and done, romanticism will turn out to be not only
worldly, but also global, and to have been so all along – marking the
beginning of a process that has only in recent years come to be recognized as "globalization." Our contemporary experience of globalization
will certainly make more sense to us if we understand it as part of a
broader historical process rather than as a freak occurrence or as
something marking the inevitable victory of one way of living in the
world. It will also make much more sense if we can understand it as a
cultural process and not merely as a socio-economic development. What
I want to contribute in this book is an attempt to map out the origins of
that process in the cultural politics of imperial modernization during the
romantic period.

This book is burdened (but also supported) by many intellectual and
political debts to scholars and writers working in a number of languages
and traditions, as well as to teachers and friends from different parts of
the world. However, this project occupies a particular position with

regard to the work of two of these scholars, writers, and teachers – Edward Said and Fredric Jameson – and I want to reflect briefly on this position because its significance has to do with the nature of the questions I have been investigating, and not just with the ways in which I have approached those questions. Jameson's work (which is primarily concerned with capitalism) and Said's work (which is primarily concerned with imperialism) helped to define the political and intellectual forcefield into which I have ventured, and which I hope to have transformed in some way.

Such a transformation, if it has taken place at all, would have to do with more than merely framing Jameson's concerns with Said's project, or framing Said's concerns with Jameson's project. Nor would it have to do simply with combining both projects (which are primarily concerned with the late nineteenth and twentieth centuries), bringing them simultaneously to bear on what might seem to be a fuzzy gray area, or even blind spot, for both, in the late eighteenth and early nineteenth centuries. Rather, if I can hope that any transformation takes place in these pages, it would not just concern the primary object of inquiry (romanticism), nor even various approaches to it (in romanticist scholarship), but also the political and intellectual forcefield defined by Said and Jameson. My claim here is not just the banal point that scholars of romanticism have much to learn from those who study imperialism and capitalism, and vice versa. It is that there is something unique about the object of inquiry – the event – called romanticism, which should force us to reconsider the ways in which imperialism and capitalism are historically related to each other, as well the ways in which they have been related to each other in and through scholarship.

This book would not have been possible without the support, encouragement, and guidance of many other friends, colleagues, and teachers. Parts of this project were first developed in my PhD dissertation in the Literature Program at Duke University, and the first rounds of writing what would eventually turn into this book were suggested during and after that process. I will always be deeply indebted to my dissertation committee (Professors Kenneth Surin, Barbara Herrnstein Smith, Marjorie Levinson, and especially Robert Gleckner and Fredric Jameson), who helped me to set this project on its feet and to move through its earliest stages; and to my friends at Duke who helped sustain me and my work, many of whom read and re-read chapters and helped me develop my ideas: John Waters, Amanda Berry, Michael Speaks, Jonathan

Beller, Neferti Tadiar, Loris Mirella, Carolyn Lesjak, Caren Irr, Richard Dienst, Cesare Casarino, and Rebecca Karl.

This book took its final shape during my first years on the faculty at the University of Chicago, and I am deeply indebted to my friends and colleagues in the departments of English and Comparative Literature, particularly Lauren Berlant, Lisa Ruddick, Miriam Hansen, Ken Warren, W. J. T. Mitchell, Françoise Meltzer, Jay Schleusener, Katie Trumpener, Homi Bhabha, Michael Murrin, and Richard Strier. My colleagues Larry Rothfield, Janel Mueller, Elizabeth Helsinger, James Chandler, and Bill Brown not only read and re-read the whole book, but very patiently sorted through drafts of re-drafts of revisions of new drafts, etc., right up to the blessed end; their encouragements, criticisms, and suggestions were always invaluable to me. I am also grateful to Wolfram Schmidgen, Fiona Robertson, Nigel Leask, Ronald Judy, and Michael Hardt for their comments on particular chapters.

Marilyn Butler and James Chandler, the editors of this series, and Josie Dixon, of Cambridge University Press, offered the support that was necessary to sustain this book over the past couple of years. Their stern criticism was as important as their friendly advice (this is true of the mysterious press readers as well, to whom I am also grateful). However, to James Chandler I am especially thankful: he had faith in this project even from its unsteady beginnings, and not only these chapters, but I myself, have benefited greatly from his patience, learning, and wisdom.

To my friends Richard Dienst, Vincenzo Binetti, and Cesare Casarino I owe more than mere words: their support, their understanding, their seemingly infinite tolerance for my endless phone calls and e-mails, as well as their advice, their criticism, and their suggestions, all helped to nourish the intellectual and political project that this book proposes. But it was that shared experience of deep friendship and community that sustained its author; that sustenance I owe to them, and especially to Cesare, the sharer of telephone consultations in the middle of the day and the middle of the night.

It was and is a different – but equally valuable – kind of community in Chicago that sustained and sustains me here: to Heidi, Vincenzo, Bill, Bernadine, Elizabeth, and above all Rashid and especially Mona I owe an altogether different kind of thanks, for the nourishment of mind, body, and soul.

Last but about as far from least as one can go, I wish to thank my uncle Edward, not only because he first marked out the terrain onto which I have adventured, but because all my adventures have taken place under his watchful eye; my brothers Ussama and Karim, whose undying fraternity goes beyond any possible acknowledgment; Christina, who made the final months of this process not only bearable but valuable beyond measure; and, above all others, my parents, Samir and Jean Makdisi, to whom this book is dedicated, because they had faith and they never lost it, because they never let the war take that faith away from them, because beneath their faith there was always unfailing love.

An earlier version of chapter 4 was published as "Colonial Space and the Colonization of Time in Scott's *Waverley*," in *Studies in Romanticism* (summer 1995); and a slightly different version of chapter 6 was published as "Versions of the East: Byron, Shelley, and the Orient," in Alan Richardson and Sonia Hofkosh, eds., *Romanticism, Race, and Imperial Culture* (Bloomington: Indiana University Press, 1996).

CHAPTER I

Introduction: Universal Empire

> The greater part of the world has, properly speaking, no history,
> because the despotism of custom is complete.
> This is the case over the whole East.
>
> John Stuart Mill, *On Liberty*

I

The Hindu legends still present a maze of unnatural fictions, in which a series of real events can by no artifice be traced. The internal evidence which these legends display, afforded indeed, from the beginning, the strongest reason to anticipate this result. The offspring of a wild and ungoverned imagination, they mark the state of a rude and credulous people, whom the marvellous delights; who cannot estimate the use of a record of past events; and whose imagination the real occurrences of life are too familiar to engage. To the monstrous period of years which the legends of the Hindus involve, they ascribe events the most extravagant and unnatural: events not even connected in chronological series; a number of independent and incredible fictions. This people, indeed, are perfectly destitute of historical records.[1]

James Mill's assessment of India's past in the opening pages of his *History of British India* (1817–36) establishes the context for the arrival of his own historicizing project and of the larger civilizing mission undertaken by the East India Company. To set to rights the chaos of India's past, and to connect factual events into a diachronic story within a rational, logical, and, above all, historical narrative: this is evidently a significant component of Mill's effort to bring history not only to British India, but to all of India (both geographically and temporally). If, he argues, the "wildness and inconsistency of the Hindu statements evidently place them beyond the sober limits of truth and history," then what is required to bring governance to the hitherto ungovernable is precisely the imposition of those very limits. Part of Mill's mission, then, is to distinguish fiction from truth, myth from reality, and unreal time from historical time, in order to supply this people without history with properly historical records, records whose epistemological foundation will rest upon a lattice-work of such dualisms. Another part of his mission, though, is to help Britain and the East India Company absorb contemporary India into the narrative of a universal history – the world history of modernization – thereby retroactively historicizing India's unruly past even as its present is brought under increasing control and order.

Thus assimilated, India and its past would exhibit the sort of order that defines the universal conception of history informing Mill's voluminous text – a conception of history that had only begun to emerge in his own lifetime, and that was still in the process of development when he sat down to write what was, he claims, the first true history of India. Mill's conception of history claims for itself the privilege not only of uniqueness, but of universal truth; for it allows itself to be thought and written only in its own sequential terms and only according to the dictates of its own units of abstract modern time. According to Mill's conception, not only was there no prior history; there was above all no prior *world history* in terms of which all other histories could be brought together and rendered meaningful.

Mill's project entails, then, the retroactive rewriting of all previous histories in terms of the narrative of the universal world history to which he claims to belong, as well as the projection of that narrative into his own time and on into the future (a future of its own making). The historical narrative into which Mill is eager to incorporate India is not so much that of British imperialism or that of capitalism, but rather the narrative of their joint transfiguration by, and convergence in, the process of modernization.[2] Paradoxically, however, the sudden appearance of such a narrative of modernization as world history anticipates the actual (and much more gradual) convergence of capitalist and imperialist practices within the process of modernization. In fact, during Mill's lifetime in the late eighteenth and early nineteenth centuries – a span commonly though not unproblematically referred to in British literary history as the romantic period – these practices had only just begun to merge and become inseparable, and at the same time *potentially* or *tendentially* global in reach.[3]

The global reach of these processes thus appears in virtual form long before it is materially consolidated in political and economic terms; in other words, the dreams of this unified world-system appear in narrative form long before it has consolidated itself and become a cultural dominant.[4] At the same time, we can also chart the simultaneous emergence of a number of *anti-histories* of this process, that is, a body of efforts to anticipate, understand, and contest these historical developments before they have actually taken place. Such anti-histories – including the one that I would argue is the earliest and most comprehensive, namely William Blake's prophecies of Universal Empire – share in common with Mill's sense of history the fact that they are anticipating a development that has not yet taken place. With this key difference: that, rather than seeking to facilitate that development, they seek to contest it.

Ironically, both the histories and anti-histories of the world-system in the early nineteenth century have the status of prophecy. However, the primary orientation of these prophecies is not the future, but rather the present in which they were produced. They are prophecies not in the usual sense, but rather in the more restricted Blakean sense. They are concerned above all with their own time, with historical and material developments that already exist, as well as possible (and impossible) future developments – including the emergence of a single dominant world-system.[5] In his form of prophecy, Mill envisages a future and a past both understood in the seamless terms of his own present: a homogenization not only of time but of all history, in which virtually everything could be made to conform and make sense (and that which could not, for example, much of the Indian history of India, would be dismissed as fantasy or impossibility or outright falsehood).

For someone like Blake, on the other hand, historical experience and time itself are never homogeneous, and one of the purposes of his kind of anti-history is to seek out the heterogeneous and the unexpected in the present, as well as to imagine the unimaginable projected into any number of possible (or impossible) futures. "Historians," he writes, "being weakly organiz'd themselves, cannot see either miracle or prodigy; all is to them a dull round of probabilities & possibilities; but the history of all times & places, is nothing else but improbabilities and impossibilities; what we should say, was impossible if we did not see it always before our eyes."[6] In Blake's oppositional form of prophecy, the present is simultaneously projected as a future and renarrated as a past, but in such a way that present, future, and past intermingle in an unresolved radical heterogeneity of time – the improbable and the impossible – which is precisely what sustains Blake's kind of prophetic vision.

Thus, the very beginning of the gradual convergence of imperialist and capitalist practices in the process of modernization provided at once the necessary and the sufficient conditions for the emergence of a new universal narrative of world history (projected both forward and backward according to the new understanding of homogeneous unilinear time that emerged with it) that is articulated in Mill's discussion of India.[7] But it also provided the conditions for the simultaneous emergence of a discontinuous constellation of attempts to resist, or to chart out alternatives to, its history – in romanticism. For it is a striking fact, which requires much further elaboration, that Mill launched his project as early as 1806, when the first generation of romantic poets was still in its prime (Wordsworth had just finished the first full draft of *The Prelude*, Southey had just published *Madoc*, Coleridge had not even contemplated the *Biographia*, Blake had just started work on *Jerusalem*) and the second generation still in its youth (Byron and Shelley had not yet published anything, and Keats, "the tadpole of the Lakes," as Byron would later call him, was not even a teenager).

The emergence of the new understanding of history was closely related to certain changes taking place at the time in British paradigms of empire and attitudes towards non-Europeans, which Mill's approach to India emblematizes. Moreover, this history, projected "forward," would henceforth be governed not only by the principles of rationality and diachrony championed by Mill, but by the ebbs and flows of the capitalist mode of production and system of exchange (both of which were undergoing momentous transformations during this period), and hence by the pulses and rhythms of what Fernand Braudel refers to as "world-time."[8] This history would, furthermore, be narrated and controlled by the most modern, most advanced, most "civilized" people in the most developed societies – those farthest ahead in what Johannes Fabian has elaborated as the stream of evolutionary Time – who, like Mill, who would claim history as their own possession in their confrontations with cultures and peoples without history.[9]

According to this view, such peoples were making the uneasy transition from a wretched state of static pre-modernity to the beginning of their apprenticeship in modernization, in which their social, cultural, and economic practices would be transformed and recoded in the transition not only from past to history, but also from custom to law;[10] from communal, clan, tribal, or despotic forms of property to private property;[11] from heterogeneous and irregular ("casual") forms of labor to the rigors of a wage economy;[12] from customary forms of payment and compensation to the strictly monetary remuneration of the hourly wage;[13] from archaic, seasonal, irregular temporal practices to the regular practice of modern clock-time;[14] from barter economies or trades-in-kind to a more strictly measurable monetary system of exchange ruled by principles of computational equivalence;[15] from highly skilled artisanal craftsmanship to an increasingly automated system of production relying only on that flow of quantified and regulated energy-in-time that would eventually come to be called "unskilled labor" but that was first broken down in William Petty's "political arithmetick" into a stream of labor-power that could (ideally) be smoothly distributed across a highly diversified production process, subject only to the forms of resistance that this appropriation of energy might encounter from the possessors of labor-power themselves;[16] from all kinds of political systems to the modern liberal democracy that would eventually (if we follow this logic to its ultimate conclusion) preside over the "end of history" about which we have heard so much in recent years.[17]

II

Britain's transition into a social formation dominated by the culture of modernization was not defined by one cataclysmic event. Rather, this process took several decades to emerge – the decades identified as the romantic period in Britain – and it took several more decades for this new cultural dominant to consolidate itself. Economically, the romantic period in Britain marked a shift from the primacy of trade and commerce towards the primacy of industrial production, and hence towards a properly modern mode of capitalism (albeit one that at the time often took only an embryonic form).[18] Politically, the period marked a rupture in paradigms and policies of imperial power, and a shift in the locus of intense imperial activity from the western to the eastern hemispheres, as well as a dramatic intensification in the exercise of state power in response to the revolutionary situation within Britain itself.[19]

However, neither the political nor the economic transition, taken on its own, can account for the overall *cultural* change that was taking place in this period. This overall change in attitudes, perspectives, relations, knowledges, and practices can be located in both material and discursive forms (including economic and political practices, to be sure, but not restricted to them). In fact, this change reminds us of the extent to which discourse – and culture – are material processes. Modernization must be understood from the very beginning as an overall cultural development, and not merely as a socio-economic process from which we might only in a secondary sense abstract either a free-floating or a superstructural notion of cultural "modernity."[20]

However, the varied engagements with the culture of modernization in Britain that we may identify as romanticism primarily took the form of an engagement not with modernization *tout court* or as such, but rather with its social, economic, and political manifestations. These in turn were grasped through their effects rather than systemically: in urbanization, for example; or the advent of machine-production; or imperial conquest; or the transformation of the countryside; or the degradation of the natural environment; or the anomie and alienation of the monad – the individual human subject cut adrift in the modern world – which inspired Keats's most passionate and disturbing Odes.

Let us consider a classic example of the often astonishing sweep of romanticism's critique of modernization. In his haunting poem, *Michael*, Wordsworth ties together (to name only a few issues brought up in the poem) the Enclosure movement; the newly significant question of debt; the development of a modern urban culture of dissolution and apparent degeneration; the erosion and destruction of traditional forms of family and social production; the possibilities opened up by emigration to the colonies; the transformation of agriculture; the emergence of a new way of thinking and experiencing time; and a new modern sense of national, as opposed to local, culture, custom, identity. It is not evident that Wordsworth thought of all these questions (which we today would readily identify as aspects of modernization) as related to one another in an overall or systematic way. But – sensitive and perceptive as he was – he was quite obviously, even if only intuitively, aware of the fact that they had something to do with each other, and were collectively to be identified as part of a "multitude of causes, unknown to former times," for which Wordsworth lacked only the systemic label that we are now in a position to supply with the benefit of hindsight.

I will argue this point at greater length in the chapters that follow, but for now I want to suggest that romanticism can be partly understood as a diverse and heterogeneous series of engagements with modernization (which here may be seen as a cause that is immanent in its effects and really has no other existence). It can also be understood as a mediating discourse, through which the multitudinous political and economic facets of modernization, many of which are mapped out in *Michael*, are related to each other to a greater or lesser extent, situated as parts of an overall cultural transformation. Romanticism was not merely a response to this transformation. It was a key constitutive element: as much as any other material development, this series of engagements contributed to the constitution of modernization as a cultural field that would eventually rise to dominance (notwithstanding this romantic critique that would accompany it to the bitter end).

We are now in a position to see that the staggering heterogeneity of romanticism was directly related to the heterogeneity of the processes of modernization. Thus, my task in this book will not be to produce a single key to "unlock" or explain the huge variety of literary and cultural output during the romantic period; such a task would in any case be not only impossible, but unnecessary. For what I am saying here is that romanticism must not be understood as a movement, a school, a style, or even a tendency. I therefore heed Marilyn Butler's warning – not the first, but one of the most persuasively argued – that we could never generate such a cohesive identity for romanticism, into which we might then insert various authors or texts.[21] "'Romanticism,' Butler writes, "is inchoate because it is not a single intellectual movement but a complex of responses to certain conditions which Western society has experienced and continues to experience since the middle of the eighteenth century."[22] I would like to follow Butler's lead and further specify the nature of this "complex of responses," and also to suggest that romanticism was never simply a "response," but a key constitutive element in those transformations.

For we, at least, *can* identify those "certain conditions" as various aspects of one overall cultural development, as signifying the emergence of the culture of modernization. If "romanticism" can make any sense as a term, then, it would have to be not as a label identifying a particular style, theme, or form, let alone a school or movement. It would have to serve as the historical designation of a number of enormously varied engagements with the multitudinous discourses of modernization, which took place in a staggering number of forms, styles, genres, and which can be linked together only in terms of that engagement and in such a way that their individual and unique traits and characteristics are respected and not meaninglessly collapsed into each other.

Such romantic engagements were dialectically bound up with modernization, and contributed to its development as a cultural dominant. In different forms, they can always be found wherever the culture of modernization is found, whether dominant, residual or emergent, in the West and in the non-West alike.[23] Strictly speaking, this is not exactly a periodizing hypothesis, except insofar as the romantic period in Britain itself marks the moment of the emergence of the culture of modernization, and hence of that whole new way of thinking of periods and periodizing and historical change that was articulated for the first time in British romanticism.[24]

While by the end of the nineteenth century the sense of world history and world-time invoked by Mill would gradually rise to cultural dominance, diffuse through and finally pervade virtually all aspects of cultural production and activity (commerce, trade, politics, exploration, as well as literary production), literature, and even more specifically poetry, emerged during the romantic period as a privileged site for the exploration of alternatives to modernization, or the celebration of anti-modern exoticism that we can see at work, for example, in the first two cantos of *Childe Harold*. Later nineteenth-century modes of understanding anti-modern otherness would rely on a different kind of epistemology, a different kind of language, and above all different ways of conceiving temporality. And while literature would retain its importance as a field for the representation and articulation of cultural identity and difference (usually but not always in the service of empire), the emphasis would increasingly shift to the novel and particularly the realist novel of development.

Of course, the nineteenth-century realist novel is the genre on which much of the most important critical work on the relationship between literature, on the one hand, and capitalism and imperialism on the other, has been focused – in, for example, the work of Patrick Brantlinger, Sara Suleri, Jonathan Arac, Christopher Miller, Fredric Jameson, and Edward Said. One of the aims of the present study, then, is to shift the emphasis to an earlier period and a different genre, in order to expand more fully our understanding of these relationships by examining them in an unstable and even explosively transitional moment.

"Most historians of empire," writes Edward Said in *Culture and Imperialism*, "speak of the 'age of empire' as formally beginning around 1878, with the 'scramble for Africa.' A closer look at the cultural actuality reveals a much earlier, more deeply and stubbornly held view about overseas European hegemony; we can locate a coherent, fully mobilized system of ideas near the end of the eighteenth century, and there follows the set of integral developments such as the first great systematic conquests under Napoleon, the rise of nationalism and the European nation-state, the advent of large-scale industrialization, and the consolidation of power in the bourgeoisie."[25] Said argues that a pattern of cultural attitudes (or structures of feeling) corresponding to this set of developments emerged alongside and accompanied the elaboration of

imperial rule well into the nineteenth and twentieth centuries. This
pattern was characterized by virtually unanimous support of imperialism and a striking lack of dissent. One of the main forms of expression of
this pattern of cultural validation of imperialism was the novel. The
history of the novel may be understood in Said's terms as the history of
imperialism itself, since "imperialism and the novel fortified each other
to such a degree that it is impossible . . . to read one without in some way
dealing with the other."[26]

According to Said, only in the climax of the "age of empire" in the
1890s, when the realist novel enters its modernist crisis, can we begin to
find a sustained pattern of anti-imperial criticism within the realm of
(metropolitan) literary production, a pattern that formed a significant
component of the modernist breakdown of the realist novel.[27] Thus,
although Said admits that the cultural ideology of imperialism never
enjoys absolute dominance within, for example, British literature, he
wants to argue that the main forms of cultural opposition to imperialism
within the metropolis itself came only towards the end, when its vision
had largely been consolidated in the decades around the First World
War; so that, until then, he says that we can speak of a *largely* if not
completely "unopposed and undeterred will to overseas dominion."[28]

However, I would argue that the romantic period in Britain marks
the earliest sustained (though largely doomed) attempt to articulate a
form of opposition to the culture of modernization – including but not
limited to imperialism – from its very beginnings. Once it is reinter-
preted as I propose, the often remarked aesthetic covergences and
parallels between romanticism and modernism can be explained in a
new way. Because of the complex and shifting engagement between
literary production and the practice and experience of modernization,
modernist literary experiments, arising partly out of the perceived
exhaustion of the realist novel and especially the *Bildungsroman* by the
early twentieth century, would return to and elaborate an earlier romantic obsession with fractured, disjointed, and disruptive temporalities, both in poetry and in prose.[29]

For romanticism appears alongside the emergence of modernization
and helps to define it culturally from its very beginnings; a process that
helps us to explain what makes the romantic period in Britain identifiable as a period. Modernism, on the other hand – though precisely like
romanticism a discourse of unevenness, and also in many of its varieties
a critique of the modern – emerges as the culture of modernization
reaches its fullest development and is on the point of absorbing or

wiping out the last vestiges of the pre-modern and the archaic in a
rapidly modernizing society.[30] The distinction between modernism and
romanticism, however, lies not so much in their engagements with
modernization (for they sometimes look uncannily similar in this regard,
though one would probably be going too far to say, "first time as
tragedy, second time as farce"), but rather in that romanticism emerges
with the beginnings of modernization and persists alongside it to the
end; whereas modernism emerges specifically at the climax of that
process and helps to constitute that climax in overall cultural terms. In
other words, the difference between romanticism and modernism lies in
the extent to which we can understand them as periodizing hypotheses;
or, rather, in the extent *to which they enable us to understand the process of
periodizing to begin with* (for otherwise modernism might just look like
nothing but a return to romanticism, albeit in a new and more intense
form because of its specific cultural and historical situatedness). Whereas
modernism, in many of its varieties, celebrates the pre- or anti-modern
and the archaic as they are on the verge of final eradication or commodification, romanticism celebrates the pre- or anti-modern at the
moment at which that eradication is just beginning. Such celebrations
are not unique to Britain, and can be located wherever the process of
modernization comes into contact with "traditional" cultures and ways
of life; it is in this sense that romanticism marks the inception of a new
culture of modernization, of which the late twentieth-century phenomenon of globalization appears as the climax.

III

Indeed, a certain fascination or even obsession with the pre- or anti-
modern (Nature, the colonial realm, the Orient) occupied the very
center of the British romantic critique of modernization. This involved
above all a new mode of understanding such anti-modern otherness
precisely because of its historical and political relationship to the emerging culture of modernization.

Even for someone writing (and voyaging) as late as Lord Byron, it was
still possible to think of the Orient, for example, not only as geographically distinct from Europe, but also as temporally and historically
unique. As I shall show in chapter 5, for the Byron of the first two cantos
of *Childe Harold* (1812), the Orient was defined and structured by its own
sense of temporality and its own sense of history, rather than merely
constituting, as it clearly already did for Mill, a subordinate element in a

larger world-history – a history narrated by Europeans, a history at the end of which stands Europe.[31] Only a little later in the nineteenth century, such a synchronic construction of the non-European (synchronic in that it is seen to exist *alongside* modern Europe, in parallel rather than in series: *anti*-modern rather than strictly *pre*-modern) would become much more difficult to articulate. For, later in the nineteenth century, the non-European, like Nature and the organic community, would be reconfigured in British narratives as that which modern Britain "might have been" or perhaps "used to be," but is no longer, having evolved into something that is not merely different, but superior. ("And this also," Marlow reminds his English audience in the opening pages of *Heart of Darkness*, "has been one of the dark places of the earth."[32])

Whereas cultural otherness had formerly been regarded in terms of sheer and even immutable difference, seen from a properly modern perspective in the late nineteenth century, anti-modern otherness would often become inferiority plain and simple, demanding that benign and nurturing program of development and improvement called empire. By the end of the nineteenth century, in a world dominated by the great European empires (which in the romantic period were just beginning their worldwide expansion) whatever alternatives to modernization a sphere of cultural otherness might offer would be strictly temporary. For the impending doom of its inevitable penetration, colonization, and incorporation into the world of modernity (i.e., its modernization) would be a haunting or perhaps reassuring imminent development.

However, this was not yet the case at the *beginning* of the dual process of colonial conquest and capitalist modernization in the early nineteenth century. In fact, the anti-modern Orient of *Childe Harold* is by no means a unique case during the romantic period. For, as I shall argue, what emerges before these later developments and specifically during this period – especially though not exclusively in literary production – is a new *mode* of understanding and representing such sites of cultural otherness, such other worlds, as the Orient. This new mode, defined in a constellation of literary works, must be understood in relation to the sense of modernization and world history clearly exemplified by Mill's book on India, which was emerging at the same time. This *specific* historical-political conjuncture is what axiomatically distinguishes this new mode from, on the one hand, any earlier British literary tradition of imagining alternative worlds (e.g., the work of James Thompson, Andrew Marvell, and perhaps above all John Milton), and, on the other hand, any previous representation or imagination of cultural otherness. After all, the notion that the Orient is Europe's other is nothing new in and of itself; what *is* new – as I shall argue – is the specifically romantic mode of understanding both the Orient's otherness *and* its relationship to other sites of alterity, other zones of anti-modernity.

This romantic mode of understanding otherness is perhaps most clearly illustrated by Wordsworth. It entails grasping romantic anti-modernity on its own terms, as the "discovery" of some of the "other worlds" being surrounded and cut off by the space-time of moderniz-ation. Here Wordsworth's notion of the spot of time (as articulated in Book xii of *The Prelude*) can be grasped as a central concept with which to understand – and an optic through which to view – the proliferation of seeming alternatives to the world of modernization that either appear or, in effect the same thing, take on entirely new significance in the romantic period and especially in romantic literature. I will explore three examples at length in later chapters: Byron's Orient, Scott's Highlands, Wordsworth's Nature. Seen as spots of time, such apparent alternatives can be understood (and meaningfully related to each other) as self-enclosed and self-referential enclaves of the anti-modern, each defined by its own unique structures of feeling and its own distinct temporality. Each is conceived as a hitherto untransformed enclave that, when discovered and colonized by the outside world, is seen to experience a fall which erases, or, rather, rewrites it by weaving it tightly into the history of the outside world.

For the spot of time is always threatened by assimilation, by incorpor-ation into that reorganization of spatial and temporal practices and institutions called modernization (new forms of production and ex-change, new ways of thinking time, new histories of the world, new territorialities, new ways of regulating flows of energy and desire). The spot of time is even threatened by the very acts of discovery and identification that reveal it to the outside world. The hidden bower in Wordsworth's poem *Nutting* is an ideal example: its existence is dis-covered, registered, and appealed to, precisely at the moment when it faces sudden and irreversible annihilation as a result of that discovery, as simultaneously celebrated and mourned in that poem. Thus the attract-iveness of the spot of time is inseparable from the inevitable destruction that is seen to follow from its discovery.

Indeed, the spot of time can serve as an ideal conceptual optic through which to view the romantic mode of representing anti-modern otherness. This is so because of the considerable extent to which the production or articulation of difference during the romantic period implied a spatio-temporal project (and not merely a thematic or aesthetic one) as the social production, practice, and experience of space and time began to change in the late eighteenth and early nineteenth centuries. This re-composition was taking place largely in terms of an antagonism between a growing abstract world-space and world-time of modernization and differential spaces and times not yet drawn into that world, and hence defined as different precisely because of their resilience – perhaps even their purity as opposed to the impurity and often disturbing ugliness of the scene of imperial struggle.[33] Viewed as spots of time, the romantic productions of space that I will examine in the chapters that follow – Nature, the Scottish Highlands, and the Orient – articulate a (futile) desire to preserve such sites of difference and otherness, to register opposition to a homogenizing system by upholding certain sites as differential loci of space and time.

Standing out as a distortion in the spatio-temporal fabric of the age of modernization, the spot of time is for Wordsworth a shelter from "the multitude of causes, unknown to former times" that were then "acting with a combined force to blunt the discriminating powers of the mind, and, unfitting it for all voluntary exertion, to reduce it to a state of almost savage torpor."[34] He humbly presents his own poetical career to the modern world as a "feeble endeavour" to resist the changes taking place by appealing to Nature as an alternative world offering the chance of even a temporary shelter or detour: *temporary* precisely because of its uneasy dislocation within the time of the modern, and yet perhaps also permanent because of the hope that it might somehow resist an otherwise inevitable modernization. In fact the spot of time stands out precisely by virtue of its supposedly permanent temporariness. As long as it is not fully assimilated into the flow of world-time and modern history, it has the potential to outlast them, to resist them by surviving as a disruption of the spatio-temporal logic of modernization, one of any number of gaps or aporias in the history of modes of production that seem to have opened up during the transition from any number of previous modes of production and never fully closed.

The persistence of such fissures within the space-time of modernization would in effect forestall the completion of the very process that is supposed to have extinguished and annihilated them. They would serve as reminders that the moment of passage from which they emerged was not fully accomplished or closed and that, paradoxically, modernity really represents not so much an accomplished state but rather a long and uneasy process of transition (modernization) towards itself: a transition *requiring by definition* the persistence of anti-modern others against which modernity can be constituted.[35] This process of transition can be seen as a struggle between what appears as a totalitarian system and a range of sometimes localized (and sometimes not) sites and zones and cultures of resistance, *beginning* though not *ending* in the romantic period. Hence this period marks not so much an open-and-closed moment but rather the onset, the beginning, of a whole range of cultural and political articulations of modernization; it defines not so much a discrete unity, but rather, as James Chandler has argued (via Hazlitt and Heidegger), the inauguration of a new way of thinking about history and the very question of "ages" and indeed of periodization itself.[36]

Thus, if the anti-modern spaces of difference first identified in romanticism are threatened with annihilation, such spaces can always (and indeed would later) be invented anew throughout the modern age. For, as, Bram Stoker puts it in *Dracula*, "the old ages have powers of their own which mere 'modernity' cannot kill." These "powers" will continue to either haunt and torment modern English imaginations (in configurations as disparate as *Dracula*, *The Moonstone*, *Jane Eyre*, and *The Sign of Four*), or to attract them, whether for their perverse horror (*Heart of Darkness*), their frank and "manly" homosociality and "savage" nobility (*The Seven Pillars of Wisdom*, *King Solomon's Mines*), their liberatory difference, their non-identity and non-conformity with the rational and the modern (*Kim*, *Eothen*), or their resilient natural innocence (*Cranford*, *Adam Bede*).

The hidden natural bowers that appear and re-appear throughout Wordsworth's poetry can be seen as spots of time – and in fact also as synecdoches for Nature in a larger sense – by virtue of their opposition to the "artificial" and unnatural world of humanity as the latter has been corrupted in the age of modernization. Wordsworth's poetical project thus logically involves not only the opposition between the natural and the modern which marks its point of departure, but above all an attempt to reconnect the human to the natural, to reconnect "man" to his own "nature." Wordsworth's kind of art is thus natural precisely in its opposition to the "artificial," the made, the fabricated, the constructed – to the very same extent as Nature (in his view) endures as all that which *has not* been made in the face of that which *has* been made. In a similar sense, poetry ("the *image* of man and nature") is outside of modern time and history just as Nature is outside of modern time and history; it is "as immortal as the heart of man." Hence

Wordsworth's project involves resurrecting "certain inherent and indestructible qualities of the human mind" and reconnecting them to "the
great and permanent objects that act upon it, which are equally inherent
and indestructible," thereby in effect short-circuiting the products of
human-made artifice (which Blake for his part would call "the productions of time").

In its perfect form, this kind of poetry would no longer be art, for the
"naturalness" of such a poem resides in precisely its lack of artifice.
Hence the most natural poetry is that which taps directly into "the real
language of men," or as closely as possible into the immediate and even
unspoken language of Nature (simple, clear, permanent, so direct as to
preclude the very possibility of mediation and hence construction and
art as well as the vicissitudes of time). Wordsworth opposes this natural
poetry – which his own work, by his own admission, only approximates
– to the built-up language and art of the modern age, the "arbitrary and
capricious habits of expression" by which modern poets "furnish food
for fickle tastes and fickle appetites of their own creation." Thus the
"gaudiness and inane phraseology" of the "frantic novels, sickly and
stupid German tragedies, and deluges of idle and extravagant stories in
verse" denounced in the 1800 Preface to *Lyrical Ballads* are the gauges of
the artificiality of modern literary productions according to Wordsworth; gaudy because they have not only been made, but overmade: so
that every production is always an overproduction, and all art is by (this)
definition unnatural.

The spot of time is the perfect mode for Wordsworth's nature poetry
because of its very opposition not only to modern time and history but
to the artificial and the constructed – to art – and hence it is no surprise
that it emerges in *The Prelude* in opposition to (in fact a refuge from) the
artificiality of London, the great center of empire. Just as the project of
empire can be understood in terms of the conquest of nature and the
imposition of rational contractual institutions on dangerous natural
tendencies, the naturalization of the artificial would represent the ultimate victory of both the spot of time and the natural poet over the
process of modernization. This almost happens in the sonnet "Composed Upon Westminster Bridge," in which London is naturalized by
being imaged as a spot of time, frozen in the quietness of dawn.

The spot of time represents a potential and persistent disruption in
the logic of continuous progressive time. Hence it offers an ideal optic
through which to read romantic articulations of anti-modern otherness. But here we come to the two all-important shortcomings of this

concept, and to two conceptual traps that any account of romanticism can fall into. First, there is no way of accounting for the history of the coming-into-being of the spot of time in any terms other than those of the very modernity against which it is defined. Second, the spot of time can only make sense as a heterotopic refuge or alternative to something larger and more powerful than itself, to which it owes its (oppositional) existence, and in terms of whose history alone it can be understood, determined, and defined. Thus its potential resistance is extremely circumscribed, even if it is not entirely eliminated.[37]

For romantic discoveries of cultural otherness were dialectically articulated in opposition to the emerging world of modernization even as the latter was being defined; they enabled that definition to begin with. This is what separates romantic "other worlds" from earlier constructions of cultural otherness, which do not take on such a dialectical form and which depend instead on less dynamic and less fluid oppositions between ontologically independent outsides and insides, distinctly *unmarried* heavens and hells. Even if Wordsworth was attempting to appropriate and rewrite Milton, he was sensitive to the unbridgeable gap between Milton's era and his own, just as he was painfully aware of the extent to which Milton and the other "Great men that have been among us" are so palpably absent from the "perpetual emptiness" and "unceasing change" that define his own age of revolution from the 1790s onwards: an absence that perhaps accounts for Wordsworth's repeated failure to recapture the spirit of Milton in such projects as *The Excursion* and *The Prelude*. Seen in this light, Blake's claim not only to have appropriated Milton but to be his reincarnation takes on new significance.

Even if it appears as a distortion in the otherwise seemingly homogeneous and abstract spatial fabric of modernization, a disruption, however temporary, in the apparently otherwise smooth and irrepressible flow of world-time, the spot of time can only be defined against the very modernization whose emergence it concurrently helps to constitute. The romantic discovery of such spots of time must be understood dialectically, not as a reaction but rather as a mutual process of constitution through which both the inside and the outside of the spot of time emerge in relationship to each other, neither priveleged with ontological priority. In being constituted dialectically against modernization, the resistance offered by a spot of time may in the long run turn out to be no resistance at all, but rather in effect an affirmation of modernization. Hence it is important to be able to see romantic spots of time as historical constructions, rather than as ahistorical essences that exist outside of time, even if there is no way to account for their historicity in their own terms, and even if they are constructions that seek (as they often do) to deny their own historicity in the first place.[38]

In any case, although the spot of time is inadequate to the task of understanding its own history, its own location outside of history still needs to be understood historically, even if it itself provides no way to do that other than by reference to the history of modernization. This necessity highlights the significance of Blake's anti-history of modernization in his prophetic books, which mark a critical divergence from the constellation represented by the other romantic writers.

I have already touched on certain aspects of this anti-history, but here I want to dwell on it a little longer and suggest certain ways in which Blake's prophetic books offer an alternative approach to the history of the period. For in effect Blake's anti-history of modernization allows us to read the history of the period against the grain *from within* and without forcing us to adopt a strictly retrospective analysis based on the accumulation of historical data and experience. The political aesthetics of the prohetic books offer us not only a variety of cultural options which were not taken up because they did not conform to the needs of the historical forces that Blake sought to oppose (whereas the aesthetic projects of the others did conform in certain fundamental ways), but also a way to prize open the cultural history of the romantic period. There is no room here to elaborate fully Blake's rearticulation of modernization, so I will present only a brief and condensed version of a far more complicated argument in order to illustrate my point about anti-history, and I will return to these questions in chapter 7.[39]

"Natural Objects always did & do now Weaken deaden & obliterate Imagination in Me," writes Blake in his annotations to Wordsworth's *Poems*.[40] But in his criticism of Wordsworth he is using the term "natural" in a very specific way, to denote a world of "vegetable" objectivity that has been (mis)understood in strictly material terms by being falsely cut off and isolated from a larger world of energy flows, to which, in Blake's view, it belongs; and from which not only Wordsworth but Blake's greatest enemies – Bacon, Newton, and Locke – have abstracted and divorced it. In Blake's view all productions, including those that we might refer to as "natural," take place in a turbulent continuum of energy flows that are given both material and immaterial form and expression by imagination and labor, as well as that combination of imagination and labor called art: "to create a little flower is the labour of ages."[41]

In this view, Wordsworth follows in the path of the great materialist prophets of sensory input and rational measurement by apprehending a world of material objectivity and individuated subjectivity in isolation from each other and from the world of energy, by opposing the human to the natural and the human mind to "the great and permanent objects that act upon it." Hence as far as Blake is concerned, Wordsworth's nature poetry represents only a variation on the all-too-familiar theme of materialist ideology, to which it offers no real alternative and from which it offers no escape, just as it offers neither escape from nor alternative to the socio-economic and political-cultural system defined by that ideology. Blake refers to this ideology, which he explicitly identifies with Newton and Locke, as the "Laws & Religions" that bound humanity "more / And more to Earth: closing and restraining: / Till a Philosophy of Five Senses was complete."[42]

In the world of time and space created according to the dictates of this ideology, its laws are enforced by its institutions of power,

> Churches: Hospitals: Castles: Palaces
> Like nets & gins & traps to catch the joys of Eternity
> And all the rest a desart;
> Till like a dream Eternity was obliterated & erased.[43]

This world is forever threatened by annihilation should the rational forces, institutions, and laws that constitute it be overwhelmed by the seething boundless energies that they seek to contain: a world governed by principles of mechanics, apprehended through the five senses, a world of unitary subjectivity in which desire is always subject to restriction and energy to the limits of rational control.

This is the world celebrated not only in Newton's and Locke's treatises but also in Wordsworth's nature poetry, one that is experienced by the individual subjects that correspond to it, one whose existence is bound up with those forms of subjectivity. Hence it is a world whose history begins and ends with the history of the form of subjectivity in terms of which it is constituted. All other possible forms of imagination and subjectivity are excluded from that history as "impossibilities," because they are indeed impossible in its terms, just as any other form of social or communal organization is inconceivable and unimaginable in its terms. Hence what we are talking about here is the coming-into-being of a whole new world, whose potential destruction would signify nothing short of an apocalypse, an "end of history," because from the standpoint of this world all time and history begins and ends with it.[44]

In this anti-history, Blake calls this world "experience" – in other words the phenomenological world – and he identifies the key figure in the struggle to contain energy by rationality as Urizen, "the great Work master"[45] and self-proclaimed ruler of the Universal Empire ("am I not God said Urizen. Who is Equal to me"[46]). Urizen is, however, more of a force than an actual being; a force that may be personified in various guises, that may take on a gendered and subjective existence, but whose real being consists in the turbulent and multivalent (hence seemingly omnipresent) condensations of the energy abstracted from and in turn confronting those subjected to his will. What is of the greatest interest is thus not so much Urizen "himself," but rather the system that he creates and enforces, that is, the Universal Empire whose coming-into-being and whose operative processes Blake transcodes and traces out in his prophetic books of the 1790s.[47] It is important historically to distinguish the Universal Empire from the narrower and more territorial British empire, to which the former is related, but which it transcends. Blake forces us to understand the history of imperialism in relation to the history of capitalism (and vice versa); this, after all, is the great lesson of David Erdman's *Blake: Prophet Against Empire*. For, indeed, if the Lambeth books of the 1790s retell the history of the creation, the creation whose story they tell is that of modern capitalism, and of the long process of modernization that began in Blake's time ("First Trades & Commerce, ships and armed vessels he builded laborious / To swim the deep; & on the land, children are sold to trades / Of dire necessity, still labouring day & night till all / Their life extinct they took the spectre form in dark despair; / And slaves in myriads, in ship loads, burden the hoarse sounding deep, / Rattling with clanking chains; the Universal Empire groans . . ."[48]). Blake writes against the advent of this process, up to and even beyond the point at which his writing breaks down into the uncontrollable and incoherent rage characteristic of much of his work.

For Blake, this Universal Empire could *only* be understood on a global scale as it redefines all space and time according to its own terms (see chapter 7). For there is something about this system that drives it to overcome all limits and to transform the entire world into itself, as it slowly encompasses the thirty-two Nations and four Continents of Blake's prophetic books. This does not exclude the possibility or the persistence of other forms of energy and desire that are not part of this world-system. In fact the project of the Universal Empire is to seek out and to contain and rewrite those other forms in terms of itself. But Blake's understanding of the Universal Empire hinges on its status as a world-system, and moreover on his sense that it could only be contested by being first understood and then resisted on a world scale, a process he seeks to begin not only in his retelling of the coming-into-being of this new world in the *Books* of *Urizen, Ahania,* and *Los,* but also in his retelling of the global struggle against the Universal Empire in the appropriately named prophecies *America, Europe, Africa,* and *Asia* (the last two constituting the two parts of the *Song of Los*).

What is important for my present purpose is not so much Blake's important status as the unique insights that the prophetic books provide for understanding the cultural and political developments of the time, that he and the other romantics sought to resist in such different ways. If for Wordsworth and the others the most adequate form of resistance involved seeking out the world-system's heterotopic others, for Blake the relationship of the system to its others is of secondary importance compared to his first priority, which is understanding the potential globality of both the Universal Empire and of any possible mode of resistance to it. For Wordsworth in particular the key mode of resistance to modern artifice has to do with resurrecting (really inventing) a non-artistic form of natural poetry. For Blake the key mode of resistance lies in taking art beyond its limit by seeking out and activating, giving expression to, those forms of energy and desire that cannot be comprehended by either the system or the forms of subjectivity which populate it, and in particular by unleashing forms of energy and desire that might overwhelm both the system and its historically unique form of subjectivity, bringing both not only to a kind of crisis, but to their explosive and apocalyptic demise. If for Wordsworth and the others the confrontation that they are witnessing is between a modern system and its anti-modern others, for Blake the process of modernization has created its others and relies upon them for their very existence, just as Urizen relies for "his" existence on "his" confrontations with the sources of the energy that he has appropriated. What is important then is not returning to those sources of energy in their present form but rather releasing them, detonating them, exploding them; and understanding how the Universal Empire represents a disruption in the world of energy, a disruption that has created the very opposition between selves and others, nature and history, inside and outside, modern and anti-modern, the people in charge of history and destiny and those condemned to follow blindly in the tracks of a system to which they can never catch up, whose standards they will never reach.

The significance of the Blakean divergence from the other romantic engagements with the culture of modernization is *not* that it embodies some kind of messianic truth, to which we must adhere. Rather, as anti-histories of modernization, the prophetic books allow us to rehistoricize the period as it takes shape and not just retrospectively. By virtue of his singular oppositional re-articulation of modernization – if for nothing else – Blake was unique among the now-canonical writers of the romantic period. His singular mode of rethinking modernization *in concepts other than its own* – concepts produced by Blake himself, whose staggering heterogeneity and fundamental untranslatability into modern rational terms anyone who has read Blake will have had to confront – will prove important to my own analysis of this period, partly, though not entirely, because it reveals the limits of the kind of anti-modern discourse in which other writers of the period participated. Blake therefore allows us a way to read the spot of time historically, against the grain, *in relation to* the world history of modernization, capitalism, and imperialism; but in an oppositional way.

The chapters that follow will examine what I regard as the key sites and locations of anti-modern otherness in romanticism. Chapter 2 presents an exploration of the heart of the emerging world-system, the city of London, as seen from the vantage point of Wordsworth; it will situate Wordsworth's spots of time in opposition to the worldliness of the imperial metropolis, and it will trace how London comes to be both the material and symbolic center of the world-system, against which all its others would be defined. Chapter 3 continues the discussion of Wordsworth and the spot of time not as a natural phenomenon but as a *human* potential for resisting the process of modernization. Chapter 4, centered on a reading of Walter Scott's first novel *Waverley*, continues the task of exploring how some of the key others were elaborated in romanticsm, showing how the large-scale redefinition of British attitudes towards the Scottish Highlands unfolding at the time could not have taken place without the colonization and appropriation of both the material and the symbolic terrain of the Highlands themselves during and after the Clearances that followed the collapse of the doomed Jacobite Rebellion of 1745 at the battle of Culloden (which was, significantly, the last battle to be fought on British soil). Indeed, this colonization reached its climax only in the romantic period; so that there is a cruel irony in the fact that Scott sat down to write *Waverley* at the very moment that the Highlands were being finally cleansed of their previous associations – as the exotic but dangerous Highlanders themselves were burned out of their ancestral homes and scattered to the corners of the earth, neither the first nor unfortunately the last people to be dispersed by modernizing colonial movements based on what Edward Said once called "an ideology of difference." To ignore the brutal fact of this non-coincidence is, I would argue, to participate in the very same colonial processes whose power lies precisely in their ability to cover up, to hide away, to claim and reinvent and re-name spaces that are not theirs, and violently to ignore what was once there.

As I suggest in chapters 5 and 6, the dramatic shift in British imaginary maps of the Orient cannot be divorced from related shifts in both colonial and mercantile/industrial networks and paradigms *and* the role that various Eastern colonial and semi-colonial spaces and societies played in the British empire in the early nineteenth century. This was in fact a role dramatically altered following Britain's victory over France in 1814–15, after which much of the world, including the Orient, lay directly open to British rule in ways that had never been possible before. Finally, in chapter 7, I will return to the imperial metropolis itself to explore Blake's imaginary and symbolic map of London as the site in which resistance to that system could be mapped. Chapter 8, a set of conclusions, will elaborate some of the theoretical and historical insights I have tried to develop in this book, in particular the relationship of romanticism and modernization to capitalism and imperialism.

CHAPTER 2

Home imperial: Wordsworth's London and the spot of time

"... London, that great cesspool into which all the
loungers and idlers of Empire are irresistibly drawn ..."
                                Arthur Conan Doyle, *A Study in Scarlet*

Universal history was born in cities and reached maturity at the
moment of the decisive victory of city over country.
                                Guy Debord, *Society of the Spectacle*

There are in our existence spots of time,
That with distinct pre-eminence retain
A renovating virtue, whence, depressed
By false opinion and contentious thought,
Or aught of heavier or more deadly weight,
In trivial occupations, and the round
Of ordinary intercourse, our minds
Are nourished and invisibly repaired;
A virtue, by which pleasure is enhanced,
That penetrates, enables us to mount,
When high, more high, and lifts us up when fallen.
                                William Wordsworth, *The Prelude*

I

Prior to his arrival in London in Book VII of *The Prelude*, Wordsworth
tries to conjure up mental images of the city's various neighborhoods
and districts (Vauxhall, Ranelagh, Westminster), as well as of specific
buildings and tourist sights (St. Paul's, the Guildhall, the Tower).[1] Once
he is swept into London's streets, however, Wordsworth's preconceived
spatial distinctions break down and dissolve, to be replaced by the flux of
a ceaselessly-changing environment, one that never stops its self-trans-
formations long enough to become a safely knowable, chartable, under-
standable place.[2] London here is, potentially, an ideal representational
site for understanding the intensely local as global: to produce some-

23

thing even approaching the status of a "cognitive map" of the city in the late eighteenth and early nineteenth centuries would somehow involve mapping the imperial world-system, of which London itself is simultaneously the beginning and the end.3 However, the spatial and observational categories that would enable Wordsworth to comprehend and emplot Nature do not work in London.4 Wordsworth's London resists being channeled into the same "knowable" spatio-temporal framework as Nature. How, indeed, could this metropolis, "where a man may wander for hours together without reaching the beginning of the end,"5 be understood? How could its greatly diversified and constantly expanding and developing space be mapped, given the extent to which the city is locked into, and partly constituted by, a complex network of relationships, exchanges, and flows taking place on what was already a virtually global scale?

Urban space here constantly slips into the conceptual and imaginary space of empire, a spatial story always in the process of being written. The urban space of *The Prelude* also represents the greatest "symptom" of the crisis of modernization – the "multitude of causes" Wordsworth refers to in the *Preface to Lyrical Ballads*. London is a spatial chronicle not only of its own and of Britain's history, but of the complex history of imperial modernization.6 This history is rendered by Wordsworth as a series of spectacles, a stream that cannot be epistemologically contained, or controlled by, or filtered through, the viewing subject. This stream of spectacles constantly threatens to overwhelm the narrative perspective of the subject, who sees without being able to frame – without being able to take that crucial step towards the sublime. It would take a different kind of perspective (one presumably transcending the limited spatio-temporal experience and coordinates of the individual subject and not necessarily commensurate with the latter) to "frame" and make sense of the stream, to see the logic and systematicity of this new abstract space, and to comprehend what appears to the individual as sheer spectacular excess. At street level and from the perspective of the viewing subject, however, that logic is nowhere to be seen; all that is left in the shower of spectacles is a terror of excess.

Ultimately, the abortive project undertaken and abandoned by Wordsworth in Book VII of *The Prelude* approaches a kind of cognitive mapping of the vast colonial network and the experience of modernization as they unfold in London. It is an attempt to see and to comprehend the imperial world-system from the vantage point of the individual subject, at street level, from within

> . . . That vast metropolis,
> The fountain of my country's destiny
> And of the destiny of earth itself;
> The great emporium, chronicle at once
> And burial-place of passions, and their home
> Imperial, and chief living residence.[7]

By the end of Book VII, Wordsworth abandons London, not because his attempt to see London fails (on the contrary, it succeeds *all too well*, and he is able to grasp far more than he concedes), but rather because he fails to frame that seeing in terms of his status as a perceiving subject who can *comprehend* what he sees.[8]

In abandoning the city, Wordsworth renounces whatever redemptive possibilities it – or at least some comprehensive knowledge of it – may have offered. As more than one critic has pointed out, his renunciation of active oppositional politics and his renunciation of London are one and the same thing. Wordsworth turns instead to the sheltering embrace, the "renovating virtue," of spots of time whose sublime purity he must himself create by removing from them any taint of the world that London represents – the world of modernization and crisis – and by restoring the viewing subject's privileged narrative and representational position, which had been destabilized and overwhelmed by the terrors of London. Wordsworth's flight from London to the spot of time (and to Nature) is thus a flight from the terror to the sublimity of individual consciousness. I will return to this process in the next chapter; but I want to begin with London, because Wordsworth's imagination of Nature cannot be understood independently of his revulsion and flight from the imperial metropolis and the crisis of modernization that the city represents.

II

London may be seen as a synecdoche for the rest of Britain during the romantic period: the space in which the histories, economies, and political destinies of England, Ireland, Wales, and Scotland were bound together into an imperial Gordian knot. The city that Cobbett referred to as a "monstrously overgrown and profligate metropolis" was by the late eighteenth century far and away the largest in Europe (probably twice the size of its nearest rival, Paris). London was swollen by the massive influx of displaced and uprooted people robbed of their old communal rights and flowing in continual streams from the rapidly

enclosed English countryside, as well as from the colonial territories of
Wales, Scotland, and Ireland. It was also *the* political and economic
center of the commercial network spanning the entire kingdom.[9] As
early as the middle of the eighteenth century, London contained perhaps 15 percent of the English population, and the city's "insatiable
demand for food and fuel transformed agriculture all over the south and
east, drew regular supplies by land and river from even the remoter
parts of Wales and the north, and stimulated the coalmines of New-
castle."[10] Without the hundreds of thousands of people walking, riding,
and stumbling into the city from the country, London's population
might have actually decreased during the romantic period (largely due
to the appalling conditions of life there[11]). The crowds wandering and
milling through the streets and fairs of Wordsworth's London were,
increasingly, not native Londoners, but refugee clanspeople from Scotland, Dalesmen from the Lakes, peasants from Ireland, farmers from
the West Riding, crofters from Wales. Once in the city – where smoke
and grime and filth saturated the air, where even the most elementary
public services (sanitation, street-cleaning, water-supply,[12] open spaces)
were unable to cope with the influx, where people used to the open
country were either living crammed into dismal slums and tenements,
or consumed by the hundreds in the great epidemics of typhoid, chol-
era, or tuberculosis that swept the ravaged urban landscape – these
people not only maintained personal and family connections with the
areas they left behind, but through their very work in the city helped
increasingly to tie those areas into London itself.[13]

They did so both symbolically, inasmuch as the spatial relations and
exchanges of London replicated those of the whole United Kingdom,
and also materially. For not only was the entire economy of England
ruled from London, but, as Fernand Braudel points out, "the capital city
created and directed England from start to finish. London's outsize
dimensions meant that other cities hardly began to exist as regional
capitals: all of them, except possibly Bristol, were at her service."[14]
London was also the center of the growing national communications
network, over which these commercial and material flows traveled.[15]
The thousands of carts, coaches, mails, and diligences which continually
poured into and out of London thus tied the national economy together,
making it not only into a national, but also an imperial economy: a
large-scale version of the incessant traffic and spatial practices that
define Wordsworth's London.

In *The Prelude*, however, London lacks the overall coherence that might result from taking an imaginary leap over the city in order to look down and see all the various spatial strands woven together into one coherent process. Rather than being defined by the "endless stream of men, and moving things," Wordsworth's London, seen at street-level, is torn apart by the pressures of this incessant movement, as though the centripetal forces draining Britain and the world *into* London "from hour to hour" are finally overcome by centrifugal powers – such as "the rash speed / Of coaches travelling far" – drawing people and "the string of dazzling wares" to the *outside*. Or rather: as if the titanic clash and endless interaction of these centripetal and centrifugal attractions and pressures left London in an endlessly-revolving "dance," a vacuum, caught and whirled around without direction, without end, and without mercy, existing simultaneously as its own place *and* as everywhere else, and hence – finally – as nowhere at all, as sheer abstraction.[16]

London and its "swarm of inhabitants," who live in their "undistin-guishable world . . . / amid the same perpetual flow / Of trivial objects," not only lose their humanity: the city itself becomes the inverse of the mythically ideal organic community to which Wordsworth wants to "return," or in other words, the space into which would be drained the hopes and products of that community – for example, the prodigal son, Luke, in Wordsworth's poem *Michael* – as well as the very notion of pre-modern community. London constitutes the heart of the network against which romantic spaces and communities of otherness would be defined. It is a growing spatial metaphor for the experience of a modern-ization that not only attracts and drains away the strength and vitality of the pre- or anti-modern spaces which are defined against it, but destroys and consumes the heterogeneous traces and relics of those spaces through absorbing and incorporating them into itself, funneling their alternative and autonomous synchronic histories into its own unilinear, universalist, and diachronic history. In this sense, London seems almost to be an anti-space, on the one hand defined by modernization and its constituent practices, experiences, and themes (alienation, loneliness, urbanization, rationalization), all of which are evoked in *The Prelude*; and on the other hand defined against the residual places in which pre- or anti-modern existence persists (the bowers of *An Evening Walk*, the hidden valley of *Michael*, the Highlands of *Waverley*, the Orient of *Childe Harold*).

It is, above all, in the people, the practitioners and producers of the space of London, that Wordsworth sees the difference between country and city. For the antagonism between country and city is located here internally, within the city, and not only in the external relations of town and country (as explored so memorably in Raymond Williams's book[17]). As opposed to the rhythm and semi-permanence of agricultural labor in the country, many workers in the swollen city could find only "casual" jobs, so that "distinct from the labourers (stablemen, street-sweepers, waterside-workers, unskilled builders, and so on) were those for whom 'casualty' had become a way of life: street-sellers, beggars and cadgers, paupers, casual and professional criminals, the Army."[18] Wordsworth's wanderings through the numberless streets of London are journeys through the seething crowds, composed largely of such "casualties." The city and the crowd in *The Prelude* are symbiotically related, produced by each other. The crowd largely constitutes London through the spatial stories woven by its individual participants (from which, again, Wordsworth distances himself as merely an uncontaminated "outside" observer), while the city is filled up by the multitude of individuals composing the crowd.

The presence of the often invisible crowd is almost always felt in this book of *The Prelude*. Roy Porter points out the "extraordinary degree of social mixing and the ease of intercourse possible in a monster town presided over not by king, court or Church, but by commerce, cultural entrepreneurship and public taste."[19] In Book VII, even after sometimes fading temporarily from visibility, the crowd suddenly snaps back into focus as Wordsworth picks out individual faces from among the throng whose movements are channeling his own flow through the avenues and boulevards of London. His movements within the crowd seem involuntary, as though he were drifting with the hidden pressures of an oceanic current; sometimes he can pull away momentarily, "into some sequestered nook, / Still as a sheltered place when winds blow loud," but then he will be engulfed and pulled "back into the throng, until we reach, / Following the tide that slackens by degrees, / Some half-frequented scene, where wider streets / Bring straggling breezes of suburban air."[20] Even though, as Mary Jacobus suggests, Wordsworth can pick out and "read" such constituents of the city, he does so only fleetingly.[21] Although he tries to, he does not read and consume the crowd, *as a crowd*, in the way De Quincey does during his own opium-inspired meanderings through a later and more pacified London.[22] Wordsworth's crowd is for the most part either registered (partly through being heard) as an *invisible* presence ("the roar continues," "the tide that slackens by degrees," "the thickening hubbub"), or separated into component faces and images that, at best, he feels only momentarily able to understand. There is little interaction between the observer and the crowd: when he reads these singled-out images, he does so only by making them disembodied (and hence safely consumable). Put back into the context of the crowd, from which they have been separated, they either fade into the background, or else the background itself looms large and threatens to overwhelm this solitary observer.

There is, indeed, a very fine line in *The Prelude* between the London crowd and its politically charged Janus-face, the mob of the revolutionary panic of 1790s London. Part of Wordsworth's ongoing effort to distinguish individual faces in the crowd is an attempt to keep the crowd from working any sudden (and not quite understood) transformation into a mob – as though to reassure himself, as he wanders through the streets of London, that what he sees is still "only" a crowd, and not yet the mob of his nightmares. Yet the "blank confusion" of Wordsworth's London crowd always threatens to slip out of his control and disintegrate even further – into the mob, for the understanding and cognitive control of which all of his classifications will be meaningless and useless. Byrd and other critics have argued that, because of the flow of images, Wordsworth's London is "unendangering and trivial."[23] But his insistence on the "same perpetual flow / Of trivial objects" is *not* a source of reassurance or comfort for Wordsworth: on the contrary, it is *precisely* because this flow has "no law, no meaning, and no end" that it constantly threatens to transform itself into the (supposedly) equally "disorderly" and "meaningless" working-class mob, from which he wants to distance himself.

From the days of the Wilkes riots through the 1780s and 1790s and into the nineteenth century, the London mob was a recurring (and for many a terrifying) presence.[24] According to some observers, London seemed to be "a great Bedlam under the dominion of a beggarly, idle and intoxicated mob without keepers, and actuated solely by the word *Wilkes*."[25] In his effort to keep distinguishing individuals in the crowd, Wordsworth tries to assimilate, one by one, the people of the mob – beggars, idlers, discharged soldiers back from the wars with France – into his map of London.[26] Indeed, much of his effort at redemption centers on this attempt, invariably a failure, to individualize people in the crowd (this is very different from Blake's "I mark in every face I meet / Marks of weakness, marks of woe . . .").[27] He can never entirely overcome his fear of the "press and danger of the crowd," however, nor his dread (finally realized in the Bartholemew Fair scene) that he might witness half the city "break out / Full of one passion, vengeance, rage, or fear... / To executions, to a street on fire, / Mobs, riots, or rejoicings."[28] Indeed, like the city that it defines and embraces, the crowd becomes an "enemy"[29] from which he seeks escape, *not* because it is an apolitical and even banal "distraction" that "shows the imaginative impulse asserting itself blindly," as Geoffrey Hartman sees it, but rather because it inspires the sort of terror in Wordsworth that also gripped Burke – who, as James Chandler has argued, ultimately figures as the "presiding genius of Wordsworth's personal and national epic,"[30] and had his own deep abhorrence of the "swinish multitude."[31]

The fear of "suffocation" (and anxiety about assimilation) that Wordsworth expresses in these passages is a fear of being overwhelmed by the people of London, and by London itself, since his account of the city is also an account of his relations to both London's people and to the people of the kingdom who constitute the crowd. As Victor Kiernan has argued, Wordsworth's relation to the people is an expression of his political commitments, which were changing dramatically during the years of revolutionary panic and reaction.[32] In the *Prelude* the crowd is nearly always an incipient mob, the embodiment of the dark side of Wordsworth's London, expressing the constant threat of disorder, and his fear of the city as an unknowable, unfathomable, and almost unmappable abyss – a vacuum torn apart by its own terrors and contradictions, ever turning the observer's mind "round / As with the might of waters."[33] And it is this fear and terror that would finally force Wordsworth to abandon his project to "humanize" or perhaps even to "naturalize" London.

The Prelude's London crowd is, however, not only a crowd of Londoners or even of Britons. What makes the city and its constitutive crowd so infinitely complex, unfathomable, threatening, and even terrifying to Wordsworth, is that all of Britain's imperial relations and connections are *also* present and expressed in the teeming streets of London, and above all in the crowd scenes of Book VII. Thus, in addition to the casualty-workers, pimps, prostitutes, thieves, beggars, merchants, mendicants, travelers, idlers, vagrants, loungers, and soldiers milling through the streets – who themselves already tie all of the United Kingdom into this, its heart – there is an overpowering overseas presence as well, in the form of peoples and commodities brought from the farthest reaches of the colonial system to London, the "vast metropolis" of empire.

> Briefly, we find, if tired of random sights
> And haply to that search our thoughts should turn,
> Among the crowd, conspicuous less or more,
> As we proceed, all specimens of man
> Through all the colours which the sun bestows,
> And every character of form and face:
> The Swede, the Russian; from the genial south,
> The Frenchman and the Spaniard; from remote
> America, the Hunter-Indian; Moors,
> Malays, Lascars, the Tartar and Chinese,
> And Negro Ladies in white muslin gowns.
>   At leisure let us view, from day to day,
> As they present themselves, the spectacles
> Within doors, troops of wild beasts, birds and beasts
> Of every nature, from all climes convened;
> And, next to these, those mimic sights that ape
> The absolute presence of reality,
> Expressing, as in mirror, sea and land,
> And what earth is, and what she hath to show.[34]

This staggering spectacle inverts the space of London, turning it inside out (like the mirror in Plato's cave) so that the entire external world and the imperial connections that have made it into a world all but ruled by Britain, can be seen all at once. The space of London itself turns into the space of empire; so that one need go no further than London to see much of the entire planet. In this initial impression of the colonial crowd, Wordsworth is still "at leisure," still able to separate the throng into its constituent faces, goods, and character-types, just as he can at times with the British crowd. One can stand at ease, "well pleased," in London, and the entire world will present itself as a more or less safely consumable spectacle.

But this is also a destabilizing and ultimately a terrifying vision. Once the colonial flood-gates have been opened, once Britain has gone out into the world, there is nothing at all to prevent the world flooding and crashing back into Britain. The trace and spatial trajectory of each British step outwards, each voyage of exploration, each colonial adventure, skirmish, acquisition, or annexation, is in Book VII precisely mirrored and reflected by a symbolic but haunting return to London of repressed imperial presences (in fact, the late twentieth-century British and French racist anxieties about immigration are only the latest version of such imperial hauntings or hangovers). Thus, the British East Indies and China trades, which opens the channels for a flow of tea, opium, spices, and calicoes, also do so for a less welcome and almost uncontrollable torrent of Lascars, Indians, and Malays (who bring with them images and sensations of the Orient, as seen, for instance, in De Quincey's opium-induced Asiatic nightmares). The slave plantations of the West Indies and America send their tribute in the form of cotton, tobacco, coffee, and sugar; but also, and in the same uncontrollable way, in ex-slaves, "Negro Ladies," and, perhaps most disturbing and threatening of all to a guilt-ridden William Wordsworth, in a stream of maimed, diseased, and crippled British soldiers and sailors – like the shadowy apparition in Book IV of *The Prelude* – now discharged and returned to haunt the island that sent them out to conquer and to die (Britain lost some eighty thousand soldiers in the 1790s war against ex-slave revolutionaries in the West Indies, where the discharged soldier of Book IV served[35]). In this nightmarish vision, the "fountain of my country's destiny" slips out of any sense of proportion and control and quickly becomes submerged by an overpowering and irrepressible flood, which, combined with the turmoil inside Britain, obliterates and overwhelms any possible sense of security, stability, or isolation.

If the space of London becomes increasingly difficult to chart, then, it is because the vastness and complexity of the world ruled from London, and the worlds constantly flowing into and swirling about *in* the imaginary space and world of London, totally overwhelm the individual subject trying to comprehend it. Wordsworth's representational crisis stems from his awareness that one cannot simply delimit and determine the space called London insofar as that space is not simply a preexisting given but a constantly re-produced system of relations and practices; and, additionally, from the growing difficulty in representing London cognitively as the center of empire, because although it was indeed the economic, political, symbolic, and cultural center, it was difficult or impossible to represent as such. For what is overwhelming here is not simply the sheer excess of material goods and other signifiers, which David Simpson has pointed out,[36] but rather the unrepresentable vastness of the world-system that has produced those objects and people and brought them to London, or in other words the very unrepresentability of the abstract space of commodity and capital flows.

The British empire of Wordsworth's day constituted a spatial system of trajectories, currents, frontiers, flows, and networks (military, political, administrative, and economic). These were not merely articulated, controlled and determined by the overarching rubric or spatial envelope called the empire, but in fact constituted it.[37] The very spatial relations and networks of which London is the center are also played out (some-times on a smaller synecdochical scale) in the city. London is thus simultaneously the center of empire and a condensed or miniature version of the entire space (of empire) of which it is the center.

Late eighteenth- and early nineteenth-century London lay at the very center of an enormous and powerful global network of trade and imperial investment and control;

A system of maritime trade currents, growing rapidly in volume and capacity, circled the earth, bringing its profits to the mercantile communities of North Atlantic Europe. They used colonial power to rob the inhabitants of the East Indies of the commodities exported thence to Europe and Africa, where these and European goods were used to buy slaves for the rapidly growing plantation systems of the Americas. The American plantations in turn exported their sugar, cotton, etc., in ever vaster and cheaper quantities to the Atlantic and North Sea ports, whence they were redistributed eastwards, together with the traditional manufactures and commodities of European East–West trade.[38]

This was the global commercial network gradually developed by the institutions of European mercantile capitalism, which slowly began to give way to the systems and structures of a nascent industrial capitalism, beginning in the romantic period.[39] By the end of the transition from mercantile to industrial capitalism, the central economic role formerly played by the old commercial centers, like London, was distributed among several interlocking centers, including prominently the new industrial cities of the north.[40]

London itself had never been *primarily* an industrial city, and although the fierce struggle between mercantile and industrial interests – best exemplified in the conflict over the Corn Laws (1812–46) – was largely played out there, it never became primarily an industrial city (unlike the northern cities of Sheffield, Birmingham, and especially Manchester, which Asa Briggs refers to as "the shock city of the age"[41]). For long after the industrial revolution, London obviously remained a crucial econ-omic center, and an increasingly important political and cultural center as well; but Wordsworth's London was at the very apogee of its mercan-tile and commercial power, still arguably the center of the world-economy being developed by Britain. The port of London during this period was at the height of its importance: the great new colonial docks were being built from 1800 to 1810.[42] London's maritime importance would later be taken over, partly as ships got bigger and needed more room, but also as markets diversified, by the Merseyside and Clydeside ports of Liverpool and Glasgow, but by the turn into the nineteenth century roughly 80 percent of Britain's foreign trade was channeled into and out of the port of London.[43] Even into mid-century, the London docklands remained a stunning sight. Engels writes:

I know nothing more imposing than the view which the Thames offers during the ascent from the sea to London Bridge. The masses of buildings, the wharves on both sides, especially from Woolwich upwards, the countless ships along both shores, crowding ever closer and closer together, until, at last, only a narrow passage remains in the middle of the river, a passage through which hundreds of steamers shoot by one another; all this is so vast, so impressive, that a man cannot collect himself, but is lost in the marvel of England's greatness before he sets foot upon English soil.[44]

By the late eighteenth century, even the mundane requirements of daily life and existence in the city (not to mention the rest of Britain) required the symbolic as well as the material interaction of the different regions and districts of the British empire. One writer of the time, struck by the significance of what was already by then the quotidian British custom of drinking tea sweetened with sugar, comments that "it appears a very strange thing, that the common people of any European nation should be obliged to use, as part of their daily diet, two articles imported from opposite sides of the earth."[45] As Sidney Mintz argues, this observation is remarkable "not for what it shows us about the English economy, already in large measure a nation of wage-earners, but also for what it reveals about the intimacy of the links between colony and metropolis, fashioned by capital," since "these additions to the diet of the English people signalled the linkage of the consumption habits of every English-man to the world outside of England, and in particular to the colonies of the empire."[46]

Superimposed on the space of Wordsworth's London we find the abstract space produced through these networks, intertwining and combining in endless play and interaction with the spatial productions of the rest of the United Kingdom. London becomes not merely the economic, financial, political, and administrative center of empire but the symbolic center as well. Turning to Bartholomew Fair,[47] Wordsworth requires the "help" of the Muse, hoping that "she shall lodge us, wafted on her wings, / of the crowd, / Upon some showman's platform." He is finally perched some safe imaginary distance over the crowd below:

> What a hell
> For eyes and ears! what anarchy and din
> Barbarian and infernal, – 'tis a dream,

Monstrous in colour, motion, shape, sight, sound!
Below, the open space, through every nook
Of the wide area, twinkles, is alive
With heads; the midway region, and above,
Is thronged with staring pictures and huge scrolls,
Dumb proclamations of the Prodigies;
And chattering monkeys dangling from their poles,
And children whirling in their roundabouts;
With those that stretch the neck and strain the eyes,
And crack the voice in rivalship, the crowd
Inviting; with buffoons against buffoons
Grimacing, writhing, screaming, – him who grinds
The hurdy-gurdy, at the fiddle weaves,
Rattles the salt-box, thumps the kettle-drum,
And him who at the trumpet puffs his cheeks,
The silver-collared Negro with his timbrel,
Equestrians, tumblers, women, girls, and boys,
Blue-breeched, pink-vested, and with towering plumes. –
All moveables of wonder, from all parts,
Are here – Albinos, painted Indians, Dwarfs,
The Horse of knowledge, and the learned Pig,
The Stone-eater, the man that swallows fire,
Giants, Ventriloquists, the Invisible Girl,
The Bust that speaks and moves its goggling eyes,
The Wax-work, Clock-work, all the marvellous craft
Of modern Merlins, Wild Beasts, Puppet-shows,
All out-o'-the-way, far-fetched, perverted things,
All freaks of nature, all Promethean thoughts
Of man, his dulness, madness, and their feats
All jumbled up together to make up
This Parliament of Monsters.[48]

Just as the London crowd constantly threatens to become the mob, the flow of colonial images, peoples and goods which Wordsworth proposes to take in (as part of the crowd) constantly threatens to turn into a deluge that will obliterate all of his standards of measurement and understanding. This flow is not just a terrible colonial *counterpart* to the dreaded English working-class mob, since it crashes through the open colonial flood-gates and mixes and interacts with the English crowd in the space of London. The space of Bartholomew Fair, in which all of London is symbolically condensed into a small zone, unites a prototypical working-class mass culture and the flow of colonial goods and peoples in London, which together produce "all perverted things" and "freaks of nature." If the Nature which Wordsworth so admires and worships is defined in its otherness against the commercial network of which London was the beating heart, London becomes not only a space of confusion. It is, once again, a space inhabited by colonial otherness, even if, paradoxically, this is the heart of the system against which that otherness is also defined.

London is unknowable because it is a space in which even the parameters of self and other become indistinguishable – so that the solitary self constantly fears being swallowed up and engulfed by the crowd – but also because it is a space in which the familiar distinctions between "here" and "there," between metropolis and colony, between east and west and north and south, become confused and blurred. The terror which proletarian and colonial Bartholomew Fair holds for Wordsworth is the terror of the dissolution of maps, boundaries, categories, and spaces – and of subjectivity itself.

III

In *The Prelude* the greatest terror of all is the threat to subjectivity, the threat to the lonely bourgeois self negotiating the streets and crowds of the giant city, always at risk of being overwhelmed by that tide of collective energy represented by the proletarian and colonial mob. In his *Confessions*, Wordsworth's young disciple De Quincey – anticipating Baudelaire – would be able to take the art of *flâneurie* to the heights of the sublime, adding the intoxication of "taking a bath in the multitude" to the pleasurable intoxications of opium, and deriving sublime pleasure precisely from the simultaneous *possibility* of being overwhelmed and the knowledge of actual safety – a possibility that he is unable to keep sight of in his Oriental nightmares, which therefore degenerate from the heights of sublimity into sheer terror.[49] But Wordsworth in *The Prelude* is unable to gain any such pleasures: the threat of the crowd is far too real for him and as a result the perspectival detachment necessary for the experience of sublimity is impossible to attain. The London crowd appears to him in Book VII as literally "undistinguishable," or in other words a mass that finally cannot be broken down into individual constituents or components:

> Oh, blank confusion! and a type not false
> Of what the mighty City is itself
> To all except a straggler here and there,
> To the whole swarm of its inhabitants;
> An undistinguishable world to men,

The slaves unrespited of low pursuits,
Living amid the same perpetual flow
Of trivial objects, melted and reduced
To one identity, by differences
That have no law, no meaning, and no end –
Oppression, under which even highest minds
Must labour, whence the strongest are not free.[50]

What is overwhelming here, however, is not so much the sheer terror of the crowd, but rather the lack of distinctions within it. Just as the swarm of objects and people, "the many-headed mass," cannot be crystalized into a whole within which one might still discern particular features or individual constituents, the "same perpetual flow" cannot be broken down into discrete moments of time and is instead perceived as a continuous blurred rush.

The solitary observer's position is therefore threatened not only because he cannot achieve any kind of visual or perspectival independence but also because he cannot regulate the "same perpetual flow" in such a way as to comprehend it by organizing the visual spectacle in a kind of chronological order, a series of discrete images. The consequent impossibility of achieving any specific conjunctures of image and time, that is, the loss of perspectival and temporal stability, precludes the very possibility of a sublime relationship to the crowd. It also denies the possibility of framing an independent and detached – and paramount – subjectivity in opposition to the spectacle of the crowd, and hence (for Wordsworth) the possibility of poetry. For, after all, Wordsworth's withdrawal from London is not just personal and political, as Kiernan and others have pointed out; it is also an aesthetic renunciation.

In his unfinished essay on the sublime and the beautiful, Wordsworth stresses the importance of time as well as of image to the experience of sublimity. According to him, the sublime develops not only out of a particular "state or condition of the mind," but also a specific conjuncture of image (or spectacle) and time.[51] "Prominent individual form," he writes, must "be conjoined with duration, in order that Objects of this kind may impress a sense of sublimity." Landscape features lend themselves to the experience of this effect of sublimity, although Wordsworth (like Kant, but unlike Burke) stresses that the sublime resides in the subject, not in the object itself.[52] It is an *experience* generated by the subject's interaction with the object given the appropriate setting, circumstance and duration, in which the perceiving subject is able to properly frame the image and suspend it (give it duration) in time; or rather, in which the subject is able to conjoin image with time. It is out of this specific conjuncture that the experience of sublimity is generated: the experience of the power of unitary subjectivity.

Like Kant also, Wordsworth adds to these specifications that there must also be "impressions of power," for "Power awakens the sublime either when it rouses us to a sympathetic energy and calls upon the mind to grasp at something towards which it can make approaches but which it is incapable of attaining," or "by producing a humiliation or prostration of the mind before some external agency." But – like Burke[53] – he is careful to stress that the sense of power cannot be too overwhelming, and cannot actually amount to a sensation of imminent personal danger to the perceiving subject. Thus he writes, "if that Power which is exalted above our sympathy impresses the mind with personal fear, so as the sensation becomes more lively than the impression or thought of the exciting cause, then self-consideration and all its accompanying littleness takes place of the sublime, and wholly excludes it."

In Book VII London finally degenerates for Wordsworth precisely into an experience of terror, rather than of the sublimity he associates with Nature: terror not only due to a sensation of imminent "objective" danger from the crowd (the constant fear of that possibility of "half the city" breaking out, "Full of one passion, vengeance, rage or fear"), but also due to the lack of perspectival and temporal – and hence narrative – stability and clarity; in other words to a crisis of subjectivity. In fact, towards the very end of Book VII, Wordsworth writes that the chaos and confusion of the proletarian and colonial crowd generate a kind of "Oppression, under which even highest minds / Must labour, whence the strongest are not free." But it is as though he seeks to reassure himself that this otherwise "unmanageable sight" is "not wholly so to him who looks / In steadiness, who hath among least things / An under-sense of greatest; sees the parts / As parts, but with a feeling of the whole." Such an elevated and composed sensibility is derived, of course, from "early converse with the works of God / Among all regions; chiefly where appear / Most obviously simplicity and power." But at this point the narrative begins to slip, from claims of (self-)reassurance that Wordsworth himself has these qualities of mind and hence can assert them in a kind of cognitive control over the maddening spectacle of London (thereby not only bringing a Natural sensibility to bear on the city but in effect naturalizing the cityscape of London), to a much less assertive withdrawal from the city and hasty retreat to "the forms / Perennial of the ancient hills."

In other words, Wordsworth's retreat from London at the end of Book VII amounts to a withdrawal from a situation in which he is unable to generate for himself a sense of perspectival and temporal control to a situation in which such control is assured; in short, to Nature – and to poetry, "the *image* of man and nature." Wordsworth is clearly evoking here an aesthetic not only of poetry, but also of landscape painting, and he is also anticipating the æsthetics of photography; though it would seem that in his terms neither of these forms is adequate to the task of representing the city. Nor, for that matter, is poetry; or rather, for poetry to be adequate to the task of representing London, the cityscape would have to be rendered in natural (or naturalized) terms as landscape.

There is, in fact, a moment in Book VII in which Wordsworth does attempt to naturalize London by trying to achieve, on the one hand, a kind of critical perspectival and temporal distance, and, on the other hand, a specific conjuncture of image and time (seeing parts as parts but "with feeling of the whole"). This moment comes immediately before the Bartholomew Fair scene. As he wanders through the streets, "oppressed / By thoughts of what and whither, when and how, / Until the shapes before my eyes became / A second-sight procession . . ," Wordsworth is suddenly struck by the only figure – the only image – that he is properly able to remove from the crowd in Book VII: lost

> Among the moving pageant, 'twas my chance
> Abruptly to be smitten with the view
> Of a blind Beggar, who, with upright face,
> Stood, propped against a wall, upon his chest
> Wearing a written paper, to explain
> The story of the man, and who he was.
> My mind did at this spectacle turn round
> As with the might of waters, and it seemed
> To me that in this label was a type,
> Or emblem, of the utmost that we know,
> Both of ourselves and of the universe;
> And, on the shape of the unmoving man,
> His fixèd face and sightless eyes, I looked,
> As if admonished from another world.
>   Though reared upon the base of outward things,
> These, chiefly, are such structures as the mind
> Builds for itself: scenes different there are,
> Full-formed, which take, with small internal help,
> Possession of the faculties, – the peace
> Of night, for instance, the solemnity

Of nature's intermediate hours of rest,
When the great tide of human life stands still;
The business of the day to come, unborn,
Of that gone by, locked up, as in the grave;
The calmness, beauty, of the spectacle,
Sky, stillness, moonshine, empty streets, and sounds
Unfrequent as in deserts; at late hours
Of winter evenings, when unwholesome rains
Are falling hard, with people yet astir,
The feeble salutation from the voice
Of some unhappy woman, now and then
Heard as we pass, when no one looks about,
Nothing is listened to . . .[54]

In these passages from *The Prelude*, the spectacle of the Beggar leads directly (and as though it required no further explanation) to Wordsworth's reflections on those rare and fleeting moments of tranquility in the streets of London. What renders the Beggar such a powerful image – unmoving himself yet moving others – is the conjuncture of his status as a silent, sightless, immobilized *image* and the label that he wears: a label that explains the man's story and that in effect stands in for the presence of the man himself, makes up for and even takes the place of the man's own speech, sight, mobility. What is moving for Wordsworth here is that the label, the story, enables the viewer at once to freeze the image of the man outside of time, a type, and to read the stories inscribed in time on the label itself.

The Beggar's own immobility is what makes possible the mobility represented by the label: his suspension in time, as image, is what enables a reflection on time, as narrative; or in other words it is this particular image that endures in time because it opens up the possibility of not only suspending this time and all time, but reactivating *other* times through narrative. The admonishment from "another world" (in any case any world other than London) is less compelling here than the realization that such images are what the mind "builds for itself." For what is being suggested here is that the mind thinks through images, that it has to construct images suspended in time, or at least images defined in time, that is, image-narratives, in order to think.

This is why the sublime, not only the highest form of image, but above all the highest form of thought, is for Wordsworth a product not of the unthinking object, but of the mind – and not of any old garden-variety mind, but specifically of refined minds, "Minds of Persons of taste," as he puts it in the *Guide to the Lakes* (from which the essay on the sublime is derived). This is clearly why, underscoring his stress on the difference between "seeing" and "perceiving," he railed against the possibility of herding masses of factory-workers through the Lake District: not only because they would be incapable of such refinement and "feeling for landscape," but also, and more importantly, because they would ruin such pleasures for everyone else.[55] The crush and terror of the crowd in London weigh oppressively against the minds of such persons, causing them to "labour" to control, to *think*, the "unmanageable sight." Seeing is a simple natural function; but perceiving here involves the act of *thinking*, of being aware and in control of the act of seeing; this apperception enables the subject's sublime awareness of himself.

The frozen spectacle of the Beggar with his appended story thus enables Wordsworth to rescue thought, however temporarily, from the chaotic rush of the streets, and to ponder other suspended images. In so doing, the scenes that spring to mind are naturally not so much images as they are times, or rather they are unities of image and time:

> ... the peace
> Of night, for instance, the solemnity
> Of nature's intermediate hours of rest,
> When the great tide of human life stands still;
> The business of the day to come, unborn,
> Of that gone by, locked up, as in the grave.

The suspension of London at night-time generates a certain kind of tranquility, and even permits a certain degree of reflection on thought and emotion recollected in tranquility. Moreover, it makes it possible to render London in the natural terms of cycles of birth and death as well as day and night (as though a city's hours of "rest," which are in fact merely the hours of a different kind of activity, could somehow conform to Nature's). The feeble salutation of the "unhappy woman" (uncannily reminiscent of the midnight harlot of Blake's "London") tears into this tranquility, but her very invisibility – the salutation is from a disembodied "voice" – protects the scene from disintegration, and she is "heard" but "not listened to."

The naturalization of the city in this in-between time of tranquility then enables the generation of a series of images in which aural as well as visual elements are incorporated together ("sky, stillness, moonshine,

empty streets, and sounds / Unfrequent as in deserts"), as though the
aural and the visual had a kind of imagistic equivalence, precisely as
images precariously balanced in this suspended no-time and no-place,
just as the rush of the daytime streets had made it impossible to separate
aural and visual elements from the "blank confusion." But of course the
aural "images" are those of silence, and in fact they serve to reinforce
the power of the visual images, as though the daytime noise and din had
somehow undermined the very stability of the visual image, which has
now been restored by the bringing to the surface of a silence not just akin
to the stillness of Nature but a silence expressed in naturalized language,
as though London could be rescued from its own modernity by being
naturalized.

These passages from *The Prelude* are strikingly and not coincidentally
reminiscent of Wordsworth's sonnet "Composed Upon Westminster
Bridge, September 3, 1802," in which the unity of distance and perspectival and temporal framing, as well as a stable subject-position vis-à-vis
the object being observed, enable the narrator to appreciate the beautiful silence of London at dawn. Once again, the combination of visual
perspective (critical distance) and the temporal stability and precision
echoed in the sonnet's title are critical to the narrator's ability to
appreciate the giant city as a suspended image; so that the "quietness
and beauty" of the scene transform the cityscape of London into a
naturalized and greened landscape ("Never did sun more beautifully
steep / In his first splendour, valley, rock, or hill"). The very form of the
sonnet – in a sense a "perfect" form for nature poetry – signals the
possibility of naturalizing the city in poetry, as though there were a kind
of relationship between, on the one hand, the "natural" object being
represented and, on the other hand, not only the regular formal stability
of the sonnet but also the form's balanced poise and even imagistic
fragility (very much as opposed to the formal and narrative chaos of this
book of *The Prelude* in particular).

But just as in the sonnet the city's beauty and tranquility are precipi-
tously suspended at that in-between time of dawn's early light (so that
there is a direct relationship between the beauty and the stillness), in the
Prelude passage the temporary naturalization that is enabled by the
spectacle of the Beggar is able to last only for as long as the "same
perpetual flow" is warded off, for as long as the image thereby frozen in
time allows the possibility of generating other images (aural and visual).
For in the city this suspension of time is strictly temporary, and the
passage continues from where we left off:

. But these, I fear,
Are falsely catalogued; things that are, are not,
Even as we give them welcome, or assist,
Are prompt, or are remiss. What say you, then,
To times, when half the city shall break out
Full of one passion, vengeance, rage, or fear?
To executions, to a street on fire,
Mobs, riots, rejoicings?

Wordsworth's attempt to green and naturalize the cityscape of London is thus not only suspended in time at the no-time of the early morning: it is also suspended between the formal and political pressure of his fear of the crowd and of the mob. Thus the reflections enabled by the temporary and fleeting image of the Beggar are quickly washed away by the resumption of the "same perpetual flow" of London's streets.

This temporary image constitutes a spot of time, though not exactly in our usual theoretical understanding of that concept – for here the spot of time functions not as a magnet for personal memories, but instead as a socially, rather than personally, constituted refuge that retains a "renovating virtue," as Wordsworth puts it in the famous passage in *The Prelude*.[56] What is disturbing about London for Wordsworth is the threat that the urban space of modernity poses to the very stability and security of his own bourgeois subject-position and hence the concomitant threat it poses to his aesthetic and political projects. It is the modernity of London that he finds so terrifying: that modernity which is signaled precisely by the crazy and undistinguishable spectacular combination, juxtaposition, and melting-together of places, figures, goods, types, images, selves, and others, even within a "same perpetual flow." Here the homogeneous time (same, perpetual, flow) of modernity offers no escape, no solace from the abstract space of capital. And it is as a refuge to the spatio-temporal flows of modernization that Wordsworth must construct a more stable, recognizable, and knowable kind of place: a spot of time.

This new understanding of the concept of spot of time, which I will elaborate more fully in the next chapter, must be framed against the seemingly endless flow of modern homogeneous time. It is precisely because of its capacity to reactivate heterogeneous time (memory, myth, history – both collective and personal) that the spot of time stands out as an assemblage disrupting the unilinear stream of modern time, the flows of abstract space. This is why the spot of time can offer a kind of refuge from the space of the modern, from the "the same perpetual flow / Of

trivial objects," and the "trivial occupations" and "ordinary intercourse" of the barren world of commodities and of capital (note how the
very language of the spot of time passage in Book XII replicates the
language of Book VII). Thus understood, the spot of time represents an
assemblage of heterogenous and unassimilable times, memories, myths,
which by its very persistence within the modern create a sense of
(alternative) space. The spot of time exists "in our existence," and not in
itself. Seen here in the very streets of London, it is now no longer a
"natural" phenomenon but rather a human potential for experience
and practice.

CHAPTER 3

Wordsworth and the image of Nature

I would enshrine the spirit of the past
For future restoration.

William Wordsworth, The Prelude

'Tis not, what it once was, the world,
But a rude heap together hurled,
All negligently overthrown,
Gulfs, deserts, precipices, stone.
Your lesser world contains the same,
But in more decent order tame;
You, heaven's centre, nature's lap,
And paradise's only map.

Andrew Marvell, Upon Appleton House

I

Let me then invite the Reader to turn his eyes with me towards that cluster of Mountains at the Head of Windermere; it is probable that they will settle ere long upon the Pikes of Langdale and the black precipice contiguous to them. – If these objects be so distant that, while we look at them, they are only thought of as the crown of a comprehensive Landscape; if our minds be not perverted by false theories, unless those mountains be seen under some accidents of nature, we shall receive from them a grand impression, and nothing more. But if they be looked at from a point which has brought us so near that the mountain is almost the sole object before our eyes, yet not so near but that the whole of it is visible, we shall be impressed with a sensation of sublimity.[1]

Wordsworth's poetics of landscape are concerned above all with images and with the production of images. This is not entirely to say that the landscape "itself" does not matter, for obviously it does. But the viewing subject's framing of the landscape in images is of greater significance in Wordsworth's guide than the landscape itself as a given or inert material object. And if the sublime represents thought at its most profound, that

45

is so because it is during the experience of sublimity that the mind is most able to exert a kind of cognitive control over the objects of perception (according to Wordsworth, the experience of sublimity has less to do with the object being viewed than with the viewing subject, who is capable of properly framing the object in spatio-temporal terms and with the proper degrees of distance and duration).[2] Moreover, the kind of images that Wordsworth elaborates in his *Guide* as well as in his nature poetry are not only visual images: they are images of time as well.

Consider for a moment how much attitudes to landscape changed in the decades leading up to Wordsworth's rediscovery of the Lake District in the late eighteenth and early nineteenth centuries. Daniel Defoe, viewing more or less exactly the same geophysical or topographical landscape as that which would later be revered by Wordsworth and the Lake Poets, sees only "unhospitable terror" in the lands around Lake Windermere:[3]

Here we entered Westmoreland, a country eminent only for being the wildest, most barren and frightful of any that I have passed over in England, or even in Wales it self; the west side, which borders on Cumberland, is indeed bounded by a chain of almost unpassable mountains, which, in the language of the country, are called Fells.

Comparing the Cumbrian mountains to the peaks of the Snowdon horseshoe in North Wales, Defoe is dismayed at seeing nothing around him, "in many places, but unpassable hills, whose tops, covered with snow, seemed to tell us that all the pleasant part of England was at an end."[4] Nor, adds Defoe, "were these hills high and formidable only, but they had a kind of unhospitable terror in them. Here were no rich pleasant valleys between them, as among the Alps; no lead mines and veins of rich ore, as in the Peak; no coal pits, as in the hills about Halifax, much less gold, as in the Andes, but all barren and wild, of no use or advantage either to man or beast."

Defoe views the Lake District in the general terms of the eighteenth-century aesthetic of "improvement" that Wordsworth would later reject. For Defoe is interested (in at least two senses of that word) in the countryside in solely material terms, for what it can *materially* offer for human exploitation. Wordsworth not only evokes a totally different aesthetic of landscape: he is ultimately more concerned with the viewing subject than he is with the landscape as such. His concern with the landscape has to do with what it offers the viewing subject in terms of possibilities for *immaterial* exploitation, rather than with the materiality or physicality of the land itself (one is reminded here of Anthony Easthope's declaration, surely not just polemical, that "Wordsworth is not interested in nature"[5]).

If for Defoe or Adam Smith or other eighteenth-century "improvers" the land is primarily a *material* mass whose value resides solely in the degree of material exploitation to which it is (or can be) subjected, for Wordsworth the land is primarily of non-material, imagistic value. And indeed for him the most imagistically valuable land is that which is least valuable, or altogether untapped, in terms of crude material exploitation (it is no coincidence, then, that the kind of large landed estates that Adam Smith criticizes in the *Wealth of Nations* for inefficiently exploiting the land are the very same estates praised by Wordsworth in the *Guide* for exactly the same reasons).[6] He writes in the very opening sentence of the *Guide to the Lakes* that "in preparing this Manual, it was the Author's principal wish to furnish a Guide or Companion for the *Minds* of Persons of taste, and feeling for landscape, who might be inclined to explore the District of the Lakes with that degree of attention to which its beauty may fairly lay claim."[7] Here, clearly, whatever degree of natural or organic beauty the landscape can offer has more to do with the taste and feeling and mind of the observer than with its own material objectivity. To an unobservant or "tasteless" viewer (presumably including a Defoe or a Smith) such a landscape would offer no beauty at all. Indeed, the very same landscape that forms the basis of Wordsworth's whole poetic career is for Defoe not worth mentioning, for, as the latter writes in his own *Guide*, "'tis of no advantage to represent horror, as the character of the country . . . ."

Much of the *Guide to the Lakes* is taken up by Wordsworth's painstaking directions for approaching particular views in order to achieve the best frame of the landscape under observation. There is a section that goes in great detail through the various approaches to the Lake District from different directions and by different routes, in which Wordsworth stresses the best approaches that allow the tourist to see the lakes through a series of successive frames, or rather as a succession of framed images.

Thus in the guidebook the framed image assumes an importance greater than the overall "real" landscape from which it is derived. Or rather, both in the guidebook and in Wordsworth's poetry ("the *image* of man and Nature"), it is not that the image of Nature simply supersedes the "reality," but that that "reality" is itself composed and defined imagistically from the standpoint of an observing subject. Images of a landscape can thus be captured and circulated not so much as abstractions from a preexisting given background, but rather as versions of that background. For that "reality" itself must be understood imagistically. Elizabeth Helsinger has argued that part of what is at stake in late eighteenth- and early nineteenth-century landscape aesthetics in England is a play of circulation and possession, in which those who are free to circulate (bourgeois tourists) are also able to possess prints of a fixed landscape, so that the purchaser of such prints "is offered visual possession of an England whose images have been placed in circulation."[8] Thus, she argues, a new understanding of property-rights and property-ownership – in which the image is understood as property – emerges alongside the traditional notion of landed ("real") property rights.

While Helsinger is of course correct to point out that such a notion of imagistic property is hardly any more democratic or less exclusive than landed property (e.g., for Wordsworth not everyone is fit to "appreciate" landscape), there is nevertheless a peculiar and somewhat understated utopian moment to this notion of image-property, namely, that unlike "real" landed property this new form of property is virtually unlimited because it is capable of multiplicity and of repeated production and circulation in the form of images. It is at least potentially open to all – a form of property that is capable of virtually infinite reproduction and infinite exploitation.

But there are two important caveats to this argument. First of all, for Wordsworth the image of landscape is tied directly to a viewing subject who is capable of producing images by the act of framing, who is capable of valorizing its "objective" reality, literally giving it value by framing it. Secondly, the image here is not necessarily only a visual image: it may be an image of *time* as well, though it is produced by framing in precisely the same way as a visual image. The production of the image and its consumption are one and the same thing, one and the same process, for the act of perception is the act of appropriation of the landscape.

In fleeing from London and seeking to "return" to the haven promised by a safe and knowable Nature, Wordsworth must himself construct that Nature imagistically. The problem that he faces, of course, is that the very same processes of modernization that had caused him so much trouble and even terror in London are also at work in the English countryside, slowly transforming it beyond recognition. His particular project then becomes one of trying to locate – that is, to frame – imagistic space-times that might offer some hope of resistance against the processes of modernization; in other words to rescue from the backdrop of a developing landscape those frames or images that defy transformation through their ability to remain as images – both visual and temporal images – against a blurred background of change and movement (the very same blurred background that virtually disabled the production of sublime images in London). Again, this does not amount to ignoring the materiality of the countryside; but it does entail searching for the appropriate frame from which to produce the necessary images. To use Marjorie Levinson's terminology, it involves "greening" a particular landscape.[9] What Levinson refers to as Wordsworth's "selective blindness," for example, can be understood in terms of finding the appropriate frame from which to view Tintern Abbey as an image.

II

A tour narrative (the form taken not only by Wordsworth's *Guide* but also by much of his poetry) is an ideal form for narrating the modernization of the countryside, for it transcribes historical process onto a background – a landscape – that it has itself produced in narrative form. William Cobbett's tour through England in the 1820s in *Rural Rides* is one instance of such expansiveness.[10] Cobbett's project involved the narration of the social and economic transformation of rural England, or, rather, the transcription of social and economic transformation in a geographic area into a narrative form. Alan Liu argues that "tours always describe motion through a land written over by history, even though they also keep history – however many pages are devoted to it – in the background as if it were supplemental to the delights of the present tour."[11] And yet, a tour, even if it presents history as "ornamental," involves the construction of a terrain onto which historical, economic, social, and political events or processes can be written. It is useful to see space itself as a tour's "background"; although the very term (background) is recognizably problematic, inasmuch as it is being actively produced even as it is being deployed as an apparently "already finished" context.

This is particularly important in view of the dramatic changes taking place in the British countryside during the romantic period. The catastrophic changes of which E. P. Thompson writes in *The Making of the English Working Class* were taking place in the changing dynamics of the social production of space in the British countryside, whose varied

landscapes were being extensively reinvented all throughout the romantic period in terms of a growing abstract space of commodification
(despite considerable resistance, as for instance the smashing of enclosure fences: a crime punishable by death). Cobbett's *Rural Rides* attempts
to chronicle the enormous scale of the transformation of the countryside
not just by mapping out the spaces in which these changes were
occurring, but by then superimposing narratives of the transformation
onto his map. "Nobody tells the tale of the labourer," Cobbett writes,
and indeed his tours, in an attempt to redress this, transplant laborers'
narratives onto the map of the socio-economic unification of Britain.[12]

To narrate the whole of this process would clearly have been impossible, so that what such narratives as Cobbett's allow us are but glimpses
into particular aspects of this process: they are therefore necessarily
incomplete and fragmentary. Nevertheless, parts of the overall transformation do stand out. The most obvious instance of this is the
Enclosure movement in England and Wales (Scotland had something of
an equivalent in the terrible Highland Clearances[13]). The process of
enclosure in England began as far back as the fifteenth century, but until
the great boom of Parliamentary enclosure in the late eighteenth and
early nineteenth centuries (especially 1793–1815), relatively small
amounts of land were involved. In the later period, however, Parliament
passed 5,286 private Enclosure Acts, which in England alone redistributed 7 million acres: 21 percent of the country's surface area.[14]

Enclosure has sometimes been separated from the broader historical
processes of which it was but a culmination.[15] It is therefore important to
see the spatial erasures and re-writings carried out by the process of
enclosure as the *traces* of the broader social, economic, and historical
forces and currents of modernization. If a simple hedgerow summons
up the notion of enclosure, it also stands as a visible spatial effect of this
change. This is particularly important since the process of enclosure
literally and materially re-drew the map of much of England and Wales,
so that, ironically, all that might be left by which to summon forth
memories of past maps and landscapes would be not only their traces
(such as the rocks for the sheepfold in Wordsworth's *Michael*), but also
the hedgerows, the lines of trees, the new roads – the visible signatures of
the *new* maps which replaced them.[16]

There were two main kinds of enclosure: of common or open field,
and of "waste" or marginal land. In either case, however, the process
obliterated most of the landmarks of the previously-existing space; the
old medieval roads were either shifted or covered over as new straight

ones replaced them ("Improvement makes strait roads," Blake writes, "but the crooked roads without Improvement, are roads of Genius"[17]); commons or large tracts of open field were parcelled out, criss-crossed by hedgerows and fences; groups of houses and sometimes whole villages would be destroyed (as commemorated in Goldsmith's *The Deserted Village*) to make way for new farmland; and the forests, copses, streams, marshes, and bogs of "waste" land were cut, drained, or diverted whenever possible. John Barrell observes:

> To enclose an open-field parish means in the first place to think of the details of its topography as quite erased from the map. The hostile and mysterious road-system was tamed and made unmysterious by being destroyed; the minute and intricate divisions between lands, strips, furlongs, and fields simply ceased to exist: the quantity of each proprietor's holding was recorded, but not among what furlongs it had been distributed. Everything about the place, in fact, which made it precisely *this* place, and not that one, was forgotten; the map was drawn blank, except for the village itself, the parish boundaries, and perhaps woodland too extensive or valuable to be cleared, and streams too large to be diverted.[18]

As space was redistributed and re-organized during the process of enclosure, its social significance was dramatically altered. In fact, that vast process, of which enclosure was but the culmination, transformed people's lives beyond recognition. This was particularly true for the countryside once its people had been dispossessed (after all, some of the land being enclosed had been *common* land) and uprooted – that is, once they had been turned into a "surplus" population and gradually forced away into the growing cities of industrializing Britain.[19]

III

What Wordsworth seeks in his own production of the space of Nature is an escape or shelter from the gigantic transformative processes of modernization that he had fled in abandoning London, and that were, of course, also transforming rural England (not to mention Wales, Ireland, and Scotland). Here, a particular aspect of the images of Nature that Wordsworth constructs becomes crucial: these are simultaneously images of time and of space. Wordsworth's image of Nature is a spot of time (like London as seen from Westminster Bridge in Wordsworth's 1802 sonnet). The spot of time, however, needs to be critically under-stood not as "natural," but rather, as I argued in the previous chapter, as a human potential for experience and practice; which is exactly what nature itself is in Wordsworth's poetry – a *human* potential.

Geoffrey Hartman has discussed Wordsworth's obsession with spots of time at great length, noting that the concept merges "sensation of place and sensation of time," so that time can be placed, or "physically" perceived or spotted.[20] Hartman sees this notion as a development of what he refers to as Wordsworth's spot syndrome, and notes the difficulties involved in this development:

It is hard to decide whether the first or second member of the partitive construction "spots of time" should be emphasized. If we derive the origin of the notion from Wordsworth's attraction to specific place (the omphalos or spot syndrome), and notice that "spot" is subtly used in two senses – as denoting particular *places* in nature, and fixed *points* in time ("islands in the unnavigable depth / Of our departed time") – the emphasis would fall on the initial word. But the natural pull of the phrase, and the fact that these spots are not only *in* time, like islands, but also creative *of* time or of a vivifying temporal consciousness, throws the emphasis to the second noun and evokes a beaconing "time-spot."[21]

Hartman, however, limits his discussion of the spot of time to a consideration of its narrative effects in Wordsworth's poetry. Various other critics have read the spot of time strictly in terms of its relationship to the poet's own private memories, which is how the concept has come to be understood for the most part in romanticist scholarship. Here I want to suggest not only that the concept forms one of Wordsworth's key conceptual underpinnings, but that the spot of time in Wordsworth's poetry defines what nature is, and how it comes to be seen as a refuge from the abstract space-time of modernization and development.

To elaborate this question, I want to discuss one very early example of the spot of time in Wordsworth's poetry, one that is constituted as an image in *An Evening Walk* by the narrator's intrusion into that poem's hidden retreat. This spot of time actually appears – *avant la lettre* – long before the explicit reference to the concept in *The Prelude*. That it appears in a poem that Wordsworth first published in 1793 and would uniquely continue to rework until 1850 – a remarkable span of time, covering his entire career – is one striking indication not only of how foundational the concept was to his nature poetry, but also of how early in his work its origins lie, namely in that decisive turning-point in Wordsworth's life and career, so often revisited by scholars, in 1792–93.[22]

However, we have now to reconsider the argument of the preceding chapter. If I am correct here in identifying the hidden bower of *An Evening Walk* as a spot of time *avant la lettre*, what this means is that the concept appears and is operative in the poetry before its explicit invocation in *The Prelude*, and even before the representation of the crisis that led to its development.[23] That crisis – the general personal and political tumult of the early 1790s – is figured specifically in Book VII of *The Prelude* in terms of the shock of the modern, and it is given form and expression in London. The revolutionary turbulence of the times is here understood not, as has often been the case among literary scholars, in and of itself, but rather as part of a larger set of cultural and political developments which together constitute the process of modernization. The subsequent representation of the crisis of modernization as figured specifically in the London of Book VII, is paradoxically given narrative form in *The Prelude* from the conceptual perspective of the spot of time.

Thus the crisis of modernization is seen in *The Prelude* retrospectively, only *after* the inception of the spot of time, which is a reaction to it. What gets registered textually in Wordsworth's early poetry (notably *An Evening Walk*, but also for example *Tintern Abbey*) is, then, not so much the personal and national trauma that he experienced in the 1790s, but rather his aesthetic and political reaction to it. Only later, in *The Prelude*, would Wordsworth return to the primal scene of that crisis in order to narrate the inception of the spot of time. Thus the reason why we cannot understand the history of the coming into being of the spot of time in its own terms is not merely because it is not up to that task, but above all because it covers up and erases the history of its own production.

> When, in the south, the wan noon, brooding still,
> Breathed a pale stream around the glaring hill,
> And shades of deep-embattled clouds were seen,
> Spotting the northern cliffs with lights between;
> When crowding cattle, checked by rails that make
> A fence far outstretched into the shallow lake,
> Lashed the cool water with their restless tails,
> Or from high points of rock looked out for fanning gales;
> When school-boys stretched their length upon the green;
> And round the broad-spread oak, a glimmering scene,
> In the rough fern-clad park, the herded deer
> Shook the still-twinkling tail and glancing ear;
> When horses in the sunburnt intake stood,
> And vainly eyed below the tempting flood,
> Or tracked the passenger, in mute distress,
> With forward neck the closing gate to press . . .[24]

From the very first word, these lines of *An Evening Walk* are charged with
tension, as a result of the repeated deferral of the event towards which
they point. This tension is carried through the passage by the narrative,
beginning with the effect of the confusing and staccato opening couplet,
which interrupts the previous flow of the poem: "When, in the south,
the wan noon, brooding still, / Breathed a pale stream around the
glaring hill." The effect is almost to objectify the noon, to make it one of
those heavenly bodies (notably the moon) which are more typically
referred to as "wan." But this strange and disturbing couplet, whose
very wording undermines itself, also contributes to the poem's tension.

The tension is also reflected in the landscape, set as it is with the
"shades of deep-embattled clouds" looming over the northern cliffs of
the scene. In addition, the animals' restlessness amplifies the tension: the
"*crowding* cattle" lashing the water with their "*restless* tails;" the "*herded*
deer" with "still-twinkling tail" and "*glancing* ear;" even the horses, in
"mute distress," "vainly" eyeing the flowing water below their intake.
Finally, the tension is also developed and channeled by the series of
barriers built onto the landscape, such as the rails that make for the
crowding cattle "A fence [a "check"] far stretched into the shallow
lake," and the gate that prevents the horses' movement.

Recalling now the earlier mention of "willowy hedgerows," "rocky
sheepwalks," and (most pleasant sounding of all) "woodland bounds,"
we begin to see that this is not at all a "natural" landscape, but one
thoroughly inscribed with the traces of social authority. This is perhaps
clearest with the rails, extending into the lake's shallow water, that pen
the cattle into their enclosures. The "rocky sheepwalks" conjure up the
naïveté of a pastoral scene, but one that is subsumed into a larger social
and economic framework, whose traces are the carefully designed
walks, which are presumably set up not only to channel the flocks from
one pasture to the next, but from the grazing areas to the slaughterhouse
and the market.

All of the other references invoke social authority and property laws
as well, though the language of the poem is carefully chosen to soften
(we could even say to "naturalize") the hard edges of this authority. A
hedgerow, for instance, is invariably the sign of enclosure: normally
quickset hawthorn, it is planted in a straight line along the boundaries of
the land allotted by an Act of Enclosure.[25] Here, however, the straight
lines of the enclosure hedges are softened, and they are transformed into
graceful "*willowy* hedgerows," anticipating *Tintern Abbey*'s "hedge-rows,
hardly hedge-rows, little lines / Of sportive wood run wild."[26] The other

main mark of property division, the line of trees (often running down roads, especially roads designed during the height of enclosure), is similarly transformed into a "woodland bound," or in other words, a wooded boundary-line. And while it is clear that the horses, sheep, and cattle referred to are private property, it needs to be stressed that the deer are as well, despite the images of "free" nature that these animals invariably conjure up. Deer were penned, to await the hunt, in carefully planned-out private parks (rendered here as "rough" and "fern-clad") which were protected not only by gamekeepers and sometimes by spring-guns, but also by the provisions of the notorious Black Act, violation of which carried the death penalty.[27]

Much of the space depicted in *An Evening Walk* is concerned not only with the inscriptions and traces of social authority, but with social and economic processes. Raymond Williams suggests that "a working country is hardly ever a landscape."[28] A working country *can* be a landscape, however, and the imaginary terrain of *An Evening Walk* is just such a landscape. But then, since the space of labor is not altogether erased, it needs to be rewritten and redrawn, either as part of the process which Annabel Patterson calls the pastoral ideology (through which the human inhabitants of rural England are reduced, she argues, to the level of "aesthetic objects"), or by absorption into the background itself, as John Barrell has suggested.[29] Later on in the narrator's walk, as the sun is declining, he notes the serenity into which the community of the Lakes is drawn at the end of the working day. Yet although "the whole wide lake in deep repose / Is hushed, and like a burnished mirror glows . . .," this repose is disrupted by the longer worktimes entailed by certain occupations – ". . . Save where, along the shady western marge, / Coasts, with industrious oar, the charcoal barge."[30] The narrator is clearly not involved in the sort of manual labour demanded of the barge crew; to his eye, it effortlessly glides and "coasts" along the lake as if no force at all were required to propel it, even though he *also* notes the presence (but makes it seem coincidental) of the "industrious oar" which, with its unseen human motor, is the barge's means of propulsion.[31]

Quickly we realize that this is not at all a time of repose. The charcoal barge passes by a steep hill:

> Their panniered train a group of potters goad,
> Winding from side to side up the steep road;
> The peasant, from yon cliff of fearful edge
> Shot, down the headlong path darts with his sledge;
> Bright beams the lonely mountain-horse illume

> Feeding 'mid purple heath, 'green rings', and broom;
> While the sharp slope the slackened team confounds,
> Downward the ponderous timber-wain resounds;
> In foamy breaks the rill, with merry song,
> Dash'd o'er the rough rock, lightly leaps along;
> From lonesome chapel at the mountain's feet
> Three humble bells their rustic chime repeat;
> Sounds from the water-side the hammered boat;
> And *blasted* quarry thunders, heard remote![32]

Not only are there scenes of and references to economic production (the boatyard and the quarry), but there are glimpses of goods being shipped to markets (the charcoal, the pottery, the timber). More significant, perhaps, is the way in which these scenes of labor have been brightened and even endowed with a certain musical quality; it takes a second look to recognize that the joy which seems to pervade these scenes comes not from the people, but from the landscape itself (the "merry song," for instance, comes from the rill). It takes yet another look to realize that the workers themselves have all but faded into and become part of the landscape. The group of potters is certainly there to be seen, and there is of course the peasant with his sledge; but after this charmingly antique figure, human agency is absorbed into the background. The loggers' wagon is moving without attendants; the chapel's bells are rung by invisible hands; the boat is being made (or repaired) by an invisible workman; and the quarry is altogether removed from the scene, so that all we have in any case are its distant sounds.

"Even here, amid the sweep of endless woods," the narrator assures us that "not undelightful are the simplest charms, / Found by the grassy door of mountain-farms." Intervening between the first sound of the quarry and its visual description are two stanzas which relentlessly insist on the beauty of the surrounding scenery. Then we finally see the quarry:

> Where, mixed with graceful birch, the sombrous pine
> And yew-tree o'er the silver rocks recline,
> I love to mark the quarry's moving trains,
> Dwarf panniered steeds, and men, and numerous wains:
> How busy all the enormous hive within,
> While Echo dallies with its various din!
> Some (hear you not their chisels' clinking sound?)
> Toil, small as pygmies in the gulf profound;
> Some, dim between the lofty cliffs descried,
> O'erwalk the slender plank from side to side;

These, by the pale-blue rocks that ceaselessly ring,
In airy baskets hanging, work and sing.[33]

The natural beauty surrounding the quarry seems to have magically lent it some of its qualities, for the coarse and rough edges of manual labor are here softened and even naturalized. The quarry is compared to an organic substance (a beehive), and its workers presumably to humming bumblebees. Their stings have been removed, however, partly because the workers and their "dwarf panniered steeds" are rendered in distant and even diminutive terms; they toil away, but are "small as pygmies." The quarry workers are happy; their labor may be "ceaseless," but it is also musical, since not only do the surrounding rocks echo and "ring," but they themselves, "In airy baskets hanging, work and sing."

The space mapped out in *An Evening Walk* has been socially organized, distributed, produced, and re-produced. It has been not merely sprinkled (or even saturated) with the traces of social, political, and economic processes: it has been formed and molded along the lines prescribed by these processes. Even the areas within it – the glens, the intakes, the meadows, the woods – which are not actually occupied by social presence, are nevertheless defined and set aside by this presence, cut up and parceled into the array of particular zones that begin to stand out in the poem's opening stanzas.

Not a square inch of the space produced (thus far) in the imaginary map of *An Evening Walk* escapes social inscription. Certain critics have compared this poem to Wordsworth's *Descriptive Sketches*: "Again a topographical poem, it serves to provide a frame for a multitude of images and sensations culled from nature, either by direct observation or via the eyes of unusually exact observers whose travel books Wordsworth had read."[34] But while *An Evening Walk* invokes the genre of the topographical poem, its topography is distinctly *not* "natural."[35]

IV

Then, while I wandered where the huddling rill
Brightens with water-breaks the hollow ghyll
As by enchantment, an obscure retreat
Opened at once, and stayed my devious feet.
While thick above the rill the branches close,
In rocky basin its wild waves repose,
Inverted shrubs, and moss of gloomy green,
Cling from the rocks, with pale wood-weeds between;

And its own twilight softens the whole scene,
Save where aloft the subtle sunbeams shine
On withered briars that o'er the crags recline;
Save where, with sparkling foam, a small cascade
Illumines, from within, the leafy shade;
Beyond, along the vista of the brook,
Where antique roots its bustling course o'erlook,
The eye reposes on a secret bridge,
Half grey, half shagged with ivy to its ridge;
There, bending o'er the stream, the listless swain
Lingers behind his disappearing wain.[36]

The obscure retreat opens up "at once," and both narrator and narrative fall into it, as by enchantment. Once we are safely inside, the branches close over our heads. We leave behind the brightness of the noon outside, the school-boys stretched out in the soft English sun, the "glimmering scene," the crashing flood of the river over which the horses stand on their "sunburnt intake." The retreat opens downwards into the depths of a rocky basin, and the preceding and longing references to hidden enclosures are here fulfilled. Just outside, the hollow ghyll is splashed with brightness, but here, snug inside the retreat, the scene is darker, quieter, softer, its colors duller and earthier than those of the outside world. Ivies and mosses cling to the rocks, and a dark, deep, gloomy green saturates the visible spectrum. Although some sunlight from the outside world is admitted here, the retreat has its own magical source of light: with its "sparkling foam," the noiseless cascade "illumines, from within, the leafy shade."

Though this obscure retreat is self-enclosed, however, it is also fragile, its fragility generated and then reinforced by the feeling of the outside weighing on the inside, threatening it, looming over it, "reminding" it always that it is at best a temporary enclosure. Feebly penetrating the gloom of the interior, the "subtle sunbeams" remind one that no matter how dark it is on the inside, the world on the outside is bright with a sunlight kept out by a few branches, by some shrubs and hanging ivies. There is also the "secret bridge" which, although it does not penetrate the fragility of the retreat, looms over it. The bridge does not exactly constitute an element of the retreat because it, like the rocky walls surrounding and defining this sheltered basin, is lifted high above it: it is "half shagged with ivy *to its ridge*."

But if the obscure retreat is a self-enclosed space, it also has a temporal structure all its own, cutting it off as much temporally from the outside world as spatially: while the retreat is *darker* than the outside world, this darkness reflects *and* produces a separate time-zone. Outside, of course, it is still high noon; but here *"its own twilight* softens the whole scene."* Indeed, it is this aspect of the retreat that is most affected by Wordsworth's gradual revisions of *An Evening Walk*: from one version to the next, it gets more and more cut off and self-enclosed, both spatially and temporally. In the 1793 version, it is not even described as a retreat, appearing instead as a "brown bason."[37] And although the 1836 version changes this to an "obscure retreat," and develops its spatial depth, it does not fully develop its temporal depth. By the final version, all the modifiers enhance the sense of both spatial and temporal enclosure. Thus, for instance, the scene's darkness comes to signify not only a spatial, but also a temporal state; while the earlier versions have "twilight shade" and then "impervious shade," by the final version the shade itself has become a result, rather than a cause, of the retreat's own temporal structure ("its own twilight").

At the same time, the obscure retreat is transformed into a spatial and temporal enclave in the poem's narrative structure and form. Structurally, the passage develops out of the all-important "Then . . ." to which the earlier part of the the poem has been leading. Just as the preceding "when . . ." clauses are temporal coordinates on the imaginary map, the obscure retreat is also emplotted in time: that is, it not only has its own internally coherent temporal structure, but it is spatially and temporally situated on the imaginary map of *An Evening Walk* by the temporal coordinate "Then . . . ." Similarly, just as earlier sections of the poem use tense-shifts as temporal registers and markers, so does the obscure retreat. For the narration is, in the movement towards it, in the past tense ("wandered . . . opened . . . stayed . . .") but, once the narrator falls into the retreat, the tense suddenly shifts into the present: "the branches close," "wild waves repose," "twilight softens." Thus the temporal terrain mapped out by the imaginary geography of *An Evening Walk* is transcoded into the narrative form of the poem, which is suddenly wrenched out of one tense and into another, just as the steady rhythm and meter of the previous passage are cut off and disrupted by the staccato and jerky rhythm in the description of the retreat. The narrator's return to the outside world is registered not only in this tense-shift to the future, but also in the narrative. Having entered the retreat's "own twilight" when it is noon outside, he lingers for a few moments, then leaves it to discover that evening has suddenly descended on the outside. It is as though his stay in the retreat had sent him through a time-warp: a few moments on the inside space translate to the passage of hours on the outside. The retreat is therefore akin to a spatial and temporal "black hole" – not, obviously, as incomprehensibly distant as an astronomical black hole, but one that shares its ability to warp space around it, and hence to distort and disable the "normal" movement of time.

The obscure retreat in *An Evening Walk* is an eminent example of a spot of time. The defining characteristic of this spot of time is its fragile separation from the social world, its persistence as a knot of heterogeneous time in a surrounding world of production and development. Unlike the spaces mapped out both before and after this passage in the poem, this space is not visibly marked by any social, economic, or political inscriptions. It is, however, negatively defined by these inscriptions, in that it is separated from them: it is, in other words, circumscribed by the abstract space of the social, but still resilient and unpenetrated. The obscure retreat's spirit of place – figured as the still-surviving charge of magical enchantment which defines it – is generated precisely by the fact that the retreat has not been drawn into either the spatial or the temporal structures of the outside world. But now we come to the obvious contradiction here, namely, that this spot of time is constituted as such, as an image, by the narrator's discovery of it; a discovery that would seem by definition to have destroyed its very purity. The point, of course, is that the spot of time never really existed in itself, but rather only in relation to that narrator, and to the very narrative intrusion and discovery that *simultaneously* preserves and destroys it as a heterogeneous site. Or in other words the spot of time is invented as heterogeneous, as anti-modern, precisely in contrast to the threat of the abstract homogeneity of the modern. At the same time, though, it offers a human potential – a "renovating virtue" – for resistance to the very homogeneity that defines it.

v

I have already described certain aspects of the process of the redistribution, re-organization, re-writing, and re-production of space during the transformation of Britain which began in the romantic period. This process was simultaneously taking place at two levels: at the level of local transformation, for instance in the movements (of people, of production) and reorganizations of space in a specific area (a village, a parish, a county) associated with an Act of Enclosure; and at a larger, properly national level. The space of Britain, considered as a whole, as a single socio-political entity cast onto a single geographical area, was being dramatically redefined during this period, and not only as a result of the Enclosure movement.

The formation of a national economy in Britain, linked to (indeed increasingly the center of) a world-economy, took place in the re-organization of the space within the national boundaries.[38] To be more exact, especially since we are talking about an island, this formation took place in the struggle to subsume certain national boundaries (those between Scotland, Wales and England) within a larger entity.[39] Space, in particular the abstract space of commodity production and circulation, must be understood here not as an end-product, but rather, as Henri Lefebvre suggests, as itself a *means of production*.[40] The redevelopment and re-invention of the space of the countryside during the romantic period may thus be understood as a struggle to impose modern means of production on a pre-modern society; modernization here involves the production of homogeneous abstract space and the attempt to paper over or incorporate heterogeneous and differential spaces and times.

The formation of a genuinely national communications network was a crucial part of this struggle. Until the late eighteenth century, British roads were not only laid out without any general plan; they were placed under the administration and care of local, rather than national, authorities.[41] Thus, it has been pointed out, "in a poor parish there would hardly be any trace of a road, while in a wealthy neighboring parish it would again reappear."[42] Many of these old roads were obliterated and replaced, in the new and more "rational" distribution of space produced by the Enclosure movement, by new roads, more carefully and deliberately planned, and above all integrated into a larger national communications network, which included roads and canals at first, and later railroads (whose arrival in the Lakes Wordsworth dreaded).[43]

Thus, alongside the Enclosure movement, we can place the turnpike movement, which was similarly legislated by Parliament, and financed the national development and administration of turnpikes and toll-roads (like the one where Wordsworth's Old Cumberland Beggar wanders) throughout Britain. Traversing these new roads, and beginning the long process of drawing the nation closer together – that is, genuinely making it into a nation, economically, socially, and politically, for transportation, after all, was the *only* means of communication, not only of goods and people, but of news, of fashions, of ideas – were the newest Flying coaches, the fast mail coaches, the stage coaches.[44] These dramatically reduced the "size" of Britain, so that, for instance, the time for the overland journey from London to Glasgow was in a few years cut from two weeks to 62 hours.[45] The first systematically produced maps of Great Britain, those of the Ordnance Survey (whose county maps formed interlocking elements in a national map), were not merely side-effects of this process, but were, rather, central elements in it.[46]

By subsuming local and regional markets and social structures into a larger national market, this process had a decisive political and economic impact. As John Barrell observes, "a good road-system would encourage every village to think of itself no longer as primarily concerned to grow its own food for its own needs, but as putting its agricultural produce into circulation, and thus as being more dependent on national prices and more part of the national economy."[47] And in turn the national communications network would bring goods from faraway places deep into the interior of Britain, so that previously exotic colonial goods such as tea, sugar, tobacco, and coffee gradually became mundane quotidian requirements. Previously isolated and autonomous zones would thus be drawn together into a network; previously isolated spaces would be brought into relation, and assembled into a flexible spatialized hierarchy, with peripheral and semi-peripheral political-economic zones feeding into the metropolitan center of this world-economy (London).

The expanding communications network enabled a gradual erosion of each particular area's sense of isolation by linking it to other regions, more often than not by articulating it as a peripheral zone in a larger economic framework. Barrell argues:

For a parish to have the maintenance of its own main road taken over by a [national] trust could well have meant that, whereas the road had been seen as serving primarily an internal need, to connect one part of the parish with another, it would now be seen mainly as connecting say one market-town to the north with another to the south, and would thus reduce the particular parish to the status of a landmark on this longer and more important journey. The parish would become less and less the centre of the area it saw around it, and more and more a part of an extended network of directions which had no centre except perhaps in the metropolis.[48]

London, the great metropolis, was indeed *the* center of Britain's national economy and its world-economy, whose relays and circuits of exchange fanned out from the city to the growing colonial network, as well as to the network of peripheral zones within the national economy itself.[49]

Even as the United Kingdom was being spatially unified during this period, even as some of its local spaces were being incorporated into larger regional and national zones, even as many spaces were losing their sense of place, were there not some spaces still cut off from this process – spaces which still clung, however surrounded and threatened, to their sense of place? This, at least, is the claim that Wordsworth makes in *An Evening Walk*: that even within an economic and social and political system through which space is divided in imaginary geography into centers, semi-peripheries, and peripheries, there are spaces which either resist such classification, or spaces which have not yet been colonized and articulated into such a system.

Fernand Braudel refers to such spaces as "neutral zones."[50] He suggests that zones of this kind "are not to be found exclusively in the really peripheral areas. They punctuate the central regions too, with local pockets of backwardness, a district or 'pays,' an isolated mountain valley or an area cut off from the main communications routes. All advanced economies have their 'black holes' outside world-time."[51] The concept of world-time is of crucial significance here, a reference to the waves and cycles of the capitalist market, which increasingly affected any zone connected to its growing world-economy, so that they would rise and fall together with the rhythmic swells and troughs of the market (homogeneous time, like homogeneous space, is far from being smooth; the structuring principle of its homogeneity is unevenness).

The notion of world-time also invokes the means of communication, which locked these different zones together into a more or less synchronized system, and through which the pulses of the market as well as political, social, cultural, and technological developments and news would be carried. A neutral zone, cut off from these ebbs and flows, would form an autonomous spatio-temporal enclave. To be cut off from the main communications routes, or even from the secondary and tertiary routes running through peripheral areas and linking them to the main arteries, would not only involve spatial isolation. It would also involve temporal isolation, being in contradiction with the temporal flows and movements articulating a particular economy into world-time, or in other words being out of synchrony with an otherwise more or less (and certainly increasingly) synchronized system – and its history. It is not that, cut off from world-time, such a zone would be ahistorical; it is, rather, that it would have its own temporal framework and rhythms, its own historical structures, its *own* history.

In Braudel's sense of the term, a neutral zone is an area lying outside the limits of the world-economy; though it is in the same sense understood as a zone of potential incorporation into that economy and into the sphere of a tendentially global modernity. As a unique zone, such a node of space-time would in other words be constituted against the outside world of modernization and development.

Such neutral zones assume great significance as they dwindle in number. That is, some of their social functions change over time. For instance, the very areas of Britain that Defoe found so horrible and ghastly in the 1720s because of their wildness became more and more socially significant in imaginary geography during the romantic period. These include most prominently the Lake District, but also the mountains of North Wales, and the Scottish Highlands – parts of Britain that remained backwaters, that still largely resisted production and cultivation, that resisted incorporation into the systems and structures of the world-economy and world-time – areas that increasingly became spatially identified as "natural."[52] Thus "Nature" comes to be seen as outside of history, or as defined against history. This idealist sense of Nature is at odds with the concept of natural history. I believe, however, that it is more productive to view Nature not as ahistorical, which is – not at all coincidentally – also how many colonized societies were viewed by their European colonizers, but rather as a spatial representation of a *different* history, one that was in imminent danger of being incorporated into the historical structure identified by Braudel's world-time, which is in this case the history of modernity and modernization.[53] This kind of neutral zone – Nature as a heterotopic space that resists[54] penetration by the modern – is thus defined as a pocket of the non-synchronic within a much larger and increasingly synchronized space-time of modernity.[55]

Such neutral zones are nevertheless socially produced, even if only by being circumscribed by what is more clearly socially practiced and inscribed space: that is, even if by negative identification. Understood in this spatial sense, Nature is "not a thing given direct from all eternity, remaining ever the same, but the product of industry and of the state of society."[56] The space of Nature is opposed to that of productively used landscape (e.g., fields, pastures, mines, orchards, fisheries) by its non-utility, by its "non-economic" status. Originally threatening, as for example seen by Defoe and other writers of the eighteenth century (and before), such space is gradually tamed, and ultimately, having been dominated, and defined precisely as that which is *not* useful, it is put to good use. In other words, Nature ceases to be recognized as a hostile power, and increasingly becomes an object for both production and consumption.⁵⁷ This definition of Nature is not only spatial: it is a constructed relational term, grounded in social and cultural contingency. Indeed, in order to see it as a heterotopic space, it is important to see the very concept of heterotopia as a relational term. That is to say, a "natural" space could involve anything from a small garden to a zoological park to an entire district; but what makes it "natural" is that it has been circumscribed and defined as such.⁵⁸ Perhaps the most striking instance of what I mean here is to be seen in the carefully planned English country house and its landscaped garden, which enjoyed an unprecedented boom both prior to and during the romantic period. For example, the country houses and gardens designed by John Nash and Humphry Repton, in contrast to those of Classical designers like Capability Brown, aspired to "a carefully arranged disorder," in which the house would be adapted to the "true character" of its "natural" background: a painstakingly planned out and physically and materially produced landscape.⁵⁹

Associated with this shift in the conceptualization of nature is a dramatic change in the notions of the picturesque and the sublime. The late eighteenth-century "movement of taste away from the landscape of Claude, the *paysage riant*, and towards the landscape of forests and mountains, was a movement from that which can be cultivated, to that which resists cultivation."⁶⁰ Without getting caught up in a discussion of beauty, however, I want to suggest that this movement at the very least marks a change in the conception of the non-human, or in other words of the Natural. Thus Nature became identified as a *place* to go to on tours, so that, as Williams observes, "the wild regions of mountain and forest were for the most part objects of conspicuous aesthetic consumption."⁶¹ The consumption of such aesthetic scenery could only be possible for the select few who possess an "elevated" sensibility, or in Wordsworth's terminology, for "Persons of taste, and feelings for Landscape."⁶² Indeed, such Nature-appreciation could not in this view be a pastime for the people as a whole. Wordsworth's horror at the prospect of a railway bringing hordes of workers from Lancaster and Manchester to the Lakes was due not only to his fear of the railway's disruption of the area's "character of seclusion and retirement." He argues that the contemplation of Nature is a solitary activity which only a few can appreciate, and that the great majority are incapable of stimulation by Natural objects:⁶³

Men as little advanced in the pleasure which such objects give to others are so far from being rare, that they may be said fairly to represent a large majority of mankind. This is a fact, and none but the deceiver and the willingly deceived can be offended by its being stated. But as a more susceptible taste is undoubtedly a great acquisition, and has been spreading among us for some years, the question is, what means are most likely to be beneficial in extending its operation? Surely that good is not to be obtained by transferring at once uneducated persons in large bodies to particular spots . . .

Wordsworth concludes that "the imperfectly educated classes are not likely to draw much good from rare visits to the lakes." His claim, however, is based as much on these specious arguments as on his fears of wrestling matches, horse and boat races "without number," and pot-houses and beer shops springing up in the District to accommodate the workers – entertainments which, he says, "might too easily be had elsewhere." Wordsworth's Nature, after all, allows escape and solace from the harsh realities of modernization.

VI

If we consider Nature in Wordsworth's poetry as a spot of time – a human potential for resistance to modernization – two questions are immediately raised and must be addressed. The first I have already touched on briefly. For the hidden bower of *An Evening Walk* can be considered a spot of time – indeed a synecdoche for Nature in a larger sense – because it is a space that the processes of modernization have hitherto been unable to penetrate, a space in which the social, the political, and the economic processes of modernization have been held in check, at least until the narrator's arrival there. And in this we come to one of the poem's profound narrative and formal antinomies. Although there is a recognition that, with the arrival there of the narrator, the retreat has been violated and hence opened up to social inscription and practice, there is a carefully encoded negation of this rupture; or, rather, the expression of a desire for the reversal – or at least the suspension – of the history of that discovery. If the scene of the retreat is constructed as a visual spectacle (in much the same way as so many bowers in Wordsworth's poetry) to be consumed by an isolated observer, then this process of consumption has to be related not merely to some "real" referent (this or that place in the Lake District). It has to be related to much larger, impinging, and contingent cultural practices, which can now be seen to have invaded and colonized the space of the retreat along with the narrator.

However, as we have seen, both in the narrative and in the form of the poem, the anti-modern space of the retreat is defined by the heterogeneous temporal structure of the spot of time; it has its own narrative time. The shift in time that takes place when the narrator enters the bower is a poetic figuration of a claim to ahistoricity. But if this is a claim to ahistoricity, it is also a claim to perpetuity. In other words, the enclave may be surrounded and threatened, but there is a subtle hope being expressed here, the expression of a desire for an everlasting and unchanging Nature, and hence for (an impossible) resilience against the history of modernization. This is a doomed desire, for the penetration of this particular bower has already taken place. The obscure retreat becomes a sacrifice ("a more benignant sacrifice"), since its incorporation into the history of modernity (its "evolution?") is rather a fall from innocence than a leap into "progress" in the Victorian sense.

Nature as a spot of time can only be revealed – that is, constituted as image – by being penetrated; and once it has been penetrated, it immediately loses its heterotopic status (is this why Wordsworth equates penetration of such bowers with violence, as in *Nutting?*). And yet, paradoxically, it is this potential loss (for the loss is poetically suspended, never actualized) that helps to constitute it as a heterotopic space. This kind of Nature cannot be mapped; for once it has been mapped it is no longer, "properly" speaking, Nature: it can only be offered as a *potential* space for the suspension of the historical processes and social practices of modernization.[64]

What is driving Wordsworth's nature poetry is not an interest in what Blake would call raw or "vegetable" nature as such, but rather his obsession with a new mode of vision and above all the new mode of subjectivity to which that vision is tied, a subjectivity that was unable to coalesce for him in the streets of London. The landscape is merely a catalyst here for his elaboration of this new mode of vision (which Blake for his part would call single vision), whose highest form is the sublime. What Wordsworth is elaborating here is a way of viewing and controlling the world: a new way of imagining and representing and even *producing* the whole world from the standpoint of a solitary observing subject.[65] This form of visuality is the mode of production of the bourgeois subject, who in turn is the key framing element – the primary ideological and cultural focal point, a cultural episteme of power – of the whole project of modern imperialism. Without such a focal point, modern imperialism simply would not have worked, or it would have taken what would be to us, its inheritors, an utterly unrecognizable form.

This brings us to the second question we must attend to. For Wordsworth produces heterotopic alternatives to or shelters from the world of modernity – spots of time – in his poetry in very much the same conceptual framework as the space-time from which he seeks to escape because it is so overwhelming. Indeed, the reason why the spot of time is "doomed" as a real alternative is precisely because it is framed in terms of the phenomenological and cognitive space of the bourgeois subject; it therefore offers no alternative at all to that form of subjectivity (although the spot of time does allow for a temporary relief from the barrage of commodities and spectacles that is so overwhelming and traumatizing to the subject).

The central contradiction here, then, is that Wordsworth seeks to construct resistance – or at least potential for resistance – to the abstract time and space of modernization on the very same epistemological grounds that modernization has itself produced and that he tries to escape from in running away from London. At the beginning of the previous chapter, I suggested that Wordsworth's flight from London to the spot of time (and to Nature) is a flight from the terror to the sublimity of individual consciousness. In either case, the conceptual paradigm of Wordsworth's poetry remains that of the individual consciousness, that of a mode of subjectivity which is perpetually (and perhaps even structurally) at odds with its conditions of existence. Ultimately, then, it is not so much the crushing triviality and deadly ordinariness of the commodity world, the barrage of spectacles, and modernization itself, that Wordsworth seeks to escape, but rather the constitutive terror of this consciousness. (Even though it does not bear on my analysis, I want to make one last thing perfectly clear: as far as I am concerned, Wordsworth was not an unwitting fool who ought to have known better than to leap out of the frying-pan and into the fire; on the contrary, he was, I believe, all too aware of these issues, and the contradiction of his simultaneous desire and terror is what drives his poetry and makes him one of the greatest writers of his age.)

What this suggests is that modernization generates a form of subjectivity that is not able to cope with or to understand the experience of the modern. In other words the phenomenological space-time of modernity is inhabited by subjects who are bound up with it dialectically (simultaneously constituted by it and constituting it in turn), and who are its necessary inhabitants, but who are at the same time fundamentally incommensurate with it. It is the terror of that very incommensurability that Wordsworth flees in fleeing London, searching for a mode of space-time outside or beyond the modern.

The question now is: what happens when a modern subject seeks out a non-modern world as an alternative to modernity? And the answer, of course, is that that subject will only ever find the modern all over again, because his conceptual/perceptual apparatus is hardwired for the framework of modern space-time; the only way to escape that framework is therefore to imagine not other spaces or times to flee to, but rather the opposite: to imagine other forms of subjectivity that will not require such constant attempts at escape to begin with.

CHAPTER 4

Waverley *and the cultural politics of dispossession*

> The clans retain little now of their original character, their ferocity of temper is softened, their military ardour is extinguished, their dignity of independence is depressed, their contempt of government subdued, and the reverence for their chiefs abated. Of what they had before the late conquest of their country, there remain only their language and their poverty.
>
> Samuel Johnson, *A Journey to the Western Islands of Scotland*

> Our geographers seem to be almost as much at a loss in the description of this north part of Scotland, as the Romans were to conquer it; and they are obliged to fill it up with hills and mountains, as they do the inner parts of Africa, with lions and elephants, for want of knowing what else to place there.
>
> Daniel Defoe, *A Tour Through the Whole Island of Great Britain*

I

It would be only a small exaggeration to say that the images that many of us associate with the Scottish Highlands have their origins in Walter Scott's first novel, *Waverley*. Scott started writing *Waverley* in 1805, though he dropped it for several years and only completed it in 1814. The novel, which is set mostly in Scotland during the Jacobite Rebellion of 1745, not only presented to its nineteenth-century readers a romanticized view of the Jacobite rebels and their leader; it offered, virtually for the first time, an altogether new series of images and representations of the Scottish Highlands. Beginning with *Waverley*, in other words, Sir Walter Scott's image of the Highlands has in cultural terms virtually taken over from and supplanted "the real thing," by which I mean something stronger than that Scott's representation has precluded other views of the Highlands.

For this raises the question, not simply of what that "real thing" was or is, but (rather) of how today's Highlands were brought into being *as* a

70

reality – or as a set of at once material and symbolic realities – at a certain specifiable moment in the violent cultural history of the United Kingdom. The questions that lie at the heart of my interest in *Waverley* are these: how is space, as a fluid and simultaneously material and political process, produced or re-produced during the process of colonial conquest? To what extent can the violent and productive process of colonialism be understood as *spatial* – as a process not merely involving the coding and recoding of conquered territories and peoples, but the virtual re-invention of the colonized territory as a space that can be put to use in various ways? If we do want to understand colonialism as a spatial operation, can we see the resistance to colonial rule in spatial terms, as an anti-hegemonic attempt either to limit or to contest the hegemonic territorializations undertaken in colonialism? The answers to these questions may depend on the extent of the spatial project undertaken in any given historical instance of colonization. But – even given that this may be a matter of degree or extent – what is for me the most urgent question here is this: what happens to a people, a history, a culture, that falls victim to a colonial project whose objective is not only to exploit its victims, but to dispossess them and claim *all* of their land in order to re-encode it, re-name it, to literally re-write it and re-invent it? What happens to the history of such a dispossessed people? And what, finally, are the relationships between the material processes of such spatial re-inventions and broader cultural processes? To what extent does symbolic production play a role in the socio-historical production of space? With these questions in mind, what I want to argue in the present chapter is that Scott's *Waverley* contributed not only to the invention of a new Highland reality, but also to the construction and colonization of a Highland past to go with it.

II

Although *Waverley* is an historical novel, it remains self-reflexive about its own (and its reader's) standpoint in the present and the future. It is "aware" of what is happening outside its own pages as it is being written, and it draws these events into itself, textualizing them and sometimes simultaneously re-writing the present as the past.[1] But, despite its obsession with the Highland past, and despite its many commentaries on the Lowland British present, it has virtually nothing to say about the Highlands of its own time.

The Highlands are blank spots on the novel's imaginary map of the present. They are blank not only because they are neither scene nor seen, but because they have been cleansed, drained of significance and signification. The novel's present-day Highlands have been emptied out, darkened, silenced, and written over as the space of the past. The events of the present, the terrain of the present, the people of the present – who were being cleared off their land and forced at bayonet-point either to bogs on the wild coasts of Ross and Sutherland or to the farthest reaches of the far-flung British empire – are neither heard, nor seen, nor is their presence registered. Their presence is, rather, almost entirely written off and written over in *Waverley*'s textual repression of the Highland present. The novel removes the people of the Highlands from its own pages and from its imaginary production of *their* space just as they were being removed in a more literal, concrete, material, and abjectly miserable way from their land, from their ancestral homes, from the glens of their clans, all of which were quickly being claimed, purged, and re-invented by politicians, by economists, by Lowland and English sheepfarmers, and by artists, poets, musicians, and writers, not least Sir Walter Scott himself.

What does it mean, though, to say that Walter Scott and *Waverley* participate in the history of the spatial reclamation of the Scottish Highlands? How can a work of fiction help to produce historical and geographical realities? The reclamation and reinvention of the Highlands took place in a number of simultaneously textual *and* contextual registers or discourses. The two overlapping and mutually-determining narrative fields that I am pointing to here are, on the one hand, the material re-production and re-utilization of the physical terrain of the Highlands during the Clearances; and, on the other, what we can call – by way of an *apposition* rather than an *opposition* to that process – the imaginary creation of a new Highland reality, a new history, a new series of images and associations, to cover over and replace the old ones as they were being literally wiped off the geophysical and cultural map of the United Kingdom. And it is in this register that I think *Waverley* can be usefully located, even though it defies any traditional encapsulation as a textual event distinct from a contextual "background."

Waverley claims the referentiality of the Highland present by laying claim to its past; that is, it claims the right to narrate and represent (or not to narrate, not to represent) its present by having narrated and represented its past. But this past is also the past of the Lowlands: the relationship of Highlands to Lowlands, as I will shortly suggest, is that of the past to the present. In other words, in its assertion of the new

national identity of Great Britain, the novel needs to associate a distinctly Scottish nationalism with the past, and hence it needs to translate
what it has so far identified as (invented) Highland "traditions" into,
more generally, *Scottish* "traditions." *Waverley*'s "postscript, which
should have been a preface," or in other words a present which has been
retrieved and saved from consignment to the past, is worth quoting at
length:

There is no European nation which, within the course of half a century, or little
more, has undergone so complete a change as this kingdom of Scotland. The
effects of the insurrection of 1745 – the destruction of the patriarchal power of
the Highland chiefs – the abolition of the heritable jurisdictions of the Lowland
nobility and barons – the total eradication of the Jacobite party, which, averse
to intermingle with the English, or adopt their customs, long continued to pride
themselves upon maintaining the ancient Scottish traditions and manners –
commenced this innovation. The gradual influx of wealth, and extension of
commerce, have since united to render the present people of Scotland a class of
beings as different from their grandfathers as the existing English are from
those of Queen Elizabeth's time. The political and economical effects of these
changes have been traced by Lord Selkirk with great accuracy. But the change,
though steadily and rapidly progressive, has, nevertheless, been gradual; and
like those who drift down the stream of a deep and smooth river, we are not
aware of the progress we have made, until we fix our eye on the now distant
point from which we have been drifted. – Such of the present generation who
can recollect the last twenty or twenty-five years of the eighteenth century, will
be fully sensible of the truth of this statement; – especially if their acquaintance
and connections lay among those who, in my younger time, were facetiously
called 'folks of the old leaven,' who still cherished a lingering, though hopeless,
attachment to the house of Stuart. This race has now almost entirely vanished
from the land, and with it, doubtless, much absurd political prejudice – but also
many living examples of singular and disinterested attachment to the principles
of loyalty which they received from their fathers, and of old Scottish faith,
hospitality, worth, and honour.[2]

The sense of urgency underlying the novel's postscript (or preface) is
derived from the imminent disappearance of the last vestiges of what the
novel identifies as the "ancient Scottish traditions and manners." The
eradication of these manners and customs is due, in the novel's scheme
of history, to "the gradual influx of wealth, and extension of commerce," and at the same time to the annihilation of the clan system in
the Highlands, as well as of the heritable jurisdictions of the border
regions' gentry. These developments, in turn, were enabled by the
victory of the Hanoverian state over the Jacobites of the Forty-Five, and
hence by the "total eradication of the Jacobite party." Thus, in the

novel's political and historical terminology, the eradication of the Highlands' social formation stands for the eradication of a now outmoded
Scottish national-historical bloc. And if the dying remnants of the previous social formation, exemplified by and embodied in the Jacobites, are
unwilling to mingle with the English, it is due not merely to their
retention of an archaic Scottish nationalism, but to the identification of
commerce and wealth – that is, modernity – with England and the
English. Here the narrator's own Scottishness is stretched to its limits;
but in comparing the development of "the present people of Scotland"
to that of the people of England since the time of Elizabeth, the narrator
is registering the fusion of the two nationalities into a new and emerging
nationalism, the newly invented "imagined community" of the United
Kingdom of Great Britain.3

The "modern people of Scotland," mingling and gradually fusing
with the English, are thus distinguished by the novel from those dying
holdovers from the days of Jacobitism, with their "old Scottish faith,
hospitality, worth, and honour," as well as their "absurd political
prejudice." The latter (especially the Highlanders) are unable to adapt
and to evolve: an evolution which is, nevertheless, experienced by the
former – the modern Scots – who can look back not only at the past, but
at the remnants of the past in the present, in order to see how much they
themselves have changed. Here the novel deploys, once again, a spatial
figuration for time: "the change, though steadily and rapidly progressive, has, nevertheless, been gradual; and like those who drift down the
stream of a deep and smooth river, we are not aware of the progress we
have made, until we fix our eye on the now distant point from which we
have been drifted." It is only through identifying a certain spatial
location with the past that "we," who are privileged to have "*been*
drifted*," can measure the temporal span of "our" drift by measuring the
distance between us and those who are not so privileged, or who are
incapable of "progress," however "gradual."

Waverley thus qualifies somewhat its earlier stance against modernization by granting it as a privilege rather than an inevitability. Its
spatialized metaphor of a river representing a "stream of time" anticipates both later nineteenth-century views of evolution as well as later
metaphorical uses of a river as the expression of slow and gradual, yet
inexorable, progress.4 Johannes Fabian has pointed out how this temporal scheme, codified through such new disciplines as anthropology,
lay at the heart of the Victorian colonial project, so that "all living
societies were irrevocably placed on a temporal slope, a stream of Time

– some upstream, others downstream. Civilization, evolution, development, acculturation, modernization (and their cousins, industrialization, urbanization) are all terms whose conceptual content derives, in
ways that can be specified, from evolutionary Time."[5] But if Scott's
novel invents this metaphor, it does so not by placing all societies on the
same "stream of time," as the post-Darwinian Victorian anthropologists
would do, but by placing some societies and individuals on the stream,
while leaving others fixed to the banks of the river, from which they
cannot move or progress – although "we" can measure "our" progress
by our growing distance from them. Such immobile and "ahistorical"
societies, and their remnants in the present, are thus reduced in this
historical evolutionary scheme to spatialized temporal reference points
for those capable of movement and progress. They remain as museum
pieces for the appreciation and self-comprehension of those who are
supposed to have left them behind.

The Highland past – and hence its present – are thus appropriated by
Waverley as the pre-history of the Scottish element of the British *jetztzeit*.
In being consigned to the pre-history of the (historical) "present people
of Scotland," the Highlanders and the vanishing remnants of the
"ancient" and Jacobite Scottish past are stripped of their own historicity, and left stranded on the banks of the river of Time. In other words,
their history, and hence their space, is colonized by the novel, it is taken
over and used for and by the Lowlander present. Indeed, what Hugh
Trevor-Roper and others have identified as the invention of Highland
"traditions" involved not only the "artificial creation of new traditions,
presented as ancient, original and distinctive," but also the process by
which these supposedly Highland traditions – the philabeg or kilt, the
bagpipes, the clan tartans – were offered to Lowland Scotland and
ultimately adopted by the Lowlanders as *their* own traditions.[6] What had
originally been devised as purely Highland traditions thus become
appropriated as the traditions of the whole Scottish nation, which the
Scots needed to wean themselves of in order to fully assimilate into the
Union with England; or, rather, which the Lowland Scots could keep as
the quaint museum-piece relics from their past, once they had been
disinfected and emptied of any political and nationalist content.[7]

The final subjugation of the Highlands, enabled, as the postscript
hints, by the results of the Forty-Five, took place at once in the military,
economic, and political pacification and colonization of the Highlands;
in the symbolic purification of the political content of supposedly Highland traditions – leaving only their emptied-out and hence reusable

forms; in the temporal colonization of the history of the Highlands; and
in the spatial colonization of the Highlands, that is, in the colonization of
the signifying and productive capacity of its imaginary terrain. Georg
Lukács has argued that Scott "was able to portray objectively the
ruination of past social formations, despite all his human sympathies for,
and artistic sensitivity to, the splendid, heroic qualities they contained.
Objectively, in a large historical and artistic sense; he saw at one and the
same time their outstanding qualities and the historical necessity of their
decline."[8] Yet Lukács, for all his claims of Scott's supposed "objectivity," is unable or unwilling to see that these supposedly "past" social
formations were not at all "past" in Scott's own time: that they were
being finally eradicated and destroyed only in the early nineteenth
century, and not – as *Waverley* pretends – immediately after 1745.

III

The aftermath of the 1745 Jacobite Rebellion did, however, establish the
historical pre-conditions for what happened later in the eighteenth
century, and on into the nineteenth. The great Highlands of western
and northern Scotland were, following the defeat of the clans at Culloden, opened up to a process of colonization. Immediately after Culloden, several acts of legislation were passed by the British Parliament to
facilitate the colonization of the Highlands, with particular reference to
the re-division of its space, which lay now under direct military rule.[9]
Thus the old feudal and clan property divisions and inscriptions were
erased as the Highlands were (spatially) literally, materially, politically,
economically, socially, and culturally redrawn and re-written, in a
manner often anticipatory of the Enclosure process in England, though
on a larger scale and usually through more brutal methods.[10] The
Highlands were looked upon as a wilderness requiring pacification and
improvement; as early as 1748, for instance, the Society for the Propaga-
tion of Christian Knowledge could say of the Highlanders that they
"were not quite civilized," and even that they were "wild and barbarous."[11] Indeed, the first acts of legislation designed to pacify the Highlands concerned not only directly political and military issues – such as
the disarmament of the clans (1747), the abolition of heritable jurisdictions (1747), and the confiscation of lands belonging to clans or to
Lowland gentry sympathetic to the Jacobites (1746) – but, all-important-
ly, cultural concerns. Thus, for instance, in a measure used very effectively during the subjugation of Wales and Ireland (not to mention India

and elsewhere), cultural forms such as the bagpipes and kilt were banned in 1747, as one of the provisions of the Disarmament Act (despite the fact that the kilt had only been invented in the 1720s – indeed, it was this act that suddenly justified the kilt's claims to cultural "authenticity," if not political potency).[12]

By the early 1780s, the Highlands had been sufficiently pacified for the ban on the kilt to be lifted (1782), and even for the confiscated Jacobite properties to be returned to their previous owners (1784), an event that *Waverley* anticipates by a few decades in the case of the Bradwardine estate. The basis of the Highland social structure – the clan system – had been destroyed by the disarming acts and the destruction of the old system of land tenure. Indeed, just as the British, following the trial of Warren Hastings, and through the Permanent Settlement Act of 1793, completely destroyed India's indigenous structure of land-ownership (by transforming the *zamindars* from revenue-collectors for the Mughal provincial governors to essentially private landlords in the capitalist sense), they destroyed the old Highland land-tenure system, replacing it with the legal and juridical structures of private property sustaining capitalism.[13]

Under the old system, the clan chief granted *tacks*, or leases, on the clan's property. These leases were held by his closest supporters, his tacksmen, who officered the clan "army" and recruited companies from their own subtenants; rents were paid in kind or in service. Having, with his clan, been disarmed, the chief no longer needed officers or fighters; and, the land having been transformed into his own private property, his clan ceased being his "people" in the feudal sense, and became tenants in the capitalist sense. Thus, as John Prebble argues, "having ceased to be a king in his own glens, having lost by Act of Parliament the power of 'pit and gallows' over the clan, he slowly realized that he needed paying tenants, not officers."[14] Not only were the clanspeople too impoverished to pay leases, but the returns that the landlord could gain from their subsistence economy were paltry compared to what returns would be made possible by large-scale "improvement," especially given the lucrative option of leasing land to English sheep-farmers.

Ultimately, sheep proved to be more profitable than the clanspeople. Under the authority of the new landlords, and enforced by the power of the state, the Highlanders were forced off their land in great Clearances that swept northern and western Scotland during the late eighteenth and early nineteenth centuries: up to a third of Scotland's population was thus uprooted and dispossessed.[15] Two of the earliest clearances, in 1782, involved land and people in Balnagowan and Glenquoich – both names that appear in altered form in *Waverley*, most notably in that Fergus MacIvor is the chief of *Glennaquoich*. The first large-scale clearance, however, took place in 1784, on the lands of Alistair Macdonnell of Glengarry, a close friend of Sir Walter Scott, and, with the Duchess of Sutherland, one of the most zealous "improvers," and – with cruel and bitter irony – the founder of the so-called Society of True Highlanders.[16] The Clearances, justified by a discourse of "improvement," then accelerated through 1792 – during which, in what proved to be the last major act of Highland resistance, the people of Ross revolted, and drove the Lowland and English Cheviot sheep off their land, until the local landlords brought in the 47th Regiment of the Black Watch and suppressed them – and on to 1814, by which time the Clearances had reached full pitch, and during which people were literally burned out of their homes by order of the Duchess of Sutherland (also a friend of Scott).

This person, who had been well instructed in economics, resolved, when she succeeded to the headship of the clan, to undertake a radical economic cure, and to turn the whole county of Sutherland, the population of which had already been reduced to 15,000 by similar processes, into a sheep-walk. Between 1814 and 1820 these 15,000 inhabitants, about 3,000 families, were systematically hunted and rooted out. All their villages were destroyed and burnt, all their fields turned into pasturage. British soldiers [actually they were Irishmen of the 21st Foot Regiment, still bitter at the the participation of Sutherland troops in the suppression of the 1798 revolt in Ireland![17]] enforced this mass of evictions, and came to blows with the inhabitants. One old woman was burnt to death in the flames of the hut she refused to leave [she was, according to witnesses, too weak to leave, and none of her family was present to save her[18]]. It was in this manner that this fine lady appropriated 794,000 acres of land which had belonged to the clan from time immemorial.[19]

Unlike the Enclosure movement in England, however, the Highland Clearances were justified not only by an ideology of improvement, but by a discourse of colonialism, in whose terms the victims of the Clearances – the Highlanders – could only be capable of "improvement" once their old way of life had been annihilated; or, in other words, once their space had been cleansed of its otherness and absorbed into the world-system of the British empire, once the Highlands had ceased being a neutral zone and had been locked into this economy as a subdued peripheral region.[20]

In addition, the Highlands' cultural associations with Ireland had to be entirely purged before their de facto union with Britain could be achieved. Indeed, an observer of the Highlands' colonial transformation in the wake of Culloden wrote in 1746:

It is remarkable that, in some districts bordering upon the Highlands, where within memory the inhabitants spoke the Irish language, wore the Highland dress, and were accustomed to make use of Arms, upon the accidental [*sic!*] introduction of industry, the Irish language and Highland dress gave way to a sort of English, and lowland Cloathing; the Inhabitants took to the Plough in place of Weapons; and, tho' disarmed by no Act of Parliament, are as tame as their Low Country neighbours.[21]

At a certain political level, the subjugation and colonization of the Highlands represented not only the conquest of a previously wild and unruly revolutionary zone, but also the reclamation of this zone from the cultural influence of Ireland, or in other words a cultural revolt against Ireland. Hugh Trevor-Roper notes that, from at least the fifth century onwards, western Scotland was "always linked rather to Ireland than to the Saxon Lowlands," and even that the Scottish Highlands were, culturally, politically, and linguistically, long seen as a colony of Ireland.[22] In other words, the Highlands had been one of those spaces referred to by Blake as the "spaces of Erin."[23] The colonization of the Highlands involved not only the appropriation of their territory (both material and symbolic), but the draining-away of their Irish influence, through which what had been culturally a virtual part of Ireland was purged of its Irishness.

To this extent, the British colonization of the Highlands, and their political and cultural annexation after 1745 (only in name had they become part of Great Britain following the 1707 Union of Scotland and England), anticipated the official annexation of Ireland itself some fifty years later. *Waverley*'s re-emplotment of the rise and fall of the 1745 Jacobite Rebellion, and ultimately its claim on the Highlands, is in this sense not only a symbolic re-enactment of the demise of Ireland after 1800, but a spatialized allegory of the colonization of a space of Irishness both outside and inside Ireland "proper."[24]

Beaten, subdued, and ultimately colonized, the Highlands became a site not only for the rehearsal of the multitudinous practices of "improvement," which would become more general throughout Britain in the nineteenth century, but also a site for the rehearsal of Britain's larger colonial project: an imaginary zone in which the spatial processes of

colonial penetration and development were practiced on a small scale
before being brought to bear on much of Africa and Asia. The languages of improvement and of colonization are brought together by the
man directly responsible for the Sutherland Clearances, James Loch, in
the conclusion to his *Account of the Improvements on the Estates of the Marquess
of Stafford*:[25]

> *First*: Nothing could be more at variance with the general interests of society
> and the individual happiness of the people themselves than the original state of
> Highland manners and customs.
> *Second*: The adoption of the new system, by which the mountainous districts
> are converted into sheep pastures, even if it should unfortunately occasion the
> emigration of some individuals is, upon the whole, advantageous to the nation
> at large.
> *Third*: The introduction of sheep farms is perfectly compatible with retaining
> the ancient populations in the country.
> *Fourth*: The effect of this change is most advantageous to the people them-
> selves; relieving them from personal services, improving their industrious
> habits, and tending directly to their rapid increase and improvement.
> *Lastly*: The improvements . . . have had constantly for their object the
> employment, the comfort, the happiness of every individual who has been the
> object of removal; and that there is no single instance of any man having left
> this country on account of his not having had a lot provided for him; and that
> those who have gone have been induced to do so by the persuasion of others,
> and not from themselves, and that in point of numbers they are most insignifi-
> cant.

The improvement offered by the Clearances, in other words, is offered
not only for the land and its owners, but for the people being cleared off
the land. Using the same proto-evolutionary and utilitarian language
that was would also be used to justify the colonization of India (particularly after 1813), improvers like Loch were arguing that the people could
be transformed and improved through the transformation and improvement of their space. This is (partly) why Michael Hechter and others
have insisted that "the incorporation of the Celtic Periphery into England can, with the partial exception of Cornwall, be seen to be imperial
in nature, rather than national."[26]

   Waverley does not so much re-order the various historical "narratives"
surrounding the Clearances as suppress them, partly by using a discourse of nationalism to describe a colonial process (as in the Postscript),
and partly by writing over the Clearances in drawing blank its imaginary map of the Highland present.[27] Yet references to the Highland
present do leak out of the novel's politicized unconscious. It uses the

same Malthusian language to describe the Highlands' overpopulation as was being used to justify the Clearances, and it contains dark hints as to what would happen to the Highlands after the failure of the Forty-Five. The Disarmament Act enters the narrative, as do the abolition of heritable jurisdictions and the confiscation of property – all of which were instrumental to the Clearances – only in reference to Tully-Veolan, and the novel carefully isolates these issues from the Highlands "proper" as they fade from view. However, Fergus MacIvor's dying wish to Edward is that he take care of the clan in their time of need; and the novel mentions that Edward "amply redeemed" his pledge, which can only mean that the clan must have desperately needed his help, for which the memory of his name lives on – not in the minds of the clanspeople, but in "their glens."

IV

Having arrived at the border of the Scottish Highlands, Edward Waverley arrives at a symbolic border dividing one world from another, and one epoch from what is posited as the next. The village of Tully-Veolan, and with it the great estate of the Baron of Bradwardine, lies in the shadow of the Highlands, which during Edward's approach "had appeared a blue outline in the horizon, but now swelled into huge gigantic masses, which frowned defiance over the more level country that lay beneath them."[28] As Edward enters the village, he becomes increasingly aware of the proximity of the border, and of the fantastic charge that this proximity carries with it, and his forward movement in space seems to take him ever backwards in time. "The houses seemed miserable in the extreme, especially to an eye accustomed to the smiling neatness of English cottages. They stood, without any respect for regularity, on each side of a straggling kind of unpaved street, where children, almost in a primitive state of nakedness, lay sprawling, as if to be crushed by the hoofs of the first passing horse."[29] The frowning mountains pose a limit to this movement in time, just as they do to movement in space: a limit that the novel posits only in order for it to be transcended, as Waverley leaps beyond it and into a space of cultural otherness. For this border is also one between cultures and nations, and although even here on *this* side of the border there prevails a sense of poverty, wretchedness, and "backwardness," we are still on the firm ground of the knowable, a ground symbolically defended from the predatory attacks of Highland raiders by the loopholes and arrowslits of

the baronial estate. Beyond the dim line of the mountains, however, not
even the awkward and broken English of the border region is spoken,
and if the Lowlanders of the border resemble Italians and the folk "of
Minerva," the people beyond are scarcely assimilable to such reassuring
European (even southern European) standards.

Edward Waverley is, of course, immediately tempted to venture into
the unknown. And, as if in answer to Edward's inquiry "whether it was
possible to make with safety an excursion into the neighbouring Highlands, whose dusky barrier of mountains had already excited his wish to
penetrate beyond them," Evan Dhu Maccombich makes his appearance: the first appearance, indeed, of a Highlander in the novel.

. . . the door suddenly opened, and, ushered in by Saunders Saunderson, a
Highlander, fully armed and equipped, entered the apartment. Had it not been
that Saunders acted the part of the master of ceremonies to this martial
apparition, without appearing to deviate from his usual composure, and that
neither Mr Bradwardine nor Rose exhibited any emotion, Edward would
certainly have thought the intrusion hostile. As it was, he started at the sight of
what he had not yet happened to see, a mountaineer in his full national
costume. The individual Gael was a stout, dark young man, of low stature, the
ample folds of whose plaid added to the appearance of strength which his
person exhibited. The short kilt, or petticoat, showed his sinewy and clean-
made limbs; the goatskin purse, flanked by the usual defences, a dirk and a
steel-wrought pistol, hung before him; his bonnet had a short feather, which
indicated his claim to be treated as a Duinhé-wassel, or sort of gentleman; a
broadsword hung upon his shoulder, and a long Spanish fowling-piece occupied one of his hands.

Evan Dhu serves as Waverley's (i.e., the novel's as well as the character's) guide into the Highlands and into the imaginary terrain of the
past. With his strength and rugged features, his air of indomitability, and
above all the latent violence expressed through his layers of weaponry
("the usual defences"), he appears here as a representative figure: more
than a spokesman, he is a personification of the Highlands. His "claim"
to be treated as a "sort of gentleman," a claim which in the narrator's
view is clearly misplaced, is really backed up not by the feather in his
bonnet, but by his broadsword and rifle. And while his "national
costume" makes him a fit national representative, the novel establishes
the represented nationality not as British, nor even as Scottish, but as
Highlander ("mountaineer") and Gaelic.

Thus, the novel re-launches itself and begins anew, as Waverley
leaves behind the relative safety of Tully-Veolan and pushes into the

vast and rugged Highlands of Scotland. When Waverley awakens on his first full day in the mountains, in the cave of the robber Donald Bean Lean, he emerges to find himself on the "wild and precipitous shores of a Highland loch, about four miles in length, and a mile and a half across, surrounded by heathy and savage mountains, on the crests of which the morning mist was still sleeping."[30] His Lowlander and English standards of measurement cannot mean much here, though, and rather than assimilating the surroundings, such standards are overwhelmed by the "heathy" – which suggests both *heathen* and *healthy* – savagery of the mountains. In his tour, Waverley appropriates the rugged landscape of the Scottish Highlands. But Waverley is an Englishman, a gentleman and an officer in the service of the Hanoverian king, intruding on the Jacobite and Gaelic heartland of Scotland; thus, as James Kerr points out, Waverley's tourism "is not a politically innocent activity."[31]

The novel begins to "slip" in between its invented background of landscape and its equally invented (i.e., produced rather than reproduced) background of Highland Nature, culture, and society. Earlier, while pausing in the border region before entering the Highlands, the narrator tells us that the Lowland borderers – the people themselves – somewhat "resembled Italian forms of *landscape*."[32] Once the novel has gained the fastnesses of the Highlanders, particularly the domain of clan Vich Ian Vohr, distinctions between natives and landscape collapse altogether, and Waverley begins to consume the culture and activity of the Highlanders just as he had already consumed their landscape. In other words, people and land are reduced not only to one another, but to the level of aesthetic objects to be taken in and consumed by the eager eye of the "tourist": the character, the narrator – and the reader.[33] It is an alienated consumption, however; and just as Waverley can appreciate the wildness of the Highland scenery only to the extent that he is charmed by (or afraid of) it, he can enjoy the great clan feast and other cultural events only to the extent that he feels a revulsion from them and from the clansmen themselves.[34]

While sitting on the banks of the loch outside Bean Lean's lair, Edward finds himself reflecting on his romantic situation, sitting "on the banks of an unknown lake, under the guidance of a wild native, whose language was unknown to him, on a visit to the den of some renowned outlaw."[35] Indeed, just as *Waverley* had established a comparison – as if to establish points of reference for the reader – between the Lowland borderers and Greeks and Italians, the novel continually compares the Highlanders not just to their "wild" surroundings, but to the natives of

Africa and America, India, and the Orient.[36] The narrator reinforces
this comparison, on the one hand by repeatedly denying that his is
anything like an Oriental tale:

Mine is an humble English post-chaise, drawn upon four wheels, and keeping
his Majesty's highway. Such as dislike the vehicle may leave it at the next halt,
and wait for the conveyance of Prince Hussein's tapestry, or Malek the
Weaver's flying sentry-box.[37]

On the other hand, however, the novel repeatedly dredges up Oriental
and Orientalist allusions, including a passing reference to Flora in her
capacity as a "dragoman" (the corrupted English version of the Arabic
word for an interpreter and guide for foreigners in the Arab lands of
southwest Asia) as she interprets the Gaelic language and folklore of the
Highlands for Waverley – and for the reader.[38] The cumbersome notes
about the Highlands and Scotland, as well as those addressing the
history of the 1745 Jacobite Rebellion, add to the novel's exaggerated
exoticism, in the same way as the notes to an Oriental tale amplify not
only its own variety of the exotic, but also its claims to authenticity.[39]

Edward Waverley's tour of the imaginary terrain of the Highlands
also involves a kind of time-traveling, in which the movement from
Lowlands to Highlands is a movement back in time (so that, with his
contrary movement, Evan Dhu appears in Tully-Veolan as little short of
a ghost from the past, just as the *cateran* raids on the Lowlands are like
vestigial hauntings from bygone days). In other words, the novel's leap
into the Highlands of "sixty years since" – expressed in spatialized terms
as an incursion into the Jacobite and Gaelic heartland – is also registered
as an imaginary leap "backwards" in time to the space of a previous
epoch. Just as the novel, then, is a spatialized "reclamation" of the
imaginary terrain of the Highlands, it also reclaims the past, through
inventing "authentic" Highland cultures and traditions. Here, however,
Scott's novel is caught up in the various movements in late eighteenth-
and early nineteenth-century Scotland literally to invent the traditions
of a mythic Highland "past." Indeed, Scott, a founding president of the
Celtic Society of Edinburgh, was a major figure in these movements,
which included Macpherson's Ossian (who has a Welsh equivalent in
Iolo Morganwg), and also the creation of "traditional" patterned clan
tartans and kilts (these were first developed – by an Englishman – in the
1720s, and firmly established only *after* the 1745 Rebellion).[40]

v

The imaginary map that underlies and sustains Waverley's tour – the "ground" on which the narrative is written, and towards which all referentiality is directed – involves the simultaneous creation and re-presentation of an imaginary terrain. It has been argued that, "whatever fictional gloss may be applied, when he is writing of Scotland, and especially of his own Border region, Scott is recording, not inventing; his vision grows out of an objective world, a place of time and the senses."[41] On the contrary, however, the novel's complex and fluid architectonic of space simultaneously constructs *and* presupposes its own conditions of existence. It does so, in the first instance, by positing a rigid dualistic structure of space, through which the narrative is channeled. This involves an opposition between the Highlands, on the one hand, and the Lowlands and England on the other. The Highlands–Lowlands opposi-tion enables (and simultaneously rests upon) a matrix of other essential-izing dualisms: thus, superimposed on this dualistic structure is an opposition between the fanciful and the realistic, the wild and the tame, the unknown and the known, the threatening and the reassuring, the turbulent and the level, the violent and the peaceful, the noble and the mundane, the heroic and the quotidian, the youthful and the mature. Other historical, symbolic, and political dualisms are similarly in-scribed: feudal against modern; myth against Enlightenment; Jacobite against Hanoverian; revolutionary against counter-revolutionary; Cath-olic against Protestant; sympathies with France against anti-French sentiment; anti-Unionist against Unionist.

Waverley's map of Scotland is also a map of time, for the opposition between Highlands and Lowlands is temporally and historically coded as an opposition between past and present. That is, the novel's Highland space does not just open up into the past, and into the archaic trappings and rituals of (an invented) tradition; it is the spatialization of the past and of this tradition. At the same time, it is the temporalization of the Highlands, registering, merging, coupling, linking, relentlessly ident-ifying the Highlands with the past. *Waverley*'s Highland space is, indeed, a Wordsworthian "spot of time." It is a *fluid* spot of time, one that can extend itself like an amoeba to enwrap and claim other areas; and one that can, conversely, be beaten back so that it can lose its hold over areas that it had once held firmly in its grip.

Written retrospectively from the standpoint of the narrative's future (i.e., Scott's present), the novel maps out the Highlands as a space that

was once unknown, that *was once* feudalistic, that *was once* violent, romantic, wild, inhabited by myth; the Highlands are reduced to a turbulent,
but, for Scott, colorful and attractive albeit dangerous past, associated
with the Jacobites, with feudalism, masculinity, backwardness, a hierarchical class-structure, Catholicism, and of course anti-Unionism. On
the other hand, *Waverley* presents the identity of the Lowlands as true
and valid not only for the past, but for the present as well as for the
future.[42] The Lowlands plus England – in other words, the modernizing
core of Great Britain as opposed to the Celtic peripheries – are thus
situated and constructed as the spaces that *were then, still are, and will forever
be* peaceful, rational, scientific, enlightened, known, and civilized; this
civilizational core, in other words, is associated with Protestantism,
progress, rationality, Unionism, capitalism, a (slightly more) fluid notion
of class-mobility, and finally with what is for Scott a supremely necessary
but nevertheless uninspiring and even boring "feminine" domesticity.
Coextensive with the overarching *spatial* opposition between Highlands
and Lowlands is an overarching *temporal* opposition between past and
present.[43]

The novel's map of space and time is supplemented with characters
who serve as markers of the map's coordinates. Each character, with the
exception of Edward Waverley, stakes out, marks, and defends a certain
slice of the novel's symbolic terrain, and hence a certain political, social,
temporal, and historical position.[44] Edward is the exception; he alone
can move through and between the novel's variegated terrains and
territories: he is the explorer, the adventurer, the traveler who in his
movements ties these symbolic territories together; for as other characters move, they necessarily stake out new terrain, so that the novel's
imaginary map moves with them. Edward – the lone hero, the monadic
traveler – is the only character who has neither a territorial identification nor a territorial limitation. The other characters are spread out in
association with the territorial identifications allowed for by the imaginary map's dualistic epistemology, with the two extreme positions being
held by Fergus MacIvor, on the one hand, and Colonel Talbot, on the
other.

Talbot is the voice of the present. An officer and a gentleman, an
Englishman, a Unionist, a Hanoverian, his territorial identification is
with the Lowlands and England. His position is solidly reinforced,
justified, validated, and relentlessly proved correct by the narrator and
the narrative, for Talbot does not just speak for rationality, progress,
Englishness, justice (he "reminds" us all that "of all nations, the English

are least bloodthirsty by nature"[45]), as well, of course, for the unity of the kingdom and nation. He speaks for what is correct and logical for and in the novel's own present: a correctness and logic inevitably validated by *Waverley's* retrospective narration, so that his "prophecies" are by definition "self-fulfilling." Talbot is instrumental in showing Waverley the hopelessness of his situation as a Jacobite, and in providing help for his escape: an escape which the novel, as a prototypical *Bildungsroman*, defines as growth and maturity that are themselves enabled by Talbot's interventions.[46] But he is also the signpost for and spokesman of the present and the future; his pronouncements on and judgments of the Highlands, Fergus, the Jacobites, the Baron, and the future of the United Kingdom are indistinguishable from the judgments and pronouncements of the narrator himself.[47]

At the other pole of this opposition stands Fergus MacIvor. Despite his Parisian upbringing, "few men," we are told, "were more attached to ideas of chieftainship and feudal power" than Fergus MacIvor, Chief of the Clan of Ivor, Vich Ian Vohr.[48] Indeed, his education has not changed his essential quality as a Highland *laird*, nor, in the novel's terms, could it have. Instead, for the most part it merely adds a gloss, a fine veneer that at first makes Fergus more "palatable" as a character, although it gradually and subtly undermines his position by reinforcing the notion that no amount of Continental education and manners could improve upon his stubbornly and immutably Highland mentality and physiognomy. Fergus is a perfect specimen of the species, plucked from what the narrator identifies as an ideal historical moment:

Had Fergus MacIvor lived Sixty Years sooner than he did, he would, in all probability, have wanted the polished manner and knowledge of the world which he now possessed; and had he lived Sixty Years later, his ambition and love of rule would have lacked the fuel which his situation now afforded. He was, indeed, within his little circle, as perfect a politician as Castruccio Castrucani himself. He applied himself with great earnestness to appease all the feuds and dissensions which often arose among other clans in his neighbourhood, so that he became a frequent umpire in their quarrels. His own patriarchal power he strengthened at every expense which his fortune would permit, and indeed stretched his means to the uttermost, to maintain the rude and plentiful hospitality, which was the most valued attribute of a chieftain. For the same reason, he crowded his estate with a tenantry, hardy indeed, and fit for the purposes of war, but greatly outnumbering what the soil was calculated to maintain.[49]

Found neither "Sixty Years" too soon nor too late, then, Fergus is the

perfect embodiment not only of the Highland *laird*, but of the precise
moment of the novel's historical setting "Sixty Years" since, or in other
words 1745: one of the many crucial turning-points for the history of
Britain, and perhaps *the* crucial moment in the history of the Highlands.
(As the description of the clan makes clear with its ominous Malthusian
language of population and resources, there are "too many" people for
"too little" land; the events of 1745, which are chronicled by the novel,
laid the historical pre-conditions for the events which were clearing the
Highlanders off their land as Scott was writing his novel.) Fergus, of
whom the narrator confides that "we should term him the model of a
Highland Chieftain," represents, like the Highland space which he
personifies, the past.[50] That is, just as he speaks for the Highlands,
identifies the standpoints and positions of the Highlands (with its myths
and legends, its romanticism and feudalism, its violence and instability,
its Jacobitism and revolutionism) and defends the Highlands, he speaks
for, identifies and defends the hopelessly beleaguered past spatialized in
and through the Highlands.

Waverley thus territorializes its political, historical, temporal, and
chronological oppositions and dualisms, inscribing them onto its imaginary dualistic map of Highlands and Lowlands. As I have already
suggested, however, the novel's Highland space is fluid: it and its
associations are capable of movement out of and away from the Highlands "properly" speaking – just as, ultimately, the Highlands can be
purged of these associations. In these terms, the Jacobite Rebellion of
1745 figures in the novel as an irruption of this imaginary Highland
space into the imaginary space of the Lowlands and England; or, put
differently, it is an irruption of the past into the present of industrializing
bourgeois Britain: both spatially, in the Highlanders' brief incursion into
the Lowlands and down into England as far as Derby; and textually, in
their arrival, through the novel, into the world of 1814 Scotland (or,
"Sixty Years" later . . .).

VI

The army and followers of Prince Charles Edward Stuart thus storm
into *Waverley*'s Lowlands like a horde of ghosts issuing forth from the
past. The novel emplots the rise and fall of the final Jacobite Rebellion of
1745 "as it actually happened" sixty years previously (although it sometimes restricts historical events to the background in its emplotment of
the events of the Rebellion into a diachronic "story.")[51] The rebellion's

vague beginning in the Highlands, where the Prince had landed with a force of half a dozen men, is transcoded into the novel in equally vague and uncertain terms.[52] It moves quickly from being a barely "audible" background murmur – with the passing glimpse at strange movements and gatherings of people, of horses, of weapons – to the highest pitch of an attempted revolution, into which the novel's characters, including its distincly English hero, Edward Waverley, are suddenly drawn. By the time Edward has joined the movement, however, the Jacobites have already taken over cosmopolitan Edinburgh, and are planning their future campaigns from there. After winning the important battle at Prestonpans (or Gladsmuir), they collect themselves and begin the long march to London, reaching as far south as Derby. Suddenly the tide begins to turn, and just as the novel tracks the beginning of the revolt in a sudden switch in tempo, it transcodes the movement's demise in the same terms. The withdrawal back to the Highlands – against the wishes and counsels of many, including Fergus – takes place very quickly, and soon the Jacobite army, its morale having collapsed, is in full retreat, thinning and dissolving as it breaks up during the march back north. Finally, the rearguard, including Edward himself, are caught up by the forward dragoons of the British army and scattered in a skirmish near Clifton. Thus Edward is once again isolated from the full movement of "history," which recedes into the background whence it had issued. Indeed, the Jacobite rebellion ends as it had begun – in the novel's background. The news from faraway Culloden[53] enters the narrative and reaches Edward only as disembodied information.

Until its final annihilation at Culloden, whatever terrain is held by the Jacobite army under Prince Charles during its doomed campaign in *Waverley* is quickly invested with the spatial forces and assemblages of the Highlands. Colonized by Highland rituals, feasts, dancing, and singing, and of course by the Highland army itself, such territories effectively *become* Highland space (space understood, of course, not as an inert material given, but as a fluid political process). In other words, places reclaimed by Jacobitism, as a political movement in support of an absolute monarchic line whose "rights" had been "usurped" by the modernizing forces of nascent parliamentary democracy after 1688, are effectively reclaimed as sites of tradition and feudalism, and are overlaid with rituals harking back to a mythic Highland past.[54]

When Edward first meets Prince Charles, in the palace at Edinburgh, the palace has been reactivated as a site of traditionalism, as if the past had been brought back to life in the dreams of the present – or, rather, as if the past had been reborn as a spatial enclave, a violent spatial irruption into the present.[55] Indeed, the feudal ritual of homage to the Prince performed by the Baron of Bradwardine – and ridiculed by the novel in a chapter entitled "rather unimportant" – is presented precisely as the re-emergence of the past in the present. The only account of the ritual is in a Gazetteer which is "quoted" by the novel: "'Since that fatal treaty [i.e., the 1707 Act of Union] which annihilates Scotland as an independent nation, it has not been our happiness to see her princes receive, and her nobles discharge, those acts of feudal homage, which, founded upon the splendid actions of Scottish valour, recall the memory of her early history, with the manly and chivalrous simplicity of the ties which united to the Crown the homage of the warriors by whom it was repeatedly upheld and defended. But on the evening of the 20th, our memories were refreshed with one of those ceremonies which belong to the ancient days of Scotland's glory . . .'"[56]

Apart from these charmingly archaic rituals, which are confined to the nobles in the palace, it is the presence of the Jacobite army in Edinburgh that profoundly enforces the Highland *territorialization* of Lowland space. The army's encampment is repeatedly described from the vantage point of "present-day" Edinburgh, as though it were being superimposed on an 1814 map of the city; or as though the novel's imaginary spatial flows could invade and even occupy the space of the present, thus militarily occupying 1814 Edinburgh by claiming a certain space on its imaginary map.[57] The Highland army's appearance in the Edinburgh of 1745 is described as though a Highland host were actually descending on the Edinburgh of Scott's own time – that is, as the ghostly apparitions of the "primitive" existence of the past. Indeed, it is above all the army that represents the irruption of the past into the present, for, apart from the vanguard (made up of the sympathetic Lowland-Jacobite gentry's tiny cavalry) it is overwhelmingly composed of "the common peasantry of the Highlands":

Here was a pole-axe, there a sword without a scabbard; here a gun without a lock, there a scythe set straight upon a pole; and some had only their dirks, and bludgeons or stakes pulled out of hedges. The grim, uncombed and wild appearance of these men, most of whom gazed with all the admiration of ignorance upon the most ordinary production of domestic art, created surprise in the Lowlands, but it also created terror. So little was the condition of the Highlands known at that late period, that the character and appearance of their population, while thus sallying forth as military adventurers, conveyed to the south-country Lowlanders as much surprise as if an invasion of African Ne-groes or Esquimaux Indians had issued forth from the northern mountains of their own native country. It cannot therefore be wondered if Waverley, who had hitherto judged of the Highlanders generally from the samples which the policy of Fergus had from time to time exhibited, should have felt damped and astonished at the daring attempt of a body not then exceeding four thousand men, and of whom not above half the number, at the utmost, were armed, to change the fate, and alter the dynasty, of the British kingdoms.[58]

This Highland *levée en masse*, this army of the people, effectively brings the people of the Highlands (in Scott's own time a people being burned off their land and scattered to the winds) into a direct and terrifying confrontation with the people of Edinburgh. This encounter takes place at two simultaneous spatio-temporal levels; for it is a confrontation between the Highland Jacobites and Lowland Hanoverians of 1745, but also symbolically between the forgotten Highlanders of the early nineteenth century and the Lowlanders trying to forget them. It is also, fundamentally, a confrontation between two different social formations (so that the Highlanders can be compared to Eskimos and Africans), and indeed the confrontation between the two armies at Gladsmuir is described as a confrontation between the "primitive" and the modern, "each admirably trained in its own peculiar mode of war."[59] Thus the disorganized and "primitive" Highland *levée* is pitched against the well-equipped British army, with its rationalized detachments and regiments, its squadrons and dragoons, its lines of battle, its artillery and infantry. The battle itself is quite brief, and the clans overwhelm the British army:

> The English infantry, trained in the wars in Flanders, stood their ground with great courage. But their extended files were pierced and broken in many places by the close masses of the clans; and in the personal struggle which ensued, the nature of the Highlanders' weapons, and their extraordinary fierceness and activity, gave them a decided superiority over those who had been accustomed to trust to their array and discipline, and felt that the one was broken and the other useless.[60]

The Highlanders' success is of course only temporary, and they are ultimately beaten back into the dark recesses of history in *Waverley*'s background, so that their temporary irruption into the space of the present is contained and even reversed. The past is thus exorcized from the present.

VII

Just as the irruption of the Highlands is spatialized in *Waverley*, this exorcism is also expressed in spatial terms, first as the containment of the irruption of the Highlanders into the Lowlands, and then as the political, military, economic, and symbolic colonization and pacification of the Highlands themselves. Historically, and at the "overtly" political level, this process involved the containment of the Jacobite rebellion, and ultimately the Hanoverian victory at Culloden, where Prince Charles's forces were finally vanquished in April of 1746, and with them whatever hopes the Highland people may have had in the Jacobite movement.[61] But this process in *Waverley* involves more than the Hanoverian reclamation of the Jacobite territories, which in any case – from the Highlands and Edinburgh south to Derby – are quickly recaptured by the forces of the (Hanoverian) state. Rather, expressed *through* this spatialized movement over the novel's imaginary terrain, there is the symbolic "resolution" of the dualistic structure underlying *Waverley*.

Thus, inscribed in the containment and then the rollback of the Highland space, there is not only the victory of Hanoverian over Jacobite, but also the modern over the feudal, the civilized over the wild, the counter-revolutionary over the revolutionary, the "feminine" do-mestic over the "masculine" adventurous, and so forth – including the victory of the present over the past. In other words, the defeat of the Jacobite Rebellion is expressed spatially in the shift of the symbolic border between Highlands and Lowlands. If *Waverley* is an historical narrative, it narrates history through spatializing it, or rather through producing historically inscribed space as a "background" upon which the novel's own narration and plot can take place: a background inscribed with a version of history which it has itself written. *Waverley* thus produces its own historical "context."[62] The novel's spatial move-ments are historical flows channeled through an imaginary terrain of its own construction.

In constructing its historical and imaginary-geographical back-ground, the novel also establishes its own politicized contour lines, of which the symbolic border between Highlands and Lowlands is of crucial symbolic significance. For if, at the beginning of the novel, the border between Highlands and Lowlands defines a boundary between different spaces and times, this border is afterwards set in motion, like a shoreline during the sweep of the tide. By the end of the novel, the borderline has been pushed back out of sight, the "old" Highlands are cleansed of their associations, and what had been the old border region – in the novel's imaginary map, Tully-Veolan – has been relieved of the proximity of the old Highland space.

Tully-Veolan, especially the great estate of the Baron of Bradwardine, is therefore used in the novel as an exemplary space, in which the novel's larger spatial – and political – movements and flows can be represented. For the Highland shadow which had once darkened the village is lifted by the end of the novel. Moreover, the Baron's own status as a feudal lord (a status enabled and sustained by the proximity of the Highlands) is revoked, and he is reduced to the status of *Mr* Bradwardine – disarmed, like the Highland chiefs, and stripped of his Heritable Jurisdiction over land and tenantry. That he is allowed to retain his estate at all is due solely to the intervention of the benevolent Colonel Talbot; but even then the quasi-magical restoration of his property (which had been demolished by the Hanoverian army) can only take place once its ownership has passed through Talbot's hands. Indeed, this passage of the estate's ownership through Talbot enables a purification of the associations of the old space. Having *once been* the center of a feudal estate, it is now merely a grand country house in the English tradition, and the Baron is astonished upon his return:

All seemed as much as possible restored to the state in which he had left it when he assumed arms some months before. The pigeon-house was replenished; the fountain played with its usual activity; and not only the Bear who predominated over its basin, but all the other Bears whatsoever, were replaced on their several stations, and renewed or repaired with so much care, that they bore no tokens of the violence which had so lately descended upon them. While these minutiae had been so heedfully attended to, it is scarce necessary to add, that the house itself had been thoroughly repaired, as well as the gardens, with the strictest attention to maintain the original character of both, and to remove as far as possible, all appearance of the ravage they had sustained.

Talbot immediately congratulates the Baron, adding that "your family estate is your own once more in full property, and at your absolute disposal, but only burdened with the sum advanced to repurchase it, which I understand is utterly disproportioned to its value."[63] The estate's sudden physical restoration is allowed by the pacification of the site's previous symbolic significance; indeed, its precise restoration, down to the last of its minutest details, suggests not so much that it had ever actually changed, but rather that its space had been symbolically and politically cleansed by an almost ritualistic passage through the modern economic system of the market. That is, the condition of possibility for the return (or the spatial reinvention) of Tully-Veolan to the person who was, after all, its original and "rightful" owner, is the commodification of its space and the objectification of its value – its sole burden being the mortgage which financed its repurchase from the past.

At the same time, the dark spell of the Highlands has been lifted from Tully-Veolan, so that the Highland line – and with it the threat of *caterans* and other raiders from the past – has been pushed back into an unbridgeable distance. Indeed, the novel does not return to the Highlands, it does not allow for the preservation of Highland space. On the contrary: once the eruption from the past has been contained, the Highlands cease to exist as a spot of time. Once the possibilities of this spot have been closed, once it has been cleansed, it is gone forever, and its imaginary terrain must be un-imagined, or rather, re-imagined in an altogether new spatial configuration (to which Scott returns in his next novel, *Guy Mannering*, set a decade or two after the Forty-Five). It cannot be transformed in *Waverley* itself.

As for the Highlanders themselves, they are trapped in their space: a space which was only ever accessible from the outside by those – notably Waverley himself – whose origins are on the outside. In other words, if the Highland space is a spot of time, it is one that can only be entered from the outside, and one that can only be left behind again, as it closes shut for the last time, by an outsider. For this spot of time allows access to another time, another mode of life and of society, whose members are apparently incapable of movement to a different time and a different mode of social and political organization. Fergus and Flora (despite their gloss of Continental taste and manners), Callum, Evan Dhu: none can make the transition from Highlands (feudalism, wilderness, the past) to Lowlands (the present and the future). Their evolution – or, more precisely, their modernization – is inconceivable as such.

Thus the Highland space produced in *Waverley* cannot be transformed: like one of those natural bowers that appear so often in Wordsworth's poetry, it can be preserved either in its original state of anti-modern difference, accessible through the magic of a spot of time, or else utterly destroyed in a "fall" into the modern; in either case, modernization amounts less to a transformative process than to a spatio-temporal annihilation and reinvention. The novel's imaginary map of the Highlands is not, strictly speaking, a map of *the* past, but rather a map of a possible past, an imaginary past that is forever spatially (and temporally) different and distinct. It is a past that can never become present because it cannot be modernized *and* remain identical to itself – it is necessarily anti-modern.

The novel, as a prototypical *Bildungsroman*, does however allow for the *ontogenetic* transformation of Edward Waverley himself. For it chronicles his growth and development from the immaturity and romance of youth to the steady rationality of adulthood. Politically, this development is coded in terms of Edward's maturation from his support of Jacobitism and its emotional and unrealistic claims to the throne, to a sober and independent outlook more congenial to Talbot and the Hanoverian and Unionist standpoint. That is, the novel directly equates his early affiliation with the Jacobite cause with an emotional and intellectual – as well as a political – immaturity. His gradual move away from the cause (which he effects without actually betraying his friends) is consonant with his emotional and intellectual growth and maturation under the guidance of Talbot. More generally, however, the novel equates Jacobitism with immaturity, emotion, irrationality, and even romantic fancy (embodied by Bonnie Prince Charlie himself) and Unionism with rationality and maturity.[64] Thus, although Waverley is shown to be the only character capable of movement from one position to the other, even at this early stage he is capable of rational insight, feeling "inexpressible repugnance at the idea of being accessary to the plague of civil war."[65] Indeed,

whatever were the original rights of the Stuarts, calm reflection told him, that, omitting the question of how far James the Second could forfeit those of his posterity, he had, according to the united voice of the whole nation, justly forfeited his own [in 1688]. Since that period, four monarchs had reigned in peace and glory over Britain, sustaining and exalting the character of the nation abroad, and its liberties at home. Reason asked, was it worth while to disturb a government so long settled and established, and to plunge a kingdom into all the miseries of civil war, for the purpose of replacing upon the throne the descendants of a monarch by whom it had been willfully forfeited?

That Edward does join the Jacobites is due partly to his emotional reaction at being (with his father) falsely accused of treason by the government, and partly to the romantic allure of the Bonnie Prince Charlie. Moreover, his attraction to the Jacobite cause is overlaid with his attraction to the Highlands and to Fergus – both, as I have already argued, embodiments of Jacobitism, feudalism, masculinity, and so forth.[66]

Here, however, the novel faces an impossible representational somersault, for *Waverley*'s Highlands do not and cannot enter the present: they remain a space apart. That is, with Edward's maturity evolving with the unfolding of the novel's plot, *Waverley*'s imaginary map confronts a representational crisis of its own making. For the Highland space does not and cannot become modern in the novel's own representational framework, and Edward must leave it behind. *Waverley*'s Highland space

is established as the space of the past, although the novel has brought
"the past to life as the pre-history of the present."[67] It repeatedly
establishes the links between certain historical events or developments
(including spurious Malthusian claims about the overpopulation of the
Highlands, as well as the abolition of the Highland chiefs' heritable
jurisdictions) and their ramifications and implications for the future (that
is, Scott's own present). Yet, once the past has been closed off, the novel
is unwilling to acknowledge the impact of these historical developments.
The space of the past cannot enter the present, even though the novel
has already traced lines of present historical development "back" into
the Highlands.

Waverley does not quite close off all references to the Highlands,
however, for even in the relentless present that closes in at the end of the
novel, there does remain one aperture into the Highlands. This is the
portrait of Edward and Fergus:[68]

It was a large and spirited painting, representing Fergus Mac-Ivor and Waverley in their Highland dress; the scene a wild, rocky, and mountainous pass,
down which the clan were descending in the background. It was taken from a
spirited sketch, drawn while they were in Edinburgh by a young man of high
genius, and had been painted on a full-length scale by an eminent London
artist. Raeburn himself (whose Highland Chiefs do all but walk out of the
canvas) could not have done more justice to the subject; and the ardent, fiery,
and impetuous character of the unfortunate Chief of Glennaquoich was finely
contrasted with the contemplative, fanciful, and enthusiastic expression of his
happier friend. Beside this painting hung the arms which Waverley had borne
in the unfortunate civil war.

The full-scale painting, hanging on a wall of the freshly reconstructed
manor house in Tully-Veolan, appears as a window to the outside
world, to the Highlands lying beyond the walls of the estate. But, as a
window, it directs the viewer's gaze to the past; as a symbolic production, in other words, it draws attention to itself and away from other
windows allowing views of the present Highlands (views which the novel
itself does not allow), it intervenes and intercedes between the viewer
and the space of the present. As an imaginary production, it disrupts the
referentiality of the "real" Highlands, and claims this referentiality for
itself.

Yet the novel does not claim the portrait's view of the past as an
"accurate" representation. On the contrary, it emphasizes the artificiality of its reconstruction of the past. The portrait involves the final
assembly of several pre-fabricated parts. The usual premise for the

production of a portrait – the subject's presence – is here not only unfulfilled, it is at several removes from the artist who assembles the images. For the portrait, produced and assembled by "an eminent London artist," is based upon a sketch of Waverley and Fergus taken (by an altogether different artist, "a young man of high genius") while they were in Edinburgh. The London artist combines elements of the Edinburgh sketch with "typical" Highland scenery, "a wild, rocky, and mountainous pass," down which a clan, also as part of the background, is charging. The portrait thus consciously and artificially re-produces a past (from which it is alienated both because of its distance and its fictiveness) by appropriating it.[69] Its claim to "authenticity" is based upon this appropriation of a past that had never "really" existed – this automatic and even tautological "seizure" of an imaginary terrain by virtue of having invented it. Whether such a past had or had not "really" existed does not matter as much as the fact that it has been claimed as a symbolic space. Once it has been claimed and mapped out, it "becomes" real: that is, it takes on political, cultural, and symbolic significance on its own terms.[70] It also becomes a contested space. The portrait's invention of the past is in this sense an allegorical restatement of *Waverley*'s own production of the past, of the space of the past (the Highlands), and of the narration of the past (its version of the history of the Forty-Five). Alongside the portrait hang Edward Waverley's weapons from the "unfortunate" civil war and the revolution whose rise and fall the novel has documented. *Waverley* thus not only spatializes the past as the Highlands: it reifies the past and ossifies history, commodifying both and presenting them as museum-piece images and aestheticized icons for consumption in and for the present and the future.

VIII

Waverley's colonial vision is never straightforward and unproblematic; its will to colonize the Highlands is partially undermined by its claims to a sentimental Jacobitism, to the trappings and rituals of a mythic Highland past. While the Highlands were being, in *Waverley*'s own present, cleaned of their otherness and brought symbolically into the present by being colonized, the novel wants to negate this process – while at the same time it is nevertheless forced to acknowledge it – and insist on their retention of a charge of anti-modern otherness. While the efforts at colonization and improvement were sustained by a colonial discourse of discipline, industry, and progress, *Waverley* counters these with a nationalist discourse and a pre-evolutionary view of otherness: one which rejects the possibility of transmutation, transformation, and development. Thus the novel wants to preserve the Highlands as a site of otherness; but the cost for this – a cost paid neither by the novel nor by its reader – is that their present cannot be admitted into the novel as a presence. *Waverley* thus simultaneously acknowledges the historical transformation of the Highlands, and negates this transformation by keeping the Highland space intact as the space of the past. In other words, it keeps the Highlands "alive" (in the past) by symbolically "killing" them (in the present).

Waverley can only cling to the Highlands as a site of difference and otherness to the extent that it can negate its loss of otherness, its fall from difference to sameness. The novel's Highlands are not only parts of Blake's "space of Erin"; rather, their claim to be parts of the space of Erin is enabled by their being – like the spaces of Erin – what Robert Gleckner terms a "residuum of 'unfallenness.'"[71] For, even though they are consigned to the past, *Waverley*'s Highlands have not yet fallen: they are held in suspense, forever on the brink of their calamitous fall from difference.

A commentator on the subjugation of Ireland in the late eighteenth century wrote: "The husbandman must first break the ground before it be made capable of good seed: and when it is thoroughly broken and manured, if he do not forthwith cast good seed into it, it will grow wild again, and bear nothing but weeds. So a barbarous country must first be broken by a war, before it will be capable of good government; and when it is fully subdued and conquered, if it be not well planted and governed after the conquest, it will often return to the former barbarism."[72] Although *Waverley* acknowledges the colonization of the Highlands, and, extending the above metaphor, its impregnation with the seeds of modernity and of the present, the novel refuses to map the "actual" modernization of the Highlands (in which, as I have been trying to suggest, it "actually" participated). The colonization of the Highlands amounts to a symbolic "implantation" with the seeds of the present social order of imperial modernization. Yet this "implantation" does not involve the fundamental transformation of the colonized space on its own terms: it involves an appropriation of this space, as a site in which modernity can be planted by force. Modernity, in this historical schema, is not something that can be achieved by the colonized themselves: it is something that must be implanted *in* them as a germ, to work its own way out and into the flow of "history." For this is the theory of history underlying such an imaginary map of colonization: historical societies are those that are in the river of history, moving in an endless flow from present to future, while colonial others are timeless and ahistorical place-markers on the banks of the river of time.

CHAPTER 5

Domesticating exoticism: transformations of Britain's Orient, 1785–1835

The vicinity of China to our Indian territories . . . must necessarily draw our attention to that most ancient and wonderful Empire, even if we had no commercial intercourse with its more distant and maritime provinces; and the benefits, that might be obtained from a more intimate connexion with a nation long famed for their useful arts, and for the valuable productions of their country, are too apparent to require any proof or illustration.

Sir William Jones, *The Second Classical Book of the Chinese*

Sir William Jones, and others, recognized the demand for a code of Indian law; but unhappily thought of no better expedient than that of employing some of the natives themselves; as if one of the most difficult tasks to which the human mind can be applied, a work to which the highest measure of European intelligence is not more than equal, could be expected to be tolerably performed by the unenlightened and perverted intellects of a few Indian pundits.

James Mill, *The History of British India*

The sea is between us. The mass of that element, which, by appearing to disconnect, unites mankind, is to them a forbidden road. It is a great gulf fixed between you and them, – not so much that elementary gulf, but that gulf which manners, opinions and laws have radicated in the very nature of the people. None of their high castes, without great danger to his situation, religion, rank, and estimation, can ever pass the sea; and this forbids, forever, all direct communication between that country and this. That material and affecting circumstance, my Lords, makes it ten times more necessary, since they cannot come to us, to keep a strict eye upon all persons who go to them. It imposes upon us a stricter duty to guard with a firm and powerful vigilance those whose principles of conscience weaken their principles of self-defence. *If we undertake to govern the inhabitants of such a country, we must govern them upon their own principles and maxims, and not upon ours. We must not think to force them into the narrow circle of our ideas; we must extend ours to take in their system of opinions and rites, and the necessities which result from both: all change on their part is absolutely impracticable. We have more versatility of character and manners, and it is we who must conform.*[1]

It is a rich irony that Edmund Burke, one of the chief prosecutors of Warren Hastings (and certainly the most outspoken), shared these principles in common with the very man whose principles of colonial administration he was trying, on charges of high crimes and misdemeanors, for his Governor-Generalship of Bengal under the East India Company (1772–86).[2] According to Burke and Hastings, India and the rest of the Orient had "stopped" developing; yet the ways in which these two great adversaries both proposed to resolve this apparent dilemma of colonial rule stand in marked opposition to the various British answers to the so-called Eastern Question that were proposed only a decade or two later in the early nineteenth century (by, for example, James Mill, Thomas Macaulay, Robert Southey, and others). This opposition, I believe, underlies a struggle between two significantly different and conflicting constructions of Britain's Orient, and, moreover, between two antithetical paradigms of British imperialism and colonial rule. What I want to suggest in the present chapter is that the romantic period marked a transitional moment between these opposed sets of colonial projects. Furthermore, I want to argue that the later paradigms – including those that pertain to what we may, with Edward Said, distinguish as *modern* Orientalism, to which I will turn shortly[3] – developed during this period through a productive intersection or fusion with other emergent modern discourses and structures, including those of racism, evolution, progressivism, and industrial capitalism. The emergence of these discourses and paradigms thus transfigured earlier notions and constructs of the Orient, as well as earlier modes of empire-building, of colonial rule, of discourses on Nature and the colonial other, and of history.

That the East had somehow "stopped developing," which (together with the duty or good fortune of imperial rule) both earlier and later views agree on, is in itself not particularly useful or important for either view. What matters instead is how to administer and govern – not to mention trade with and understand – populations in such a state. And it is on this point that the radical disagreement arises. Burke very shrewdly uses a spatial figure, the sea, to illustrate the gap between Britain and its colonial subjects in India. The sea, he argues, simultaneously separates and unites the two countries; the political, economic, military, and cultural ties between metropolis and colony are drawn through the sea and the endless tide of shipping that cleared British ports each week for Bombay and Calcutta, taking with them news, information, manufactured goods, troops, and supplies; and bringing back the bounty of colonial wealth: cotton, silk, textiles, calicoes, tea, spices, knowledge, and the profits from the East India Company's monopoly (from 1773) on opium sales to China. And yet, Burke says, "the sea is between us," thus "forbidding, forever, any direct contact between that country and this." The sea is hence also an obstacle, which can be crossed in one direction but not in the other (or, rather, by one party in *both* directions). It figures as a gap in status and development between India and Britain, simultaneously a material and a metaphorical barrier. Just as, according to Burke, the Indians cannot – purely on account of their own limitations – cross the material sea and travel to England, India itself cannot cross the great metaphorical divide of development to become like Britain. Instead of what will appear in more modern accounts as the great stream of time and of evolution (so cogently discussed by Johannes Fabian[4]), Burke here posits an immense ocean, which by its nature does not flow in one direction like a river, but which remains stationary: a massive, enormous, and permanent barrier.

Since Indians cannot travel to Britain, and since India cannot develop towards or into Britain, Burke argues, it is morally required that Britain keep an eye over who goes to India from Britain, in order to "protect" India and Indians from the likes of Warren Hastings. In a larger sense, though, what Burke wants to insist upon (and indeed what Hastings himself had not only insisted upon but had made into colonial policy) is the "fact" that, since the metaphorical journey of development from east to west cannot be accomplished ("all change on their part is absolutely impracticable"), what is paramount is that the imperial move from west to east be guided by the "limitations" imposed by eastern concepts. In terms of colonial administration, Burke says that this means that "we must govern them upon their principles and maxims, and not upon ours."

Of course, neither Burke nor Hastings questions for a moment that Britain *should* rule India; rather, the question is *how* it should rule, for whose ostensible benefit, and on what terms, and how it should manage its relations with the peoples of India and the Orient which they are made to "represent." According to Burke, the East India Company derives its authority not only from the British Parliament, but from the Mogul empire itself. He argues, however, that the Moguls, due to their weakness (which was, not coincidentally, partly fostered by the East India Company), are incapable of controlling the rapaciousness of the Company, and hence that it falls to the British Parliament to act as enforcer, in the name of Britian and its Constitution as well as in the name of the Moguls and of the people of India – and indeed in the name of the universal "rights of man."[5]

For it is, fundamentally, in the name of the otherwise silent Indian people that Burke proposes to speak, just as it is in their name that he proposes that Britain have dominion over them, saying that "at length justice will be done to India."[6] Yet the colonial mission which Burke envisions is *not* one of transformation and improvement, of which India is simply not capable. Indeed, that India is not as "developed" as Britain does not by any means suggest for Burke that it *ought* to be as developed as Britain, let alone that it is Britain's duty to improve it (just as, according to Burke, the landed classes in Britain neither could nor should help to improve the condition of the nascent working class, the "swinish multitude" who were "utterly incapable of amendment; objects of eternal vigilance"[7]). On the contrary: India is and will forever be the way it is; in its very otherness it is immutable and unchangeable. However – and this is what makes Burke's so radically different from later conceptions of Britain's imperial project – there is nothing wrong with this otherness *on its own terms*, and "we" must accommodate "ourselves" to "their" status, radical difference, and immutable otherness, not the other way around. "My Lords," Burke insists, "these Gentoo people are the original people of Hindostan. They are still, beyond comparison, the most numerous. Faults this nation may have; but God forbid that we should pass judgement upon people who framed their laws and institutions prior to our insect origins of yesterday. With all the faults of their nature and errors of their institutions, their institutions, which act so powerfully on their natures, have two material characteristics which entitle them to respect: first, great force and stability; and next, excellent moral and civil effects."[8] Elsewhere Burke says that the Indians, whom he distinguishes from Africans and native Americans (who are "an abject and barbarous populace," made up of "gangs of savages"), are a people "for ages cultivated and civilized, – cultivated by all the arts of polished life, whilst we were yet in the woods."[9]

Burke's impassioned (and often quite hysterical) speeches on India are characterized by an underlying tension between, on the one hand, his universalistic claims about the trans-cultural and univocal "nature" (and hence "rights") of humankind; and, on the other, his repeated invocation of a version of polygenesis as well as the contemporaneous scientific (and, I would argue, *political*) concepts of preformationism and anti-mutationism, according to which "improvement" in level and status, whether for species, for individuals, for societies, or for classes, is impossible.[10] (Here Burke's views on class structure are once again of great significance; his belief in the immutability of India and its inability to change its status vis-à-vis Britain has an almost exact equivalent in his claims that the working class of England should and must accept its permanent and natural subordination to the higher classes.[11])

While, for the most part, Burke insists upon the static immutability and everlasting difference from England of India and Indian culture – an immutability which for him merits great respect for that culture – he also invokes the possibility of mutation and development (as in the case of Britain, which developed out of the "the woods" of its "insect origins of yesterday"). Moreover, he vehemently denounces the notion of "geographic morality" and insists that "the laws of morality are the same everywhere," because all human beings and societies share certain fundamental qualities and rights – qualities and rights that implicitly deny the possibility of totally separate spheres of existence, separate histories, separate destinies.[12]

In other words, Burke's attitudes towards India and the Orient oscillate between, on the one hand, an extreme kind of cultural relativism; and, on the other, contradictory claims to and invocations of certain trans-cultural and universal laws and tendencies of humankind. The former view is, in Burke, related to preformationist scientific concepts.[13] According to such concepts, there is a wide though static range of human types, an extension of the animal world's great chain of being (near the top of which, just beneath the angels, stand all the human types in ascending order), some perhaps higher than others on the chain, yet not capable of mutation to a higher or lower level.[14] Thus the *ontogenetic* development of an individual organism (in a process known as "evolution" before the nineteenth century changed the usage of that term) takes place only to a certain fixed or predetermined level, and never beyond it. Ontogenetic transmutation to a higher stage of development, like *phylogenetic* transmutation to a higher species-form, is inconceivable in these terms.[15] And yet, at the same time, Burke anticipates the possibility, if not quite the *inevitability*, of social "evolution" and of the concept of national "development" according to which all societies could be placed on a temporal slope, a "stream of time" leading to and culminating in Eurocentric modernity.[16] These contradictory claims and concepts are thoroughly intertwined in Burke's attitudes towards India, and indeed in a broader set of British attitudes towards the Orient in the late eighteenth and early nineteenth centuries.

"In the eighteenth century," writes Maxime Rodinson, "an unconscious sense of Eurocentrism was present but it was guided by the universalist ideology of the Enlightenment and therefore respected non-European civilizations and peoples. With good reason it discovered universal human traits in their historical development and their contemporary social structures."[17] According to Rodinson, the Eurocentrism that would find its "place" in the nineteenth century and the universalism of the eighteenth century are "naturally" opposing tendencies, and he argues that Enlightenment universalism would give way to a belief in the hierarchical separation of cultures.[18] Now what I am arguing here proposes exactly the opposite: that the universalist tendencies which (as Rodinson observes) emerged from the Enlightenment would gradually transfigure the very notion and possibility of separate social/national development (which has an analogue in the scientific paradigm of fixed types) and lead towards the construction of a universal evolutionary "stream." In the meantime, the kind of respect that Burke extends to Indian civilization is derived not merely from what he sees as its sheer difference from England, but also from the non-applicability to India of what would become (only a little later on) the simultaneously Eurocentric and "universal" tendency towards development, improvement, and modernization.

That this not-yet-universal tendency and its attendant principles, maxims, laws, and truths do not, for Burke, apply to India renders Britain's colonial mission in India ambiguous, and even dangerous because of the threat of that ambiguity and the obscurity – the *sublimity* – of the colonial mission. Yet the absence of universal laws and rules through which to "read" and understand India makes it that much more important, according to Burke, that the British try to discover the specificities of India's own principles and maxims (hence his call for the administrators of the empire to "take in their system of opinions and rites, and the necessities which result from both"). India's difference from England, India's unknowability, and the dangers and ambiguities of colonial rule thus become conflated in Burke's speeches.

Sara Suleri argues that Burke's India is a fundamentally unmappable space (and hence sublime, to the extent that it is overwhelming and defies the understanding of the constructed English subject). She suggests, moreover, that, when Burke invokes the sublimity of India, "he seeks less to contain the irrational within a rational structure than to construct inventories of obscurity through which the potential empowerment of the sublime is equally on the verge of emptying into negation."[19] This sublimity of empire draws its power precisely from what Burke sees as the inscrutability and unreadability of India. "In the colonizing imagination," Suleri adds, "the Indian sublime is at its most empty at the very point when it is most replete, dissolving the stability of facts and figures into hieroglyphs that signify only the colonizer's pained confrontation with an object to which his cultural and interpretive tools must be inadequate."[20] Burke's respect for the cultural difference of India is inextricably caught up with his fear of India and, moreover, with his fear on behalf of what he sees as the "extreme youth" of so many of the Company's colonial administrators in India, whom Burke judges to be vulnerable to the pressures placed upon them both by their positions of power and by their inability to resist the "dark" side of native customs and habits. And, finally, Burke's belief in the immutability of India is premised upon the "fact" of its indecipherability, its resistance to British and European constructs and categories of knowledge, which are never able to contain it.

Whereas Edmund Burke's respect for the cultural difference of India is derived from his fear of the sublimity of colonial rule in India, for Sir William Jones – perhaps the leading Orientalist of the late eighteenth century – it was knowledge of India, in addition to the subcontinent's sheer and still unbridgeable difference from England and Europe, that empowered his attraction to that other culture. Jones, a scholar and judge in the Hastings administration in Bengal, elaborated conceptions of Orientalist knowledge that paralleled Burke's and Hastings's views of empire in the East. For Jones's Orient was not only as immutable as Burke's; it contained vast intellectual treasures, knowledge of which could, in his view, be "exchanged" for European ideas and scientific concepts.

Jones argues that, by virtue of its sheer difference and utter otherness, the "infinitely diversified" East has a great deal to offer Europe. The Orient, according to Jones, is "the nurse of sciences, the inventress of delightful and useful arts, the scene of glorious actions, fertile in the productions of human genius, abounding in natural wonders, and infinitely diversified in the forms of religion and government, in the laws, manners, customs, and languages, as well as in the features and complexions of men."[21] What Jones proposed to do, through the agency of his Asiatick Society of Calcutta, which he founded in 1784, and through the publication of *Asiatick Researches* (beginning in 1788), was to establish an intellectual analogue to the extraction of material wealth from the Orient, and from India in particular, in the discovery and then the translation and circulation, not only of European knowledge about the East, but above all of the indigenous cultural, literary, artistic and scientific productions of the Orient "itself."

The purpose of his vast project, originally proposed by Warren Hastings himself, was thus on the one hand to extract and circulate this knowledge of the Asiatic other; and on the other hand to use this knowledge to facilitate imperial control over India (which was obviously Hastings's main concern). As Javed Majeed points out, these two aims were inextricably related to one another for Jones, whose knowledge of indigenous Indian laws and Sanskrit was used not merely to communicate with local judges but to render them totally redundant and replace them *in their own element, their own language, their own code of law and juridical principles.*[22] In other words, Jones's project involved not merely what Gauri Viswanathan refers to as "reverse acculturation,"[23] but an attempt to virtually simulate and even to replicate the other, to understand the other "from within," to contain the threat of otherness not by transforming it but by reproducing it in a controlled system. Javed Majeed points out Jones's desire "to tap the sources of a pure 'orient knowledge,' both to undermine the authority of the sacerdotal classes and to redefine the ancient constitution of India, which he believed had been fragmented and dispersed for centuries."[24]

But although Jones's knowledge of the colonial other and his participation in the colonial project are thoroughly intertwined, they are not quite coextensive. While much of his work on Asiatic languages, literatures, and histories centers on an attempt to put his knowledge of India directly to work for Hastings and the East India Company (the assumption being that Indians would forever be the same, so that the only way to rule them would be to know them sufficiently to judge and understand them on their own terms), there was an "excess" of knowledge that served no immediate administrative purpose.

Indeed, quite apart from the usefulness of his Orientalist knowledge to the imperial administration, Jones argues that "disinterested" knowledge of the Orient is valuable on its own terms as well, precisely because it constitutes knowledge of difference and otherness. Thus, in an essay on the poetry of Asia, he extols the virtues of Oriental literatures, not only comparing them to the works of Greece and Rome, but in some sense elevating them "above" the European classics. "I must request," he writes in the conclusion to this essay, that

in bestowing these praises on the writings of Asia, I may not be thought to derogate from the merit of the Greek and Latin poems, which have been justly admired in every age; yet I cannot but think that our European poetry has subsisted too long on the perpetual repetition of the same images, and incessant allusions to the same fables: and it has been my endeavour for several years to inculcate this truth, that, if the principal writings of the Asiaticks, which are reposited in our public libraries, were printed with the usual advantage of notes and illustrations, and if the languages of the Eastern nations were studied in our great seminaries of learning, where every other branch of useful knowledge is taught to perfection, a new and ample field would be opened for speculation; we should have a more extensive insight into the history of the human mind; and we should be furnished with a new set of images and similitudes; and a number of excellent compositions would be brought to light, which future scholars might explain and future poets might imitate.[25]

This new field is conceptually analagous or homologous to the other commercial fields that were being pursued and exploited by the great mercantile Companies. Just as Europeans would benefit from the discovery and extraction of new material commodities in the colonial realm – tobacco, cotton, silk, sugar – they would (and did indeed) benefit, and on the same terms, from the discovery and commodification of such new sources of inspiration or versification. And yet, in this conception, the great value of such an intellectual commodity lies not merely in its beauty, its inspiration, its charm, but in its sheer difference from the standard European classics. Raymond Schwab takes (and stretches) this point so far as to argue that, "both geographically and historically, what had been lacking through the centuries and what would come to dominate everything was cultural dissonance, a sense of *the dissident.* The known world had been wholly classical before 1800. Or, in a sense, it had been a classified world. Homer was simultaneously the essential beginning and the culmination."[26] Thus Jones began to develop and expand his knowledge of this dissident East, working closely with Indian scholars and sages whom he both respected and admired, and giving in "exchange" knowledge of European scientific principles and techniques.[27]

In other words, there were both cultural and economic benefits to be obtained from this state of immutable difference among human groups, benefits that, indeed, could not be obtained without such an absolute sense of alterity and the various "ideologies of free trade" that help to constitute it. For the very logic of the East India Company (chartered in 1600), which brought Britain and British interests to India to begin with, had been predicated upon the lucrative commercial exchange of exotic goods – and hence the commodification of difference – with this other society. The original mercantile aim of the Company had been, as

Ramkrishna Mukherjee observes, to obtain and secure a monopoly over this supply and the exchange of Indian and British goods. Their problem, indeed, had been what to "exchange" in return for Indian commodities (the East India and especially the China trades had been steadily draining Britain's supply of silver and gold; the "solution" was simultaneously to develop the opium trade with China to pay for Chinese tea and silk, and to subjugate India in order to obtain Indian goods at little expense).[28]

Mercantile capitalism, with its emphasis on the circulation rather than the production of goods – through monopoly wherever possible, which the various British Companies[29] as well as others, like the Dutch East India Company (VOC), were invariably granted by their home governments – sought the preservation rather than the transformation of otherness, even if this "preservation" involved (with cruel irony) the ruthless annihilation of anything that impeded its intensive exploitation.[30] Industrial capitalism, on the other hand, stresses production and the productive trasformation of otherness, beginning with the crude material of Nature itself, and hence the relegation of circulation, which then becomes merely a moment of production rather than the end-in-itself that it was for the various trading Companies and for the empires they helped to build. The struggle between these two forms of capitalism, from its beginnings in the romantic period, intensified during the debate over the Corn Laws (1812–46), and was ultimately "won" by the institutions and structures of industrial capital. The latter's "victory" was marked, on the one hand, by the abolition of the Corn Laws, and on the other hand by the gradual substitution of exotic colonial goods by cheap industrially engineered and produced commodities (e.g., the replacement of cane sugar by beet root, the substitution of synthetic textiles for raw cotton, etc.); as well as by the abolition of the mercantile Companies' monopolies on trade (1813 for the East India Company), and then the total abolition of such institutions as the East India Company itself (following the doomed Indian Rebellion of 1857).

The form of imperial control associated with mercantile capital generally involved the acquisition of key trading posts and the control over essential caravan routes, navigable rivers and channels, ports, and a few points of production or extraction.[31] Thus, as Eric Hobsbawm points out, for much of the early history of British imperialism, the British were content to hold strategic points crucial to their global trading interests, such as the southern tip of Africa, Gibraltar, Ceylon, and Singapore (founded just after the Napoleonic wars); "on the whole, with one crucial exception, their view was that a world lying open to British trade and safeguarded by the British navy from unwelcome intrusion was more cheaply exploited without the administrative costs of occupation."[32] The crucial exception to which Hobsbawm points was of course India; but even here the British presence was small by later nineteenth-century standards, and until the mid- to late eighteenth century, the British dominiation of India was based on control of shipping lanes and of a few key ports and inland garrisons and settlements.[33] However, it was also in India that British imperial attitudes and policies began to change dramatically, away from those held by Burke, Jones, and Hastings.

Indeed, just as Edmund Burke's attitudes towards India are characterized by a tension or contradiction between his insistence on, first, the untranslatable and immutable specificities of India's culture and civilization, and, second, his repeated invocation of certain "universal" qualities of humankind, so indeed are Jones's. For while Jones stresses the (intellectual, aesthetic, and commercial) value of the sheer and untransformable cultural and civilizational difference from Britain of India and the rest of the Orient, his work on Oriental history and, above all, on the nascent field of Oriental philology was part of a much larger process of "discovering" and tracing certain linguistic, historical, cultural and social continuities between the Orient and Europe. These continuities would ultimately not only contradict but also finally discredit the notion of separate (polygenic) spheres of existence and contribute instead towards the emergence of universally applicable "laws" of evolution and development linking – rather than permanently separating – Asia and Europe.[34] While it may indeed be the case that philology was the first discipline to be based on the emergent concept of evolution,[35] it is important to stress that for scholars like Jones in the late eighteenth century, there was no sense of progress associated with the growth and expansion of the various branches of a language "family."[36] Nevertheless, in tracing the cultural and historical links between Europe and the Orient, Jones contributed to the emergence of a new sense of temporality and of history in early nineteenth-century Britain. According to this new vision, history is constructed as a unilinear stream teleologically pointing "towards" modernity and Europe, into which other histories are incorporated as subordinate elements in a larger universal History – a History henceforth to be narrated and controlled by Europeans.[37]

While the respect shown by Burke and Jones to India and Indian culture is related to their perception of the Orient's utter distinction from (and synchronic, rather than diachronic, relation to[38]) Europe, the growing British resistance to this sense of immutable and untransformable cultural dissonance drew its strength from an insistence on the new construction of history and appeals to certain universally applicable forces and currents (as with the historicism of Herder and Hegel). And while their stress on India's non-transformability (not to mention the value and attraction of its cultural "dissonance") is an indissoluble aspect of Burke's and Jones's views of India, the emergent conceptions of the Orient stress the fundamental importance of alteration and "improvement" to the productive global transformation of difference which was central to the emergent forces and institutions of industrial capitalism.

By the early nineteenth century, as I have already said, British attitudes towards, policies in, and above all inventions of the Orient had been turned upside-down; so that by the 1830s, for instance, new advocates of imperialism, such as Macaulay, could declare without any hesitation not only that earlier imperialists such as Jones and even Hastings were naïve and misguided, but that "a single shelf of a good European library was worth more than the whole native literature of India and Arabia."[39] The exoticism of difference and otherness had begun, as it were, to fade, in association with major shifts in both the paradigms of empire and versions or visions of the space of the Orient, as well as fundamental shifts in scientific and social theories (intertwined from at least Malthus onwards[40]) of evolution and "progress." The Company's 1757 victory at Plassey, for one, had already signalled the development of new forms of imperial investment and control in India, which accelerated through the eighteenth century (e.g., the Regulating Act of 1773, the India Act of 1784), culminating in a major overhaul of imperial policy after the trial of Warren Hastings and on into the nineteenth century.

The extraordinarily long trial of Hastings, which ran for a full seven years from 1788 to 1795, has, not surprisingly, been identified as one of the great "trials of empire" and of the colonial project itself, in which Hastings's own status as the accused became less and less relevant as the proceedings dragged on.[41] That Hastings was eventually acquitted and exonerated was, indeed, not of any particular interest to the debates surrounding the trial. As Suleri points out, not only did the charges against Hastings represent "the first exhaustive compilation of colonial guilt to emerge from the colonization of India," but "the issue of his guilt or innocence was obsolete, almost totally irrelevant to the trial proceedings themselves."[42]

What the trial brought up for thorough consideration, however, included the administrative policies of the East India Company in Bengal, but above all the relations between Britain and the subjects (and victims) of its empire in India. One of the issues that had brought the corruption charges against Hastings was the question of whether or not England ought to transform and "improve" India. Hastings himself, like his enemy Burke and his colleague Jones, opposed such a policy; and one of his principal accusers, Philip Francis, a Company official, argued strongly that Indian laws and institutions should be uprooted and replaced with more "rational" and "advanced" British laws. Even before the conclusion of the trial, such policies, which had been vigorously prevented by Hastings during his own administration, were put into effect by the Permanent Settlement of 1793, which, for instance, at one stroke transformed the *zamindars* – the Mogul tax-collectors (over whom the Company now had power) – into landlords in the capitalist sense, and their previous area of responsibility into their private property; so that the people under their control suddenly became their paying tenants, at exactly the same time as the Scottish Highlanders became the tenants, and then quickly the ex-tenants, of their clan chiefs, through similar legislation in Scotland.[43]

Cornwallis, Wellesley, and other governors-general also introduced policies to "begin" the "education" of the Indians, although as Gauri Viswanathan has argued, "England's initial involvement with the education of the natives derived less from a conviction of native immorality, as the later discourse might lead one to believe, than from the depravity of their own administrators and merchants."[44] Viswanathan points to the long debates in the late eighteenth and early nineteenth centuries between the so-called "Orientalists" of Hastings's following (who believed in the sort of "reverse acculturation" proposed by Burke and Jones, and argued that Company administrators should be trained to fit into native "ways of life," and were able, through a rearguard action, to keep missionaries out of India until as late as 1813) and the so-called "Anglicists," who called for the transformation of Indian social and cultural institutions and who pressed for the increasing education of the natives and the "improvement" of their morals. Viswanathan argues that, since Anglicism was dependent on Orientalism for much of its ideological program, the two positions should be considered "not as polar opposites, but as points along a continuum of attitudes towards the manner and form of native governance, the necessity and justification of which remained by and large an issue of remarkably little disagreement."[45]

As I have already suggested, the debate over Indian education both informed and was informed by much larger debates and transitions. By the end of the Napoleonic Wars in 1815, Britain "had gained the most complete victory of any power in the entire history of the world, having emerged from the twenty years of war against France as the *only* industrialized economy, the *only* naval power – the British navy in 1840 had almost as many ships as all the other navies put together – and virtually the *only* colonial power in the world."[46] By the 1820s, only the struggling Ottoman empire stood between Britain and India, and the East ceased to be, from imperial Britain's point of view, so much a place as it was a question – the Eastern Question – to be "answered," of course, by Britain's foreign and colonial policies in the region. In the Levant, Britain's "answer" was to preserve the Ottoman empire for as long as possible, to thwart Russian and French designs on the Balkans and west Asia; a policy that, even if it angered Shelley, Byron and, other advocates of Greek independence, more or less lasted until the Crimean War in the 1850s.[47] Farther to the East, in India, there began taking place the shift in imperial and colonial administration that I have indicated above.

Now no longer the immutably different space governed by Hastings, "defended" by Burke, and fervently studied by Jones, the Orient became a space defined by its "backwardness," its retardation; no longer a region or a field offering materials for extraction, exploitation, and exchange, it became a field to be rewritten and transformed; it became "undeveloped," a region whose "development" suddenly became the European's burden. The Orient, in short, became a backward, debased, and degraded version of the Occident; having lost its immutable alterity as a member of "another species," so to speak, it became recognized as a member of "our species," and one that in the fantasies of colonialism and colonization needed to be "raised" and "improved" until it became "like us"; or, rather (as with James Mill and the Utilitarians), wiped clean and re-written until it became what "we" would ideally be (if only we could be wiped clean "ourselves").[48]

The once so impassable sea that Burke envisioned between Europe and *his* Orient gradually narrowed into an evolutionary river, shaped and defined by a powerful upwards current.[49] Increasingly (though not exclusively), cultural difference could no longer be accepted, let alone appreciated or valued; it became something that Europe had a "duty" to "improve" – and hence to seek out, penetrate, uproot, eradicate and destroy. The Orient became something not to learn from, as Jones had argued, but to instruct. Thus James Mill, in *The History of British India*, notes not only the "rudeness of Hindu civilization," but, attacking Jones for his credulity, he insists that England has the obligation to overcome this rudeness, to help India on its "progress towards the high attainments of a civilized life."[50] In a work that would later inspire Macaulay as well as a whole generation of experts in India, Mill disputes Jones's claims about the veneration, learning, and wisdom of Hindu sages capable of offering profound "truths" to Europe. For, writes Mill, "under the glossing exterior of the Hindu, lies a general disposition to deceit and perfidy"; indeed,

Such, in many of them, is their imbecility of mind; so faint are the traces of their memory; so vivid the creations of their imagination; so little are they accustomed to regard truth in their daily practice; so much are they accustomed to mingle fiction with reality in all they think, and all they say; and so innacurate is their language, that they cannot tell a true story, even when they are without any inducement to deceive.

To this sweeping condemnation of the Oriental type, Mill adds this astonishing footnote, as "proof" of what he means:

The following is a case so analagous as to afford some instruction. "He that goes into the Highlands with a mind naturally acquiescent, and a credulity eager for wonders, may come back with an opinion very different from mine; for the inhabitants, knowing the ignorance of all strangers in their language and antiquities, perhaps are not very scrupulous adherents to truth; yet, I do not say that they deliberately speak studied falsehood, or have a settled purpose to deceive. They have inquired and considered little, and do not always feel their own ignorance. They are not much accustomed to be interrogated by others; and seem never to have thought upon interrogating themselves; so that if they do not know what they tell to be true, they likewise do not distinctly perceive it to be false. – Mr. Boswell was very diligent in his inquiries; and the result of his investigations was, that the answer to the second question was commonly such as nullified the first." Johnson's Journey to the Hebrides.[51]

It is clearly not coincidental that Mill should mention the Highlanders (who by his time were being uprooted and cleared from their ancestral homes by the very forces of modernization, rationality, and civilization of which he speaks so highly). The very fact that he could think of the Highland clans and the Indians in the same terms, that he could use "evidence" supplied by the one as "proof" against the other,[52] suggests that the two types are remarkable not so much in their similarities to each other, but in their radical difference from the third – equally constructed and invented – character-type he in invoking here by way of opposition: the cultivated, rational, honest, clean British Utilitarian whose apparent duty it was to stand as an example to Indians, High-landers, and other Others of the "proper" way "to be."[53] For Mill, this propriety could not merely be taught through example; it had to be enforced through disciplinary apparatuses like Bentham's Panopticon, which he says could be put to good use in India in "hospitals for the [degenerate] mind."[54] Thus, through the elaboration of this new vision of the Orient, the region becomes not merely a backward and undeveloped version of Europe, but a degenerate and perverse – sick – version of Europe, plagued with all the characteristics of Richard Burton's Sotadic Zone; that is, with all the associations of European "illnesses" and "weaknesses" (*and* "pleasures") – perversion, sodomy, pederasty, imbecility, irrationality, deceit, perfidy, innacuracy, and laziness.[55] This Orient is then a perfect "patient" for European treatment, as Mary Poovey suggests in her reading of Florence Nightingale's discourse on the medical "treatment" of India, in which the subcontinent is reduced to the level of a sickly patient who needs to be nursed (i.e., colonized and civilized) by a benevolent and matronly Great Britain.[56]

Thus, in the early nineteenth century, a new version of Orientalism began to emerge, through which the Orient was altogether reinvented. This new Orientalism emerged in a dialectical, mutually enforcing, and symbiotically related association with the new paradigms of imperial rule exemplified by both the Utilitarian and "Anglicist" educational and institutional policies for India;[57] with the nascent institutions of indus-trial capitalism and its attendant discourses of productive transform-ation and development; with bourgeois constructions of class, centered on mobility and fluidity, and of gender, centered on dualism and opposition;[58] and with rapidly unfolding but still emergent social/scien-tific theories of evolution, transmutation, and race. These "discourses" fused together in the imperial realm, contributing to the emergence of new attitudes towards – and indeed versions and productions of – Orientals and the Orient as a space of opportunity.

The claim that I am making here involves an extensive elaboration of what I see as some of the central arguments of Edward Said's *Orientalism*: first, that the Orient does not exist "as such" and was brought into existence by Europeans at a certain moment in European cultural history;[59] second, that that existence has been continuously renewed in a political and historical process; third, that the modern version of Orientalism emerged in the late eighteenth century and is *conceptually, politically, and culturally distinct from and discontinuous with earlier versions*;[60] and, finally, that Orientalism is *part of* the process that brings those fluid and dynamic identities, "the Orient" and "the Occident," not into *being*, but into an endless *becoming* – and, coextensively, into a constantly changing and dialectically constituted historical relationship with one another. There are certain moments in the book in which Said undermines what I take to be these, his most important points (e.g., by claiming that Orientalism "distorts" the "real" Orient,[61] by claiming that Orientalism has certain unchanging "essences,"[62] by claiming that Orientalism has a continuous history from ancient Greece until today,[63] etc.). But I believe that his central claims withstand the text's shortcomings; and what brings those claims together is Said's challenge to the politically charged opposition between representation and reality, text and context. Orientalism's "representations" help to produce the very realities that they claim merely to be faithfully re-presenting, so that, as Said puts it, these texts (and all others) are "worldly" events, participating in the production of reality. [64]

William Jones and Edmund Burke simply do not fit into – and are in fact antithetical to – that disciplinary version of Orientalism which Said has designated as modern (and which is exemplified by figures such as Mill and Macaulay). In other words the shift to a specifically modern version of Orientalism marks so radical a break from older versions of that discontinuous and heterogeneous discourse that one cannot speak unproblematically – as Said sometimes does – of a continuity of Orientalism across that break, which has been designated as the romantic period in Britain. This, at least, is what I want to propose, in the remainder of this chapter and in the chapter that follows.

At that transitional moment – the romantic period – when Orientalism overlapped and gradually fused with other integral processes of modernization (modern imperialism, industrial capitalism, evolution, modern constructs of race and gender), an altogether new discourse on otherness came into being. The "Orientalism" that Said spends so much time discussing in his book really only emerges from this new formation, which began to develop in the late eighteenth century, and which was more or less intact (though still changing) by the 1820s and 1830s.[65] But the various tendencies, trajectories, assemblages, intensities, and desires of this new formation are no longer separable (if they ever were), except perhaps provisionally and heuristically, into separate "discourses," and mark instead a turbulent, heterogeneous, and discontinuous "continuum." The old discourse of Orientalism was, in other words, radically transfigured as it merged and productively fused with the modern discourses of evolution, racism, industrial capitalism. This fusion marks the emergence of the Universal Empire of modernization – that overall cultural process which would rise to dominance into the nineteenth century – into which Orientalism was assimilated during this period as one discourse among others. This is what separates romantic Orientalism from all previous Orientalisms and pushes us to see it as part of a broader transformation in modern European discourses of otherness.

In other words, what I am delimiting here is a fundamental political and epistemic shift from an Enlightenment "discourse" of otherness to a more properly modern and evolutionary one: a rupture symbolically marked by the contrast between, on the one hand, Burke and Jones, and, on the other hand, Mill and Macaulay (read as exemplary figures). This transition, in part, contributes towards the ambivalence, anxiety, and uneasiness of some of the writers in this period, in very similar ways to those in which it contributes towards the realignment of British colonial and imperial policies, fantasies, and ideologies. This is not to say that Enlightenment or romantic attitudes, fantasies, desires, and tropes do not appear much later in the nineteenth century, or even on into the twentieth, for they do. But following the emergence of what Homi Bhabha calls "the discourse of colonialism" (though again I would qualifiy this as distinctly the discourse of *modern* colonialism), such attitudes and tropes would be largely residual afterglows.[66]

Billie Melman, contesting what she describes as Said's "androcentric" account of Orientalism, proposes "an alternative, gender-specific discourse on the Middle East, one which evolved alongside the dominant discussion, which nowadays is described as Orientalism."[67] Melman argues that "in the eighteenth century there emerged an alternative view of the Orient which developed, during the nineteenth century, alongside the dominant one. The new view, which is expressed in more diverse images that are in many ways more complex than the orientalist *topos*, is found in the mammoth body of writings by women travellers to and residents in, the Middle East."[68] Part, though not all, of the distinction that I have been making in these pages between pre-modern and modern Orientalism, Melman argues in terms of an opposition between male and female writing on the Orient. As a result, historical shifts and ruptures *within* each of the gendered paradigms that she distinguishes, as well as historical overlaps and continuities *between* her two paradigms, are almost totally obliterated. Thus, many of the signs that she argues are characteristic of "women's" domesticating Oriental-ism can be found in James Mill, in Robert Southey, in Thomas Macau-lay, in William Jones, in Edmund Burke.[69] Gender constructions and identities do indeed have important roles to play in the shifts in modes of Orientalism, but Melman ends up decontextualizing gender and dehis-toricizing it. But despite all this, Melman's book, which is based on readings of a huge range of women's texts, throws open an important avenue for discussion. In her conclusion, Melman argues that by the end of the nineteenth century,

The Orient came to be the opposite of a rational and rationalizing West, superior and identified as "masculine." The oriental female apothosized that Orient's "otherness." But, as I hope I have shown . . . the image of the different was never monolithic and, certainly, not androcentric. Women travellers, missionaries and writers did not perceive the oriental *woman* as the absolutely alien, the ultimate "other." Rather oriental *women* became the feminine West's recognisable image in the mirror. The *haremlik* was not the *ne plus ultra* of an exotic décor, but a place comparable to the *bourgeois* home. And even alien landscapes were domesticated and feminised, by evangelicals and non-evan-gelicals alike. Of course, the reconstruction of the Orient cannot and *should not* be separated from the construction of the notion of Empire and from modern Imperialism. Nonetheless the processes outlined in this book should be related primarily to the *Bildung* of individuals, the evolution of class culture and to concepts of gender and feminine sexuality.[70]

The trouble with this assessment is that it was not historically confined to English *women*'s attitudes towards the Orient, although this tendency towards the (imaginary) domestication of the other constitutes a central pillar in the modern ideologies of empire that began emerging in the early nineteenth century. In this sense, the "civilizing mission" of modern British imperialism can be seen as one of planetary "domestica-tion," through which England's unfolding domestic sphere could be extended to the entire world – or rather, through which the entire world could be absorbed into the bosom of gentle English domesticity. Despite her important insights into this, Melman is methodologically trapped by her insistence on this domesticating outlook as a peculiarly *female* phe-nomenon; whereas I would argue that it is a specifically *modern* phenom-enon, characteristic of later nineteenth-century discourses on the Orien-tal other.

In this sense, the civilizing virtue that the later empire ascribed to itself is actually one of a class- as well as gender-oriented "domestication," through which crude and unsophisticated others could be tamed and slowly raised to the heights of a (constructed) feminine and bourgeois English domesticity: an ideal which Nancy Armstrong argues was constructed around the modern bourgeois subject, who, she suggests, was "first and foremost a woman."[71] In addition to the more familiar construction of a violent and punitive imperialism (which is always "lurking in the wings"), the process of colonization could *also* be presented to the world (and to England itself) as one of gentility, domesticity, affection, and nurturance: "To have found a great people sunk in the lowest depths of slavery and superstition, to have ruled them so as to have made them desirous and capable of all the privileges of citizens, would indeed be a title to glory all our own."[72] The mission that Macaulay here defines as that of the British empire is, indeed, *exactly* analagous to the role of the bourgeois household in preparing individual citizens for the hard realities of the public sphere; only the "home" for Macaulay is a British colony – a colony ideally constructed as a large-scale bourgeois "*intérieur*," so that the discourses of race, class, and gender become inextricably connected.

Here Mary Poovey's suggestive reading of Florence Nightingale is particularly illuminating. Poovey argues that, in the period following the failed Indian Revolution of 1857, Nightingale persistently presented India as if it were the "brute" working-class soldier whose "treatment" (which was more than a strictly-speaking "medical" treatment) she deals with in her notes on nursing during the Crimean War. Thus, Poovey writes, "the two discourses actually employed exactly the same terms in different social registers: the patient (read: India, the poor) is really a brute (a native, a working-class man) who must be cured (colonized, civilized) by an efficient head nurse cum bourgeois mother (England, middle-class women)." She adds that "the ultimate goal in both projects is a tidy society where there is 'no waste of material or force or space,' where 'we learn to have patience with our circumstances and ourselves,' where 'we become more disciplined, more content to work where we are placed.' In both cases, surveillance, discipline, and good administration are the keys to this transformation; in each case, a housewifely, regal, classless woman presides."[73] Thus, just as a constructed gender discourse could be mobilized for an assessment and justification of class constructs and attitudes, "conquest and colonial rule could also be written as the government of love, which was superintended by a motherly monarch."[74]

In the next chapter, I will consider at greater length some of the implications of this emergent modern Orientalism and particularly its intersection with discourses of "improvement," transformation, and domestication. In the meantime, I want to reiterate that this new formation never went unopposed by alternative constructions and images of the Orient and of British imperialism. Certain romantic writers, such as Byron (whom I will consider more closely in the next chapter), radically opposed such a cult of domesticity and its translation into imperial ideology. For Byron, the Orient was precisely a place from which to escape such ideologies and their attendant privileging of the modern and the European. In particular, Byron's Orient ("the greenest island of my imagination," he once wrote[75]) was a place to which one could flee from English domesticity, from Christianity, from modernity: a space from which one could critique these emergent constructions, and in which one could celebrate alternatives to them (not least the unrestrainedly masculine, which also underlies Scott's libidinal investment of a pre-domesticated/"feminized" Highlands, as well as the avowedly male homosociality of "the East"). By the middle and late nineteenth century, such views as these would be residual reminders of a different construction and representation (and libidinal investment) of the Orient; but they can be found, for instance, in Kipling's *Kim*, in Conrad's *Lord Jim*, in Burton's *Narrative of a Pilgrimage to Mecca and Medina*, in Lawrence's *Seven Pillars of Wisdom*.

Perhaps the shift that I have been describing here is related to the distinction that Anne Mellor and others have suggested, between the loosely defined conceptual structures of "masculine" and "feminine" (*not* male and female) romanticisms, and particularly for the cultural project underlying the shifts in the patterns and ideological justifications for nineteenth-century British colonialism (some of which I have just suggested).[76] Mellor makes a provisional distinction between the ideologies of a "masculine" romanticism (which she argues is partly predicated on the constructed assumption of an often violent antagonism between self and other) and a "feminine" romanticism (predicated on a construction of self that is "fluid, absorptive, responsive, with permeable ego boundaries," and hence a constructed self that can assimilate its other). Might there be a correspondence between what Mellor calls this "masculine" romanticism, which is not at all restricted to male writers, and certain non-transformative notions of empire (e.g., William Jones, Edmund Burke); and, on the other hand, Mellor's "feminine" romanticism, again not restricted to women writers, and later (modern) views of empire (e.g., Nightingale, Macaulay), which stress the maternal and nurturing duties of Victorian Britain towards her colonies? If this is the case, then what Mellor proposes as a secondary or subaltern cultural form or literary/ideological structure in the romantic period ("feminine" romanticism) would, together with its attendant constructs of fluid and absorptive subjectivity, shift to prominence in the Victorian period. Admittedly, this actually goes far beyond what Mellor argues, and even distorts her argument altogether by recontextualizing it and reorienting what seems to be the originally privileged or dominant ideology of "masculine" romanticism (with its attraction to immutable difference). The latter can now be seen to have gradually faded away into the nineteenth century, as one mode of imperialism replaced another.

In one sense, this shift also marks a transition from the symbolic production of difference to the symbolic production not so much of identity as of a practically infinite range of hybridities;[77] signaling the end of a quest for otherness and a troubled beginning of a new quest for sameness. With this double transition, the Orient ceases to be a site of immutable difference, and becomes instead a space to be cleansed, purged, and re-written – a symbolic space for the representation and contestation of Western and European concerns, values and desires, rather than their unchangeable and libidinally charged opposites. In the next chapter, I will consider this spatial reinvention of the Orient and of the colonial other in greater detail, through two emblematic literary texts: the second canto of Byron's *Childe Harold's Pilgrimage,* and Shelley's poem, *Alastor; or, the Spirit of Solitude.*

CHAPTER 6

Beyond the realm of dreams: Byron, Shelley, and the East

> The settler makes history and is conscious of making it. And
> because he constantly refers to the history of his mother country, he
> clearly indicates that he himself is the extension of that mother
> country. Thus the history which he writes is not the history of the
> country which he plunders but the history of his own nation in
> regard to all she skims off, all that she violates and starves.
>
> Frantz Fanon, *The Wretched of the Earth*

I

James Mill writes in his *History of British India* that "whatever is worth
seeing or hearing in India, can be expressed in writing. As soon as every
thing of importance is expressed in writing, a man who is duly qualified
may obtain more knowledge of India in one year, in his closet in
England, than he could obtain during the course of the longest life, by
the use of his eyes and his ears, in India."[1] Mill argues that the entire
reality of what was for him an "object" called "India" can be defined by
being captured in writing, just as its territory had been defined by being
captured by the armies of the East India Company. He is "correct" to
the extent that imperial rule from London relied upon the minute
documentation of the endless activities of the Company in India, so that
what was being judged and decided upon by the directors in London
were not the material activities themselves, but rather the documents
produced alongside them – not, in other words, the "realities," but the
"representations." During the course of the late eighteenth and early
nineteenth centuries, not only the British empire itself but the territories
over which it had or sought dominion – as well as their peoples – were
reinvented. A series of Oriental realities was produced, partly through
the discursive networks on which Mill places such heavy emphasis.
Frantz Fanon once wrote that it is "the settler who has brought the
native into existence and who perpetuates his existence."[2] And yet

neither the native nor the settler is or can be a static being: caught in the violent "dialogue" of imperialism, settlers and natives, Europeans and others, have been – and still are – ever-changing and turbulent, non-identities rather than identities.

As Edward Said has argued, the Orient "as such" only exists – and has only ever existed – as a spatial construction endowed with a series of facts, essences, histories, etc., a space that could be known, controlled, exploited, and developed by Europeans.[3] Byron's Orientalism has often been compared to Shelley's, but while the two poets undoubtedly have much in common, I believe that it is of crucial importance to distinguish between Byron's East – as produced in the first two cantos of *Childe Harold* (1812) – and the vision of the East first produced by Shelley in *Alastor; or, the Spirit of Solitude* (1816). Underlying each of these versions of the Orient there are radically opposed concepts of empire, of Oriental-ism, and of history – concepts that would become more defined in Shelley's (and, though to a lesser extent, Byron's) later works.[4] What I want to propose in the present chapter is that the Oriental space developed in *Alastor* represents a reclamation of an Oriental terrain from previous visions and versions of the East and its incorporation into the emergent space-time of modernity. Thus it not only anticipates the paradigms of Orientalist discourse associated both with James Mill and with late nineteenth-century English Orientalists (many of whom were inspired by Mill's *History*) but it contributes to the historical production of the Orient as a space for European knowledge, discipline, and control. The version of the Orient that is produced in *Childe Harold* II – the Orient as refuge from and potential alternative to modernity – was contested and redefined in later spatial productions; its critical and imaginary terrain had to be seized, cleansed, and totally re-organized and re-invented. The Oriental space produced in *Alastor* symbolizes the beginning of that reclamation, the production of a new Orient that the poem "discovers," which would later be embellished, developed, aug-mented, and improved in succeeding visions and versions of the East.

II

Even if Byron never ventured farther into Asia than the eastern outskirts of Istanbul, he had certainly ventured to the "Orient." For in the first two decades of the nineteenth century, Albania and Greece were merely outlying provinces in a far-flung Asian empire. Europe did not simply grow gradually "less European" towards the East, as Victor Kiernan has argued, for the very identity of a geographical or spatial entity called Europe was still in the process of development.[5] Nevertheless, at a certain point, "European" travelers crossed an indefinite symbolic "frontier." For Byron, that frontier was the Albanian coastline, which he first viewed from the decks of the Royal Navy frigate that carried him eastwards from the British colony of Malta. As his alter ego Childe Harold wanders on that shore, he finds "himself at length alone, / And bade to Christian tongues a long adieu; / Now he adventured on a shore unknown, / Which all admire, but many dread to view."[6]

Harold's arrival in the East represents a passage across a multidimensional "border" into the space and time of the Orient, a space-time that has its own distinct pattern of temporal ruptures and losses, but, on its own terms, is a discrete spatial-temporal sphere, different from that of the West which Harold leaves behind. Thus the space-time of Byron's Orient exists alongside that of the Occident, in apposition to it, rather than as a rupture contained by – or within – an otherwise homogeneous Western *jetztzeit*. This East is then not simply a repository of some mythical Western "past"; it exists as its own space, on the fringes, perhaps, of a power that threatens it with annihilation, but nevertheless still clinging to its own life, its own structures, its own meanings, distinct from the homogenizing modernity of the West – and hence profoundly attractive to exiles attempting to flee that modernity. Byron conceives the historical relationship between East and West in synchronic, rather than diachronic, terms. Indeed, he could conceive of the Orient as a spatial alternative to Europe precisely because he sees European and Oriental histories as distinct – as synchronic *histories*, rather than as one diachronic *History* narrated and controlled by Europe.

"Byron's is a poetry of trajectories," Bernard Blackstone argues; "we travel far afield, but always on a return ticket. *The Ancient Mariner*, not *Alastor*, is the paradigm of *Childe Harold, Lara, Mazeppa, Don Juan*."[7] As a self-constituted pilgrimage (even if in the end it proves to be aimless), *Childe Harold* has its basis in what Johannes Fabian argues is the concept of "sacred" as opposed to "secular" time, depicting a movement *towards* some central spatial objective from elsewhere. According to Fabian, the creation and development of secularized time was inextricably caught up with a gradual shift in European concepts of travel, away from an outmoded version in which travel involved a movement *to* the centers of religion (e.g., Rome, Jerusalem, Canterbury) *from* everywhere else; and instead towards a notion of travel *from* the new centers of learning and power (London, Berlin, Paris – acclaimed in later Eurocentric views as "capital" of the nineteenth century itself) *to* "places where man was to find nothing but himself."[8] In this new topos of travel, the old model of Judeo-Christian time was simultaneously secularized and gradually universalized, so that time became a more or less uniform natural essence, pointing to and "culminating" in a (nevertheless developing) modern Europe. This new sense of time was fundamental to the formation of a properly evolutionary temporality, through which difference was understood as, or expressed in terms of, temporal distance from a standard point of reference (modern Europe).[9] In a "quest," like that of *Alastor* (to which I will turn shortly), which has no delimited spatial objective, the movement represents a turn outwards, away from the center, and in search of some outside fulfillment. But *Childe Harold's Pilgrimage*, by contrast, implicitly affirms a belief in, or a claim to, sacred (or at any rate pre-modern) time. Childe Harold, in leaving Europe, leaves behind the slowly-universalizing temporality of modernity and enters a synchronous structure of time, space, and history; not a *pre-modern*, but an *anti-modern* Orient.

Byron's meditations on Greece in canto II are interwoven with his "discovery" of the space of the East. The text of his musings on Hellenic antiquity is shaped by the context of the Oriental world within which he finds the ruins of ancient Greece; at the same time, this context itself is altered by Byron's nascent philhellenism. The Greek ruins of *Childe Harold* II are inseparable yet distinct from their Oriental surroundings – so that Byron's discovery of what Robert Gleckner terms "the ruins of paradise"[10] and Harold's contact with the Asiatic other are in symbiosis: the one is written in terms of the other. And yet the contemporary Orientals in Byron's vision seem not to see the ruins, or at least not to pay them any heed. From their standpoint, the days of Hellenic antiquity are as remote as they are from Byron's – even if they do not participate in the modernity whose homogenizing sameness drove the Englishman into his exilic search for alternatives to it, a search which eventually brings him to their world.

For the space-time of the contemporary Orient that canto II produces is neither modern nor ancient; it is as distinct from the ruins that mark its terrain as it is from Europe, as though these ruins had been left there by a society whose lost heirs have not yet come to claim their heritage. The history of this space, in other words, is alien to the people currently inhabiting it; or, rather: the space-time of Hellenic antiquity is somehow buried beneath the space-time of Byron's contemporary Orient, figuratively existing in a planar dimension whose ruins protrude through the

latter, marking and scarring it in places – marks and scars that Byron
can emplot on his imaginary map of this contemporary Oriental space,
whether or not they are seen, felt, and recognized by the natives. His is a
pilgrimage, however, not an excavating archaeological expedition; and
though he points out and traces the "ruins of paradise," he does so not
in order to retrieve them, but in order, once again, to "remember" the
imaginary past in which they were produced and for which, hence, they
are memorials: "Come – but molest not yon defenceless urn: / Look on
this spot – a nation's sepulchre! / Abode of gods, whose shrines no
longer burn."[11] Byron's anxiety pertains not to the spatial zone that he
has discovered (the Orient), but to the scattered relics of a space that
once was, or in other words, a previous spatial production of the
(Hellenic) East. His admonition is, moreover, directed not at the "ignorant" Greeks and Turks – ignorant insofar as they apparently ignore the
ruins – but at Lord Elgin and his antiquary relic-collectors.

The dark sepulchral tone of canto II is thus restricted to the dreamlike
"memories" and memorials of Greece, rather than to the living Oriental
pageant of the present (although his admonition "not to molest" may
also be applied to the Oriental space, rather than solely to the ruins).
The ghosts and specters haunting the tombs and temples do not torment
the Orientals, by whom they are not seen. They are, rather, the private
projections and possessions of the European tourist, even if they are his
as an individual, and not simply as a European, for not all Europeans
acknowledge or feel the sepulchral gloom that pervades Byron's Greece.

Although there is a sense in canto II that the ruins of paradise ought to
be exclusively appreciated by those who hold a cultural claim to a right
of inheritance (i.e., modern Europeans, not the "fallen" Greeks, and
certainly not the Turks), this sense is tempered by Byron's insistence on
the sepulchral nature of the ruins. The canto's claim is that the relics of
Greece ought to be preserved just as graveyards and tombs are preserved, as relics and reminders of a previous age forever irretrievable from
modernity, and not as treasured kindling for some Promethean fire of
European cultural renewal (which I will argue is what they would
become for Shelley and others after 1815: see below). Greece is finally,
utterly, and irrevocably dead, though its traces are immortal; it can be
remembered, perhaps, and its passing can be mourned, but it can never
be revived or excavated from the crushing historical weight of the other
civilizations that have come to claim its terrain.

The death of Greece is redeemed, though, by the Oriental presence
on its terrain. Byron's and Harold's thrilling contact with this other

civilization easily rivals Byron's "memories" of Hellenic antiquity; so that the space of Hellenic "memories" and that of Oriental contact both afford zones of escape from modernity. Canto II thus structurally distinguishes – and even segregates – Harold's expedition from what we may term Byron's philosophical and political musings on Greece. The version of Oriental space that the canto produces is both structurally and spatially separated from the monuments of antiquity against which it is juxtaposed. Harold's arrival in the Orient takes place after crossing the symbolic frontier (the Albanian coast) dividing East from West, Europe from Asia. But the ruins of paradise are neither "here" nor "there"; separated from modern Europe by a gulf, they are also opposed to the contemporary Greeks and Turks, whose spatial structures and assemblages are superimposed upon them.

Harold's pilgrimage is thus twofold: on the one hand, it is a trip to the space-time of Hellenic antiquity; and, on the other, it is a journey to the East. The canto begins with the first journey, "rewinds," then begins again with Harold's arrival in the East; the two dimensions of Byron's East (Hellenic and contemporary) occupy the same space, the one displacing the other. Access to either dimension requires a leap across the frontier and away from the space-time of modernity and modernization. The contradictory and even mutually-exclusive relationships connecting the space-time and history of modernity with the space of (on the one hand) the Hellenic past and (on the other) the Oriental present are not at all coincidental to Byron's anxious production of these spaces. In his mourning for the Hellenic past and in his indignant attack on Lord Elgin, Byron is affirming or positing an historical and cultural continuity between modern Europe and not only ancient Greece but the rest of the (pre-modern) Levant; yet in constructing (and turning to) the contemporary Oriental Levant as a space distinct from modern Europe, he is affirming a rupture and dislocation between East and West, Orient and Occident, Asia and Europe – as spaces with synchronic histories, rather than one diachronic history.

When I say that Childe Harold's pilgrimage is twofold, what I mean is that Byron narrates a voyage to two different and mutually-exclusive spatial-temporal constructs (that he himself produces): first, the Levant as the cultural and historical ancestor of Europe; and second, the Levant as the space and territory of the Oriental other. The first is an affirmation of a diachronic historical continuity between modern Europe and ancient Greece, while the second is an affirmation of a synchronic historical separation between modern Europe and an anti-modern

Orient. In other words, the first implies the re-possession and the appropriation of the space of the Levant for a Eurocentric vision of history, in which Europeans claim to assimilate other peoples, cultures, and histories into the history of modernity – a history to be narrated and understood from the standpoint of Europe; while the second implies the coexistence of distinct though related cultures and histories, spaces, and times.

Byron's anxiety here stems from his simultaneous participation in both projects – viewing the East as the site or birthplace of Europe's great cultural heritage, while at the same time viewing the East as a site into which one could escape from modernity, a site from whose vantage point one could critique both modernity and Europe itself. For while Byron views the East as such an alternative synchronic space, he sees its possibilities and its very existence (as such a space) threatened by its appropriation and re-constitution in European colonial projects – colonial projects he both participated in and at the same time opposed and contested.

For Byron arrived in the Levant along with the first wave of intense European colonial activity in the heart of the Muslim world, and his first trip to the East took him not only to the very fringes of Europe, but close to the freshly captured – and at the time still hotly contested – easternmost European possessions on and off the Mediterranean coasts of Africa and Asia. These territories, including Sicily, Malta, and the Ionian islands as well as Egypt and Syria (from 1798 to 1801), were neither the first nor the most valuable European colonial prizes, though they represented the beginning of the intense European imperial investment in the region. On the other hand, they were unlike all other colonial territories inasmuch as they were virtually extensions of Europe, lying within quick and easy reach across the various straits and channels of the Mediterranean.

During his sojourn in the East, hence, Byron was never very far from the scene of colonial rivalries. In spite of the rapidly-unfolding European involvement in the region, however, Byron's 1809–11 Levantine tour was a voyage into territory still largely "unknown" and "unexplored" by Europeans, and Gibbon's famous remark about Albania ("a country within sight of Italy is less known than the interior of America") still held true in Byron's time, at least from a Eurocentric standpoint. The Levant was – for the most part – still neither occupied nor firmly controlled by any of the various competing European powers. In 1809, still mired in the war with France, Britain was unable and unwilling to fully commit itself to large-scale interventions in the area, except where the French directly and immediately threatened the overland routes to India (most notably in Egypt).[12] The Ottoman empire was, despite its weakness, still intact, and certain semi-independent Ottoman provincial governors would become or were already major forces to be reckoned with even on their own. Britain's main imperial policy in the region, at least until the end of the war with France, was to back up the steadily-weakening Ottomans in order to safeguard the approaches to India from both the Russians and the French. The Ottoman territories, from North Africa to Palestine and from Palestine to the Balkans, were held in a kind of political vacuum: a space still decidedly "Oriental," but one which no longer posed a significant threat to Britain. Hence it was an ideal space to tour the exotic East without, on the one hand, having to see the obvious deployment of British imperial power needed to keep it under control (as in India); or, on the other hand, feeling threatened by what even some contemporary critics *still* refer to as "the austere ferocity of Islam."[13] While the integration of the local economies of Southwest Asia and North Africa into the capitalist world-economy would radically and permanently transform the region, beginning after 1815 and accelerating in the 1830s, they were not yet fully locked into the Eurocentric structures of capital. In other words, while this region *would become* crucially important to, and dependent on, European industry from the 1830s onwards – when, for example, the intensification of cotton production in Egypt and silk production in what is today Lebanon would gradually force Egypt and Lebanon into dependence on the textile industry of Lancashire and the silk industry of Lyon – the Ottoman Levant was in Byron's time still largely a "neutral zone" lying outside industrial capitalism's circuits of unequal exchange.[14]

At length, Harold bids to Christian tongues "a long adieu" and "*finds himself*" alone. Canto II has been called "Byron's 'self-discovery' canto," or the poetical narrative space in which Byron "invented the myth of himself."[15] It is, as both McGann and Blackstone observe, not coincidental that Byron's self-discovery or self-invention – for they are one and the same – takes place in the fantastic Orient produced in *Childe Harold* II. In the very process of producing an Oriental other, Byron has to produce an image of himself: a narrative persona of himself as a man, an Englishman, a European. Even if one of the aims of Childe Harold and of Byron's flight and exile from England in 1809 was to escape the realities of his self-identity and his status as an Englishman and a modern European, his voyage to the Orient only forced him into greater awareness (or, rather, the "discovery") of those identities and realities. His despair stems in part from the realization that any attempt to escape self-recognition only strengthens it, especially in the narrative field of the other. For it is when he is most overwhelmed by the surrounding presence of others – in and among whom he tries to lose himself – that Byron can declare, "This is to be alone; this, this, is solitude!"[16] Byron's alter ego, Childe Harold, is even more lonely than Byron was on his Levantine trip, since the entourage of servants, followers, and friends that had journeyed with Byron from England is nowhere to be found in the pages of the *Pilgrimage*. Indeed, Harold's existential loneliness is an important structural and thematic component of the Albanian narrative – a narrative of a single European's visual discovery of the Orient and its mysteries. Childe Harold's pilgrimage is necessarily a private, if not quite secretive, tour; his tourist's "consumption" of the landscape and people of the East (in an imaginary space of his own equally private production) is a deeply personal, private, and even selfish affair, to which no other tourists or wanderers can be admitted. Indeed, the narrative of Harold's pilgrimage to the East takes place almost entirely in a visual register, and hence his consumption of the Orient is doubly private in that it takes place through and in his own eyes (". . . let me bend mine eyes / On thee . . .").

The very privateness of this visualized touristic consumption is of more importance, in and of itself, than the space that it consumes. Moreover, the uniqueness of the consumed space does not matter as much as its radical difference from the modernizing culture and historicity of the tourist: a difference that, on its own terms, makes the distinction between, for example, Scottish Highlanders and Albanians (compared in Byron's poetic vision) fade into obscurity. The attraction of these other cultures, in other words, lies first and foremost in their sheer difference from the standard of emerging European modernity, and only in a secondary sense in each culture's unique features. In another sense, however, the radical alterity of a particular anti-modern culture could be rendered more comprehensible by comparison to one more familiar – but still different; or, inversely, a culture that might otherwise seem to be dangerously "familiar" could be distanced (from "us") by a comparison to a more unfamiliar group. Thus, although in *Waverley* Walter Scott repeatedly uses Oriental allusions and references to accentuate or exaggerate his Highlanders' radical difference from some standardized Lowland-English culture of modernity, Byron makes his Albanians seem more knowable by assimilating them to the familiar alterity of Highlanders: a group that, for all that remained of its exoticism in Byron's time, had already been purged of whatever hostile threat it might contain in the aftermath of Culloden.[17] Hence, just as Oriental allusions are repeatedly invoked in Edward Waverley's tour of the Scottish Highlands, the Highlands and Highlanders are repeatedly invoked in Byron's stanzas on Albania. Such reassurances notwithstanding, the central parts of canto II are about contact – beyond the safety delineated by the frontiers of modernity – with an otherness whose appeal would possess Byron for the rest of his life, and whose influence would shape his poetry more profoundly than by merely offering him exotic thematic material.

Byron never ventured farther east than the western territories of the Ottoman empire, Greece, Albania, and Turkey; yet, as I have already suggested, he did not need to in order to "discover" the wonders of the East. In canto II of *Childe Harold*, Albania – the westernmost and northernmost of those territories – is the most significantly Oriental, or, to use Said's term, Orientalized space. Indeed, Byron's spatialized vision of the East and his production of an Oriental space is largely confined to Albania, although that confinement does not by any means prevent Albania from standing for and representing the "Oriental" nature of spaces farther east. On the contrary; in *Childe Harold*'s imaginary map of the East, Albania is a synecdochical space for the representation of the greater Orient; the former's exoticized character-types (the despot, the eunuch, the harem-girl, the janissary) and spaces (the harem, the emir's palace, the mosque) are not only "found" in the rest of the Orient: they are specific cases or illustrations of the Oriental "truths" and essences that would be generalized through the later nineteenth century by the institutions and discourses of modern European Orientalism.[18]

This imaginary Oriental terrain can never be defined, let alone invested and captured, insofar as it defies encapsulation in a single field of vision; rather, its spatial–visual field is defined by the infinite series of barriers that not only invite, but necessitate discovery. The rich and colorful Oriental collage describing Ali Pasha's enclave is a visual encapsulation of the sights, colors, odors and sounds of the Orient. It is a complex space, marked and defined by a honeycomb of walls, courtyards, doors, gates, passageways, layers within layers. The most impenetrable space – that of the harem – is not seen by Childe Harold, who merely pauses outside its "silent tower," though the ultimate voyeuristic vision of the harem's "sacred" space would later be famously provided by Byron in *Don Juan*. Nor is Ali Pasha himself encountered in these stanzas; he remains an unseen presence, whose invisible power nevertheless invests all the activity and bustle that Harold does indeed encounter. Apart from the flow of "typical" Oriental types in a "many-hued array" – slaves, eunuchs, santons, etc. – Ali Pasha's domain brings together exotic and exoticized people from all over the Orient: Tartars, Moors, Nubians, Indians, Turks, and, more locally though no less exotically, Greeks and Albanians as well. Over this "motley scene" of preparations for feasts and battles – this crowd of "strange groups" adorning Ali Pasha's corridors of power, this collage of smokers and players and prayers arguing and talking and babbling in a mix of Eastern tongues, this moving panoply of Oriental shapes and colors – floats the muezzin's distant call to prayer, rendered here in *very* Anglicized terms, "There is no god but God! – to prayer! – lo! God is great!" Byron's visual and spatial portrait of the Orient is an alluring series of images of the exotic Orient drawn by a charmed and attracted European "caught in its spell." Once again, Byron here anticipates later developments and uses of colonial imagery and visuality in the nineteenth century, as for instance in the Great Exhibitions of the second half of the century, which, in part, render the experience of colonialism in iconographic and visualized – and, later on, cinematic – terms.[19]

The space of Ali Pasha's enclave in Albania is an exemplary and representative space; "defining" the Orient, it is "purely" Oriental in the sense that the purest essences of the Orient are spatially and visually represented in it. Yet, precisely because of its Edenic quality, and despite the protection and insulation afforded by the layered boundaries separating it from the impinging outside (Western/modern) world, this perfect and exemplary space is threatened with penetration, "discovery," and destruction by the forces against which it is momentarily and even fleetingly defined. Robert Gleckner argues that the reader's final impression of Ali Pasha's enclave "is of an Edenic, sublime land surrounded by the awe-inspiring, terrible, and destructive power of the Pasha, a panoramic image of one of Byron's major themes, the ruins of paradise."[20] The isolation of this Oriental space, however, is as yet an *unruined* paradise, not one that has been destroyed, pillaged, and only then touristed. Ali Pasha's paradise, in other words, is encircled and threatened by outside penetration, but the enabling condition for Harold's (and through him Byron's) entry into that space is that its essential property as an exemplary Oriental space not be physically touched, materially altered, or tangibly affected. This is strictly a visual tour of an imaginary space, leaving no trace of its own passage on the terrain that it voyeuristically describes. Thus the lone European who ventures silently into the realm of the Oriental other virtually lifts himself out of his own voyage, and the process of self-discovery once again slips into one of "selfish" self-negation. The Orientalism of Byron's production of the Orient is therefore not simply visual or even thematic – its distinction between East and West is simultaneously a spatial and an *epistemological* structure.[21]

While the threat of destruction is the price to be paid for visiting this forbidden Oriental space, the reward, on the other hand, is the viewer's access to a pristine, and Edenically inviolate otherness. The space of this otherness, whose silent Western viewer/voyeur can observe almost without being observed, once again becomes a "theatre" for individual Western discovery of self (a discovery whose significance for Byron in particular has been pointed out by Jerome McGann and others), or for the freedom and refreshing independence of a lonely Western tourist.[22] At the same time, Byron's Orientalism – quite apart from its litany of authenticating devices and references – claims to re-present to Western readers the multitudinous realities of the East in its scenes and images that are not only taken from the land of the other, but even reproduce (at a distance) the experience of that otherness on its own terms. Marilyn Butler argues that Byron tended to respect "the autonomy of other cultures, but was inclined to admire them precisely for their otherness, their unreformed 'romantic' features."[23] Indeed, Byron's Orient seems to be the Orient's Orient – the real Orient "out there," and not only some vaguely-realistic figurative landscape produced by a Western imagination.

For, ultimately, Byron's attraction to and obsession with the East is driven not only by a deep-felt interest in non-Western structures and spaces, but also by the desire (however chimerical) to experience the East "as such," on its own terms and in its own sphere of existence – a sphere preferably, for Byron, protected from European incursion and imperial investment. Butler points to the central importance of Southey in the early nineteenth-century literary production, and especially to what she argues are "the reappearances of Southey's structures and images in the nineteenth-century literature of colonialism, high and low, beginning with Shelley and Byron."[24] She insists, however, that much of Byron's poetry, including *The Giaour*, can be read as an explicit contestation of Southey's interventionist and evangelical attitude towards empire, as exemplified in *Madoc* (1805) and *The Curse of Kehama* (1810).[25]

Drawing upon a contrast between Byron and later English writers on the Orient (e.g., Burton, Thackeray, and Disraeli), other critics, including Patrick Brantlinger, have discussed what they see as Byron's "anti-imperialist message," a "message" predicated upon the contrast that they establish with the paradigms of imperialism supported by the later figures.[26] That Byron did not share the kind of imperial attitudes expressed by Disraeli and Burton does not, however, necessarily mean that he opposed imperialism altogether.[27] Indeed, it seems to me that the question at hand is not *whether* a politics of imperialism underlies Byron's vision of the East in *Childe Harold* II, but rather what kind of politics it is.

"Fair Greece!" Byron writes in canto II, "sad relic of departed worth! / Immortal, though no more; though fallen, great! / Who now shall lead thy scatter'd children forth, / And long accustom'd bondage uncreate?" The next stanzas propose two answers to this question. On the one hand, and in striking contrast to what a Burton, a Disraeli, or a Lawrence might answer, Byron insists that only the Greeks can free themselves ("Hereditary bondsmen! know ye not / Who would be free themselves must strike the blow? / By their right arms the conquest must be wrought?"). On the other hand, he is certain that "ne'er will freedom seek this fated soil: / But slave succeed to slave through years of endless toil." Thus, the sepulchral tone of the opening stanzas of canto II – in which Byron mourns for the ruins of paradise – is, at the end of the canto, tied not only to Byron's analysis at the time (for it would later change) of the prospects for Greek rebellion against the Ottomans, but to his views of the Greek nation and the Greeks themselves. These views, in turn, are inextricably caught up with Byron's uneasy and ambivalent early attitudes towards empire and towards empire-building in the "boundless East," as he was writing in the years before the triumphant victory of 1815: a victory that would forever alter British attitues towards the rest of the world. Among the notes to canto II, Byron has a lengthy reflection on Greece and the Greeks:

The Greeks will never be independent: they will never be sovereigns as heretofore, and God forbid that they ever should! but they may be subjects without being slaves. Our colonies are not independent, but they are free and industrious, and such may Greece be hereafter.

Byron continues:

The English have at last compassionated their negroes [NB: only the slave trade was abolished in 1807, not slavery itself], and under a less bigoted government, may probably one day release their Catholic brethren; but the interposition of foreigners alone can emancipate the Greeks, who, otherwise, appear to have as small a chance of redemption from the Turks, as the Jews have from mankind in general . . .

To talk, as the Greek themselves do, of their rising again to their pristine superiority, would be ridiculous: as the rest of the world must resume its barbarism, after re-asserting the sovereignty of Greece; but there seems to be no very great obstacle, except in the apathy of the Franks, to their becoming a useful dependency, or even a free state, with a proper guarantee; – under correction, however, be it spoken, for many and well-informed men doubt the practicability even of this.

It is well known that Byron would not only later change his views of the Greeks and their rebellion against the Turks, but that he would give his own life in their cause. Nevertheless, at this earlier moment (at least up to his return to England in 1812), he was clearly doubtful both about the Greeks' "national character" and about their chances for freedom. Byron here neither advocates Greek independence, nor does he call for immediate British intervention in the cause of a struggle whose prospects he believes are hopeless, or, at best, doubtful.

Byron's assertion, earlier in the canto, that there is no hope for a recuperation or regeneration of the Hellenic monuments is by the canto's end tied to his assertion that the Greeks of his time have lost virtually all claims to their fabled Hellenic ancestry. Like Africans and Irishmen, he argues, contemporary Greeks are "afflicted" with certain "ailments" (principally moral ones) as a result of their treatment and their historical condition. Yet his position in the notes is not that England ought to intervene and "enlighten" these "degenerate" colonial or semi-colonial peoples, let alone that England has some moral duty to do so, but – at the most – that England might take it upon itself to remove the conditions that led to their "degeneration," through the abolition of slavery, through Catholic relief, and by ending the foreign domination of Greece. Although "only" foreign intervention could force the Ottomans out of Greece, such intervention could never truly liberate the Greeks; on the other hand, Byron is clear that ending the foreign domination of Greece might benefit England (because it would alleviate the prospects for French and Russian intervention which would destabilize Turkey).

At most, Byron argues, Greece might be turned into a colony or protectorate under the benevolent guidance and care of a power like Great Britain. Thus Byron resigns himself to an ambivalent argument –

the Greeks can only be free by freeing themselves, the Greeks cannot
under their present conditions free themselves, therefore the Greeks will
never be free – whose main thrust is not simply to defer intervention, but
to assert that, if one day the Ottomans might be pushed out of Greece,
on the whole it would be better for England if France and Russia were
not behind the Ottoman defeat and the new Greek "state."

Byron does not, however, call in any way for British intervention
elsewhere in the Ottoman empire or in the rest of Asia. His fascination
with the otherness of the Orient is predicated, as I have already mentioned, on its inviolate non-Westernness as much as on its own pure and
essential Easternness – indeed these are, for him, one and the same. His
belief (such as it is) in the Greek cause is not based upon assumptions of a
wider British imperial destiny or mission in Asia and the world; rather,
his equivocal support for English intervention in Greece is based as
much upon his desire to keep the rest of the Ottoman empire intact and
free of Russian and French interference as it is upon his belief in Greek
liberty.

Byron's weakly stated and deeply ambivalent philhellenism of 1812, in
other words, has little to do with notions of innate European superiority
over Turks and Muslims, and even less to do with a broader European
mission civilisatrice in Asia. Indeed, Byron is very careful not to make
sweeping pronouncements about Turkish or Oriental degeneracy, or to
declare their "need" for moral "improvement," development, and
evolution. "It is hazardous," Byron writes in his notes, "to say much on
the subject of Turks and Turkey; since it is possible to live amongst them
twenty years without acquiring information, at least from themselves. As
far as my own slight experience carried me, I have no complaint to
make; but am indebted for many civilities (I might also say for friendship), and much hospitality . . ." He goes on to say that

the Ottomans are not a people to be despised. Equal, at least, to the Spaniards,
they are superior to the Portuguese. If it be difficult to pronounce what they are,
we can at least say what they are *not*: they are *not* treacherous, they are *not*
cowardly, they do *not* burn heretics, they are *not* assassins, nor has an enemy
advanced to *their* capital. They are faithful to their sultan till he becomes unfit to
govern, and devout to their God without an inquisition. Were they driven from
St. Sophia tomorrow, and the French or Russians enthroned in their stead, it
would become a question whether Europe would gain by the exchange.
England would certainly be the loser.

Byron's knowledge of the Turks is here defined in negative terms, rather
than as the sort of positive knowledge that was already being advocated

by James Mill; with the lack of such positive knowledge, there is a lack of explicit proscriptive or prescriptive emphases, and hence no effort to correct the deviation or the abnormality of another civilization. On the contrary; as a spatial production, the East is for Byron not only a refuge from modernity – that is, a space from which to flee modernity – but also a space from which to critique modernity and the West itself.

Byron's Oriental space, in other words, offers liberatory possibilities for the critique of Western, European, English concepts, taboos, norms, and standards – political, social, sexual, poetical, economic, and cultural. The concept of imperialism underlying Byron's early Orientalism is hence torn with anxiety. Sometimes in favor of intervention, and sometimes not, it is as though he were aware that Ottoman independence – and hence the kind of "pristine" or even Edenic Oriental realm that the Ottoman domains provided for Western tourism – could, paradoxically, be maintained only by a British intervention that would eventually undermine and erode it. Not seeing any need for a productive transformation of a cultural system that he in many ways finds admirable, Byron wants to preserve it intact, though it becomes increasingly clear that such "preservation" would be as fictive as declaring a regularly maintained country park in England to be "natural." His desire to keep this space of non-Western and anti-modern otherness intact is thus contradicted by his increasing awareness that to do so would only accelerate its penetration by the West and by the forces and structures of modernization; such otherness would henceforth only be toured in the imaginary spatial productions of a poetry which might preserve it as an alternative space forever. Or else it would be abandoned altogether with a return to Eurocentrism – the sort of Eurocentrism advocated and typified by Shelley, but also by the later Byron, the Byron of *Childe Harold* III and IV, whose destination is no longer the East, but Italy – the "heart" of modern Europe.

III

Following hard on the tracks of its Visionary, *Alastor* takes us on a journey deep into the vast expanses of what Byron called the "boundless East."[28] Like *Childe Harold* II, *Alastor* faces the dilemma of having to create its own object, that which it wants simultaneously to describe and to "represent." It does so at a crucial historical juncture, in which the multiple conditions of that rapidly developing "object," the East – its location, its figurative and material possibilities, its value, its history, its peoples, its usefulness, its rule, and, above all, its relation to "the West" and to Europe – were undergoing momentous changes. *Alastor*'s map of the East has no real referent: it does not and cannot simply "represent the Orient," a region and a space that did not and does not exist as such, but that had to be endlessly reinvented by its symbiotically related opposite term, "the West," during the long and bloody history of imperialism. Inhabiting the form of a travel narrative, Shelley's poem is in large measure informed by the shock of (imaginary) encounter on the imperial frontier, a region in which, as Mary Pratt has observed, "Europeans confront not only unfamiliar others, but unfamiliar selves."[29] Torn by the anxieties of colonialism and of oppression, *Alastor* is a profoundly disturbed meditation on empire.

"The philosophical traveller, sailing to the ends of the earth, is in fact travelling in time; he is exploring the past; every step he makes is the passage of an age."[30] Joseph-Marie Degérando's observation, made in 1800 following his excursion from Europe into lands inhabited by "savages," provides a strangely appropriate description for *Alastor*'s Visionary. In the prime of his youth, the Visionary – just such a philosophical traveler – leaves "his cold fireside and alienated home / To seek strange truths in undiscovered lands." His thirst for knowledge is at first satiated by what he can grasp through intercourse with Nature and the magnificence of "the external world." But the charms and intellectual treasures of a sweet and domestic Nature are quickly exhausted, and the Visionary takes his search into lands "undiscovered" not by people, but specifically by Europeans. He pushes away from the tranquil scenes of domestic Wordsworthian Nature, and towards the (Byronic and Southeyan) realm of the foreign and distinctly non-European: "Many a wild waste and tangled wilderness / Has lured his fearless steps; and he has bought / With his sweet voice and eyes, from savage men, / His rest and food." Having pursued like her shadow "Nature's most secret steps," the Visionary leaves behind the familiar world of squirrels and deer and begins his fantastic adventure back in time, not only to Eden, but to what came long before. At the end of the poem, once he has reached the very heart of the East, the so-called "cradle" of (Western) civilization, and still in pursuit of the phantasmatic and elusive "veilèd maid" of his dreams, the pitch and velocity of his journey accelerate "beyond all human speed." A tiny boat carries him on to his destiny at the very origins of time: "Nature's cradle, and his sepulchre." This cyclical inversion of time, in which a cradle is also a sepulchre, in which the beginning is also the end (oddly reminiscent of

Wordsworth's "the child is the father of the man"), is accomplished precisely through the translation of a forward movement in space into a backward movement in time. For, propelled by a supernatural whirl-pool, the quasi-magical boat is indeed a time-machine of sorts, taking the Visionary *up* the cavern of a river which pours *down* into the Caspian sea:

> Seized by the sway of the *ascending stream*,
> With dizzy swiftness, round, and round, and round,
> Ridge after ridge *the straining boat arose*,
> Till on the verge of the extremest curve,
> Where, through an opening of the rocky bank,
> The waters overflow, and a smooth spot
> Of glassy quiet mid those battling tides
> Is left, the boat paused shuddering.[31]

Having reversed and rewound time, having defied the laws of gravity and of physics, the Visionary's boat arrives at the source of space and time (to which I shall return a little later). This dizzying upward and backwards journey bears a synecdochical relationship to the entire poem's spatial–temporal flow, especially that of the section preceding this mystical last stage of his journey. For even before this apotheosis, each of the Visionary's steps towards the East is signaled as a troubled step "back in time." The passage recounting his travel to and arrival in *Alastor*'s Orient is worth quoting at length:

> His wandering step
> Obedient to high thoughts, has visited
> The awful ruins of the days of old:
> Athens, and Tyre, and Balbec, and the waste
> Where stood Jerusalem, the fallen towers
> Of Babylon, the eternal pyramids,
> Memphis and Thebes, and whatsoe'er of strange
> Sculptured on alabaster obelisk,
> Or jasper tomb, or mutilated sphynx,
> Dark Hiopia in her desert hills
> Conceals. Among the ruined temples there,
> Stupendous columns, and wild images
> Of more than man, where marble daemons watch
> The Zodiac's brazen mystery, and dead men
> Hang their mute thoughts on the mute walls around,
> He lingered, poring on memorials
> Of the world's youth, through the long burning day
> Gazed on those speechless shapes, nor, when the moon

Filled the mysterious halls with floating shades
Suspended he that task, but ever gazed
And gazed, till meaning on his vacant mind
Flashed like strong inspiration, and he saw
The thrilling secrets of the birth of time.[32]

These passages, "set" in the Levant and northeastern Africa, are of course only the beginnings, the westernmost leading edges, of *Alastor*'s map of the East, for the Visionary will penetrate deeper still, beyond Arabie and Persia, beyond Kashmir, beyond the Caucasus, beyond the Caspian and Aral Seas. This eastward movement (the opposite of Keats's "westering") involves a complex and subtle temporal play. On the one hand, the Visionary has arrived in the space of Oriental and Hellenic antiquity, intact and laden with its tombs and palaces, its memorials and sphinxes, its columns and its halls. On the other hand, he has not quite gone back to the *time* of antiquity; or, rather – paradoxically – he has *and* he has not. Time has stopped: nothing has changed in this mythic Orient, nothing has altered the Roman temples of Baalbek, the Phoenician palaces of Tyre, the temples of Athens, the towers of Babylon. The "eternal" pyramids are as they were when Cheops was entombed; Tyre has neither grown nor changed since Alexander's siege; Jerusalem's temples remain as they were left by the city's last pillagers or pilgrims; the Parthenon stands silently awaiting its sacrificial trains; Memphis, once the united capital of Upper and Lower Egypt, is frozen, its palace of Apis remaining as it was – though all of these places are desolate and depopulated, at once preserved and emptied out. And yet, of course, time has moved on: these are ruined temples, open wastes, fallen towers, mutilated monuments.[33] In other words, these "awful ruins of the days of old," these "memorials to the world's youth," have somehow been frozen in time – as though nothing has changed and no one has lived here since some vanished moment of antiquity – and yet they have also been inscribed by the movement of time and the passage of the ages: they are ruins, they are memorials. *Alastor*'s map undermines and contradicts itself. If this *is* a move back in time, why are these temples and palaces not alive, rather than being dead? And if this is *not* a move back in time, then where are the living people of the present? How can great and living cities – Athens, Tyre, Jerusalem – be reduced to ruination and to waste, to the eternal silence of death?

The difference between this vision of the Levant and that of *Childe Harold* II is striking, for this is ostensibly the same landscape in which Harold finds both the same ruins *and* the civilization that has developed in the Levant since the temples and palaces were destroyed. Where Harold sees the ruins of paradise mingled with the signs and peoples of the contemporary East, however, the Visionary sees only ruins – not only because the narrator has effectively obliterated the people of the present from the Visionary's field of vision, but *because this is indeed not the Orient toured by Childe Harold.* Having been reinvented, it is an altogether different space, one that cannot be reconciled with the latter, but that can only take its place – for these visions and versions of the East are mutually exclusive and all demanding.

Thus, while Byron and Childe Harold retrospectively mourn the passage of time from their inescapable standpoint in the present, viewing the Levantine ruins as the traces of pre-modern and bygone times, Shelley's East is always already in ruins, the flow of history – impossibly and paradoxically – having inexorably moved on to the future, in order to leave behind ruins, and at the same moment having ground to a halt in some fixed and immutable space of the past. "The waste where stood Jerusalem" presents the exalted city itself as at once preserved as a trace, and simultaneously canceled and blasted out of existence, its inhabitants written over and hidden away, vanished refugees banished from their land. "The eternal pyramids" are eternal, living forever before and after, and yet at the same time they are consigned to the oblivion of the past. Such ruins are in one sense the "concretization" of history, bearing in their very materiality the inscriptions of the passage of time, that is, the movements and flows of historical events. Temples, castles, memorials, columns, statues, tombs stand as place-markers on imaginary maps, the signposts of spots of time which open up from present and future moments to past ones – each is a space that has been temporalized. The spots of time in *Alastor*'s map of the East are, however, fleeting and illusory, sometimes reactivating and reanimating the glories of the past – so that the Visionary can literally "see" the birth of time – and sometimes falling short and yielding nothing but mute and non-signifying memorials, piles of barren and silent rocks. While each of the signposts on the map ("Tyre," "Memphis," "Babylon," "Jerusalem") might open to a different temporal level, none allows for the reactivation of events, so that they finally succeed one another as a series of flashes which flatten out into a more or less uniform time and space of a "past" seemingly without history.

There is a certain order of succession, however, for they form a series that describes a gradual curve, an inverted "fertile crescent," first towards the southeast (Athens–Tyre–Baalbek–Jerusalem–Babylon) and then towards the south (Babylon–Giza–Memphis–Thebes[34]– Ethiopia). At a more abstract level this series also describes a temporal trend, with every shift south or east marking a corresponding move "back" in history, that is, roughly from Ancient Greece to Phoenicia to Sumer to Ancient Egypt. Yet this temporal hierarchy breaks down and dissolves, not least because each of these civilizations had (spatially) moved out of its area of origin and (temporally and historically) mingled with the others. Again, *Alastor's* map is undecided and unclear, and what we are left with is a more or less haphazard spatial identification of the Orient with the past, a will to render the East past, despite the awareness that Athens and Tyre and Jerusalem live on into the poem's own historical present, the one in which Childe Harold encounters them. Shelley's vision of the East is ruthlessly violent, for he symbolically depopulates a space in order to establish the possibility (or even inevitability) of its reclamation as part of some suddenly invented "Western" heritage. For *if* this journey to the Orient is a journey back in time, its condition of possibility is the annihilation of the present Orient, which is necessarily reduced to desolation and ruin, not to life and "living history" but to spatialized and ossified, "dead" history – or rather to a place altogether without history (i.e., outside the diachronic and universal history of modernization and Europe).

Emptied of their peoples, the living cities of the Orient are rendered as tombs of the dead, frozen museum-piece images, icons of antiquity – as if Tyre and Athens and Jerusalem exist not for the sake of their own peoples and cultures, but for the sake of the European explorer who "discovers" them, indeed as if they would not exist at all without this explorer and discoverer who, even if he does not actually bring them into being, at least confirms their existence (as "dead civilizations," as more than one contemporary critic has put it). These cities, in other words, exist as signs to be read and suddenly understood, like statues or columns or paintings, by the European explorer, the "philosophical traveller": marks upon a suddenly aestheticized landscape.

Alastor, however, again undermines itself, for the Visionary does indeed encounter one inhabitant of the present Orient on his eastward journey:

> Meanwhile an Arab maiden brought his food,
> Her daily portion, from her father's tent,
> And spread her matting for his couch, and stole
> From duties and repose to tend his steps: –
> Enamoured, yet not daring for deep awe

To speak her love: – and watched his nightly sleep,
Sleepless herself, to gaze upon his lips
Parted in slumber, whence the regular breath
Of innocent dreams arose: then, when red morn
Made paler the pale moon, to her cold home
Wildered, and wan, and panting, she returned.[35]

But the Arab maiden is (paradoxically) out of place in this Orient, a disruptive eruption, interfering with the Visionary (who resolutely ignores her as if she were not there at all), just as the phantasmic Arab horseman intrudes on Wordsworth's dream of the East in *The Prelude*. The maiden is not part of the (dead) past, she shares the present with the Visionary. Or does she? She can see him; but does he see her, does he recognize her presence? Their encounter is non-synchronous, not as if they were in separate spatial compartments, but on the contrary as if they "share" or overlap in the same space but at different times, and hence as if they do not share it at all. She is like a ghost from the past who remains unseen and whose presence goes unrecognized in the present; she is there and yet not there; she is in the Visionary's time and yet not in it, she is simultaneously absence *and* presence, a kink, a distortion in an impossibly convulsed and twisted imaginary map. The maiden is like one of Byron's voluptuous Eastern women, but where Byron's Eastern poems are tales of encounter with the other, *Alastor* is a narrative of non-encounter. While the maiden, hence, cannot be accommodated or reconciled with the map, and remains an intrusion on its surface, *Alastor* is nevertheless uneasy in its treatment of the peoples of the East, principally their representative, this maiden who falls in love with the Visionary and who tends him, feeds him, clothes him only to be mutely and carelessly unacknowledged as he moves on in search of his ideal and phantasmatic love – a gesture of which the Narrator is highly critical.

The ruins of the East are silent and deserted, places where dead men hang their *mute* thoughts on the *mute* walls around. Byron's Childe Harold, in Greece, mourns for the fact that "these proud pillars," which to him are laden with all the meaning of Hellenic antiquity, "claim no passing sigh; / Unmoved the Moslem sits, the light Greek carols by."[36] In *Alastor*, though, Orientals are not just unmoved – they are altogether absent from the stupendous ruins of the days of old, where the "speechless shapes" of the East are finally unveiled, unlocked, understood by the silent gaze of the European, upon whom alone inspiration can flash and to whom alone visual and graphic meanings can be transmitted from these memorials of the past. *This* Orient, in other words, is a vacancy and an absence to be filled in (a "land without a people," to cite the planners of a later episode in the region's colonial history) to be brought to life by the European, who alone can fulfill its hidden potential and make this symbolic desert "bloom." Unlocking this Orient's potential wealth, both material and figurative, in other words, fundamentally requires the intervention of Europe, without which this wealth would go unappreciated and hence unexploited.

In his 1820 essay "A Philosophical View of Reform," which is often taken to be the poet's greatest political statement (though indeed its explicitly imperialist orientation usually passes unnoticed), Shelley argues that "the Turkish Empire is in its last stage of ruin, and it cannot be doubted but that the time is approaching when the deserts of Asia Minor and of Greece will be colonized by the overflowing populations of countries less enslaved and debased, and that the climate and the scenery which was the birthplace of all that is wise and beautiful will not remain forever the spoil of wild beasts and unlettered Tartars."[37] This view of Britain's and indeed Europe's colonial project contributes also to the shaping of *Alastor's* map of the East, though in the poem it is to a certain extent qualified and undermined. In either case, the appreciation of the Orient's monuments comes to stand for the awareness and productive exploitation of its *other* resources, so that what European intervention accomplishes is not the *creation* of wealth, but its actualization and realization, its redemption. In his "Philosophical View of Reform," Shelley goes on to argue that the introduction of "enlightened" European institutions, literatures, and arts into Egypt "is *beginning* that change which Time, the great innovator, will *accomplish* in that degraded country; and by the same means its sublime and enduring monuments may excite lofty emotions in the hearts of the posterity of those who now contemplate them without admiration."[38] Without this European impetus, time would not be able to accomplish anything; or, rather, it is the arrival of Europe in the Orient that activates "History" and allows time to begin moving and accomplishing "historical" and modernizing change there – *the very change from which Byron, for his part, had turned to the Orient as a refuge in* Childe Harold II.

Alastor's map of the East emplots the creation of an altogether new Orient through the arrival there of European influence and empire. This is at once a spatial creation, insofar as a new Oriental space has been "discovered," and a temporal one, insofar as this new Orient is determined by the beginning of a new temporal structure: not the time – or timelessness – of the old Orient toured by Childe Harold, but the time of the "new" Europe (which would not include places like the Scottish Highlands, Ireland, Sicily, etc.), or in other words the time of modernity from which Harold and Byron had fled. Shelley's poem charts out a polymorphous and multidimensional Orient, only one "layer" of which is occupied by its Visionary. It constructs a spatialized map of time that effectively opens a fourth dimension, which for want of some more appropriate language I find myself forced to describe three-dimensionally as the "layers" and "levels" of an imaginary map. The Visionary's push into the East involves the penetration into and literally the discovery of a previously hidden – *because not yet invented* – layer of the Orient, a layer that *Alastor* "peels" away from other versions and visions of "the" Orient. What the poem maps out is thus a new space-time of the Orient, "outside" or "underneath" of which other Orients (i.e., the Orients inhabited, lived, and experienced by others and by European tourists in search of an Orient of difference) still manage to "exist," though they are inaccessible to the Visionary, just as *his* Orient is spatially and temporally forbidden to these others. The Arab maiden is a troubling and even transgressive figure who undermines and threatens the coherence of this structure: she is a refugee, a vagrant in space-time who floats in between the different dimensions of *Alastor*'s East, coming to "haunt" the poet in his own private Oriental space, only to finally give up and return to her father's tent, or in other words, to her "proper" space, that Orient where she "belongs."

Alastor concerns itself with and limits itself to the Orient that its Visionary has discovered, explored, appreciated, and, above all, understood. The "living" Orient of the poem's own present, as opposed to the "dead" Orient of ruined temples and palaces, is not seen (just as the Visionary does not really see the Arab maiden). Thus when the Visionary explores the "waste where stood Jerusalem," or the deserted and dust-blown ruins of Tyre or Athens or Memphis or Thebes, it is *his* own Jerusalem, his own Tyre, Athens, Memphis and Thebes, that he sees – Oriental spaces upon which he meditates and ruminates. There are other visions and versions of these places, inhabited (though apparently not appreciated) by others. *Alastor*, a travel narrative of sorts, commemorates a certain type of tourism in which the tourist is "free" to consume the objects of his contemplation in his own private way, though unlike Childe Harold's tourism, which involves a private voyeuristic consumption of the otherness of the (contemporary) Orient. On its own terms, *Alastor*'s vision or re-vision of the East is *the* East, which is being "faithfully" re-presented to its Western readers. In other words, *Alastor*

makes a claim about the universality and the truth of its vision and representation of the Orient. Its Orient is the Orient; there is no other. Or,
the Orient which *Alastor* discovers – that is, invents – is not just cut off,
isolated, and placed in radical opposition to other versions of the Orient:
it is linked to, and placed in continuity with, a larger vision of the world
which lies to the west. *Alastor*'s East does *not* exist in isolation from some
putative West; if it dives underneath other layers of the Orient, it does so
partly in order to establish connections and continuities between *its*
Orient and what lies to the west of this Orient, as though this (equally
invented) West had seeped or pushed eastwards along with *Alastor* to
claim this other Oriental space as its own, as part and parcel of the space
that it had left "behind" – as an extension, or better yet, a colonial
possession, of the West and of Europe.

   In this sense, *Alastor* maps out a temporal colonization coinciding with
and complementing European spatial and material colonizations of the
Orient in the late eighteenth and early nineteenth centuries. On the one
hand, this involved the process that Johannes Fabian has identified as
the simultaneous secularization and universalization of time (see section
II, above).[39] On the other hand it involved a colonial reclamation and
appropriation through the invention and spatial production of a certain
version of the Orient as Europe's source of origin ("the birthplace of all
that is wise and beautiful"). Not merely the "cradle of civilization," but
the site, the scene, of Europe's heritage, this space suddenly needed to
be understood and explained in terms of a (fabricated) historical and
cultural "continuity" with modern Europe. It was gradually appropriated by the universalizing European claims that time and history are
uniform natural "essences" that point to modernity and to Europe.

   What *Alastor* does, then, is to re-orient the East in terms of this newly
developed universal essence of time. I say re-orient, because the other
Orients (or older visions and versions of the Orient), including that of
Childe Harold, cannot be accommodated in this newly produced configuration of the East. Indeed, this Orient – *Alastor*'s East – has to be
fundamentally reinvented in a recuperative gesture that removes it from
the claims of the other Orient. One can posit a temporal divide separating these Orients from each other, as I have already suggested, the
dimension of the East which the Visionary discovers and explores being
neatly cut off from and made inaccessible to Orientals themselves, so
that the Visionary is free to appreciate and understand it on his own.
What I am arguing involves the production of an analogue to Frantz
Fanon's great dictum that "the colonial world is a world cut in two."[40]

Alastor's map of the East is not only an intervention in the Orient and hence (which is to say the same thing) in the imaginary terrain produced by Orientalism; it produces a new version of Oriental space-time that must be placed in radical opposition to previous European conceptions, versions, productions, of this space, not least that of *Childe Harold*. Its logic of separation and division is not solely spatial, but simultaneously spatial and temporal. The natives, the Orientals themselves, are consigned to their own version, their own space, their own time – none of which concern *Alastor* or its Visionary, as they are displaced beyond the poem's rigorously self-imposed limits and remain ghosts hovering on the edges of the poem, haunting it. They exist on the multiple other sides of this interdimensional frontier: in the Orients of Beckford's *Vathek*, of Southey's *Thalaba* and *Kehama*, of Byron's *Corsair*, of De Quincey's opium-induced Asiatic nightmares, in the worlds of European penetrations and visits to the Orient of the other, as opposed to this newly invented "European" Orient. And yet, of course, both these Orients are produced, and policed, by Europeans – by the Orientalists, the colonial administrators, the armies of occupation. This amounts to something more than what Fabian terms the "denial of coevalness," through which Europeans distinguished themselves from their colonial interlocutors according to their supposed relative positions on the stream of evolutionary time, so that European ventures into the colonial realm were seen as voyages "back" to the time of the other.[41] Thus the clash of cultures on the imperial frontier is also a clash of temporalities: this newly invented Orient, and hence this whole new set of relations between Orientals and Europeans (which is what the Orient and Orientalism always imply and delineate, as Said argues), could thus be opposed to older versions, older and now-subsumed "layers" of this imaginary map of the imperial domain.

In the meantime, this new Orient could be excavated and explored, could be recuperated, redeemed, put to good use, saved from itself and from degradation and waste. And indeed its inhabitants could and even had to be reinvented as well. They had to be re-Orientalized.[42] Europe's colonial project could change to a benevolent mission of salvation, by which the Orientals could be given aid and allowed, through "catching" what Shelley called a "contagion of good," to break out of the prison of their old space and hence into "our" world, "our" world history, and the stream of evolutionary time which is warily patrolled by "our" gunboats. While this vision of the colonial mission anticipates the Victorian conception of empire, in Shelley it is still premature, as if the terrain on which its great drama will eventually unfold has only just been captured, and hence is still composed of ruins and deserts in urgent need of repopulation and reconstruction. In a long and careless, though impassioned, paragraph of his 1820 essay, Shelley writes:

Revolutions in the political and religious state of the Indian peninsula seem to be accomplishing, and it cannot be doubted but that the zeal of the missionaries of what is called the Christian faith [allowed into India for the first time as late as 1813] will produce beneficial innovation there, even by the application of dogmas and forms of what is here an outworn incumbrance. The Indians have been enslaved and cramped in the most severe and paralysing forms which were ever devised by man; some of this new enthusiasm ought to be kindled among them to consume it and leave them free, and even if the doctrines of Jesus do not penetrate through the darkness of that which those who profess to be his followers call Christianity, there will yet be a number of social forms modelled upon those European feelings from which it has taken its colour substituted to those according to which they are at present cramped, and from which, when the time for complete emancipation shall arrive, their disengagement may be less difficult, and under which their progress to it may be the less imperceptibly slow. Many native Indians have acquired, it is said, a competent knowledge in the arts and philosophy of Europe, and Locke and Hume and Rousseau are familiarly talked of in Brahminical society. But the thing to be sought is that they should, as they would do if they were free, attain to a system of arts and literature of their own.

The arrival of Europe in the Orient thus suddenly and even violently wrenches the latter into "the" stream of history. Not only does it begin the process of freeing the Orientals literally from themselves (from their culture, their social institutions and organizations), but it begins their gradual and total re-development, through which they have to begin from nought, leaving behind the cultural products of their past only to hope for the vague possibility of some day developing "their own" arts and literature. What has been used up and rendered outmoded in Europe, including for instance Christianity, thus has some usefulness and applicability to this region which can now aspire to cultural, philosophical, economic, and political handouts, aid, and encouragement from Europe. Whereas Byron turned to the East, in *Childe Harold* and his Tales, as a space towards which to escape – and from which to critique and contest – modernity and its claim on the space of Europe, this newly produced Eastern terrain is effectively an extension of Europe, no longer an opposite, but a space which Europe could colonize and thus use to re-produce itself. In other words, the supposedly specific, cyclical, and even centripetal time and history of the East can now be opened up and channeled into the uniformationist, unilinear, and universal time and history of modernization and development.[43] I have already said, however, that *Alastor* is not quite so straightforward as this later summary of the dubious benefits of colonization. If the latter is reminiscent of a retrospective history of contact on the imperial frontier, *Alastor* represents a first glimpse at a new space that would be elaborated in later visions of the East, including Shelley's 1820 Essay.

These possibilities of the new East exist not merely for the Orientals themselves (if at all), but for the Europeans who have captured this terrain by the act of having defined it. Greece, in particular, becomes a site which had to be cut off from its Oriental affiliations and completely redeemed as a part of Europe, thus pushing the imaginary frontier between East and West further east, towards Turkey. In a now often-quoted claim, Shelley argues in the preface to *Hellas* (1821):

The apathy of the rulers of the civilised world to the astonishing circumstance of the descendants of that nation to which they owe their civilisation, rising as it were from the ashes of their ruin, is something perfectly inexplicable to a mere spectator of the shows of this mortal scene. We are all Greeks. Our laws, our literature, our religion, our arts have their roots in Greece. But for Greece – Rome, the instructor, the conqueror, or the metropolis of our ancestors, would have spread no illumination with her arms, and we might still have been savages and idolaters; or, what is worse, might have arrived at such a stagnant and miserable state of social institution as China and Japan possess.

And yet, when he was writing those words, in 1821, Greece was still a part of the Ottoman Empire, and hence merely one of the many parts of the Orient which Europeans were gradually beginning to claim for themselves. As he announces in *Hellas*, the modern Greeks ("descendants of those glorious beings whom the imagination almost refuses to figure to itself as belonging to our kind"), through their revolution against the Turks, are somehow reinventing themselves, rising as reincarnated Europeans from the ashes of Oriental despotism: "Greece, which was dead, is arisen!"[44] And yet in this reinvention lay opportunity not only for the Greeks, but for the other Europeans, who could now establish their claims to an "authentically" Greek (as opposed to Egyptian, Persian, or Arab) heritage. Indeed, this reclamation and recuperation of "our" heritage establishes, on this Romantic Hellenophilic (or, rather, Hellenomaniac) view, not only a claim to some past, but the basis for security for the future, almost a renewal, or rather re-beginning of time and of history; "The world's great age begins anew, / The golden years return, / The earth doth like a snake renew / Her winter weeds outworn."[45] This is precisely the standpoint on Greek renewal and rebirth – a reawakening of Hellenism – denied and rejected by Byron in *Childe Harold* II and its notes (see above), which instead insist on the final death of Greece, albeit as one that ought to be commemorated.[46]

Elsewhere in the East, Europeans were laying their claims to have derived their heritage from certain "pure" strains of Indic civilization, leading ultimately to the construction of an "Indo-European" language family, civilization and race, supposedly distinct from the taints and impurities of Africa or the rest of Asia. This newly discovered Orient, however, had first to be separated from the old Orient (i.e., other "layers" of the imaginary map), and purged of its influence, whether through the fires of revolution (as in Greece) or through the discipline of archaeological or philological research (as in India). Thus, as Martin Bernal has suggested, in the late eighteenth and especially the early nineteenth centuries, Europeans began to fundamentally re-cast their relations with and to the Orient, selectively claiming heritage from this or that corner of the East, while separating these putative heritages from less convenient or desirable cultural, historical, and political attachments and associations (e.g., the enormous influence of Egypt on classical Greek culture, or the interpenetration of Indian cultures with Arabic, Persian, and Chinese civilizations).[47] Indeed, the Orient itself, as a space of material, discursive, and figurative opportunity, had to be entirely re-invented and re-discovered. It had to be altogether re-produced, and Orientals, born "anew," had to begin their "progress" from scratch, the cultural productions and achievements of their previous incarnation being not merely devalued but, in the course of their new development, inappropriate, as the outworn remnants of a bygone age. As Shelley puts it in his essay, they could now only "aspire" to arts and literature "of their own," like good pupils who have plenty of potential and yet have not actually produced anything to show for themselves. For (as I have already said) in Shelley's terms, the arrival of European influence "begins" the change that time "will accomplish." Until then, time was unable to accomplish anything: not only had the Orient "stopped developing," but time itself had stopped there, and had thickened and congealed into endless and everlasting ruin and decay without or outside of history. Yet even if it opens up into the "new" Orient, *Alastor* marks a transition between Orientalist structures and paradigms, and the supposedly displaced other returns in the form of the Arab maiden, a haunting presence who is recognized by the Narrator and not by the Visionary – as though the Narrator could see the "old" Orient inhabited by this other, whereas the Visionary can only see the ruins and temples of the "new" Orient which are there for him to understand, to know, and to map on his journey and his quest into the Orient.

Perhaps for obvious reasons, I have not been concerned in this reading of *Alastor* with an examination of this quest itself, or in other words with an examination of the poem's narrative. Instead my analysis has been restricted to the terrain on which the narrative takes place, a terrain that has more or less been taken for granted in recent scholarship, much of which uncritically reproduces Shelley's vision of the East as a tantalizing imaginary space, which serves – for us as well as for the poet – merely as a necessarily silent surface for (Western) inscriptions and interventions. For insufficient critical attention has been given to the imaginary terrain on which the Visionary's (I use Earl Wasserman's terminoloy to avoid confusion[48]) quest unfolds. Instead, critics have focused on the nature of the quest. Thus, Wasserman's reading of the poem has become one of the central landmarks on the terrain of these critical debates, and whether more recent critics try either to support, to attack, to refine, or to develop Wasserman's careful and nuanced reading of the quest, the poem's historical ground – and, again, the terrain on which the quest is written – recedes farther and farther from view. That is to say, this "critical" terrain supplants the imaginary Oriental terrain produced in the poem as a basis for readings and re-readings of *Alastor*. The main issue at stake in the critical discussion of the poem has recently shifted towards a debate over whether *Alastor*'s narrator and the Visionary are two different characters (which is what Wasserman proposes), one character struggling with himself, two different versions of the same persona (as Christopher Heppner argues), or indeterminate identities (the position taken by Martyn Crucefix and Frederick Kirchhoff).[49] For all the critics' disagreements about the similarities or differences between the Narrator and the Visionary, they seem to be virtually unanimous in their view of *Alastor*'s representation of the Orient, almost entirely taking for granted the poem's assumptions about Asia and the peoples and civilizations that happen to be there – whose existence and history make it difficult, in my view, to take Shelley so easily and uncritically at his word. Harold Bloom, for instance, writes simply that the Visionary "moves on to the foothills of the Caucasus, retracing in reverse the march of civilization,"[50] a march that in this view "obviously" took a westward course, reaching its height in Europe and America, so that the Visionary, going back in time, goes back to the

cradle of (ultimately a Western) civilization. Heppner writes that the
Visionary tours the ruins of "Nature and past culture"; Strickland says
that the voyage is to "dead civilizations . . . away from civilization
altogether"; while John Reider, offering his reading as "a politicizing
supplement to other interpretations," has little differences with other
critics on this point. In the poem's own terms, of course, these critics'
claims have truth-content; but it seems to me that one must question not
merely the poem's narrative, but its very terms and conditions of
possibility. My own reading of *Alastor* proposes that the quest and the
terrain on which it unfolds are not coincidental to each other and must
be read together; a detailed reading of the quest, which lies outside the
scope of this chapter, must be informed by a reading of the terrain, by
placing both in an historical and historicized perspective.

   The Narrator's reappearance and intervention in the text of the
poem highlights the Visionary's death and the total failure of his quest.
Up to that moment, however, the Narrator's involvement complements
the Visionary's voyage. It is the Narrator who translates the spatial
production of the East undertaken in the poem into visual terms, and
hence it is structurally and formally through the device of the Narrator
that the Visionary is placed on *Alastor*'s map of the East. Until that final
moment, therefore, the Narrator and the poem both enable and participate in the Visionary's quest through and across the space of the Orient.
The Narrator's "reversal" of position – even if it had been anticipated
and prepared for in the Preface and the opening lines of the poem itself –
retroactively and retrospectively unravels and condemns the Visionary's
quest. *Alastor* produces an imaginary map of the space of the East and
then consumes it. It puts it forward and then withdraws it and cancels it
out. Put in slightly different terms, the quest that takes place – a quest for
a self-projected and self-confirming other (in other words, a version of
the self *itself*) – is enabled and sustained by the terrain on which it takes
place, that is, the particular version of the space of the East that the
poem itself produces. In simultaneously producing this terrain and
narrating the quest that it finally condemns, the poem rewrites and
destroys itself.

   Alastor produces a version of the Orient in which otherness has been
all but obliterated (save for its traces and vestigial hauntings, for
example, the Arab maiden), and in which a search can take place for
images and reflections of Europe; this new Orient is thus no longer a
refuge offering and containing the other, it is a cleaned-out slate ready
for European colonization and inscription – even if these processes are

condemned by *Alastor*'s Narrator. In *Childe Harold* II, Byron produces a spatial version of the Orient as a refuge from modernity; he and his alter ego venture into that space in search of otherness, and precisely in search of the sort of exchange and reciprocity with otherness that the Narrator of *Alastor* affirms. Against *Childe Harold*'s dreams of an immortal, everlasting and immutably different East, Shelley's poem puts forward a vision of the East as a space for European redemption in evolution and in progress, in the development and improvement of others who turn out to be merely inferior versions of "ourselves."

CHAPTER 7

William Blake and the Universal Empire

They are mockd, by every one that passes by. they regard not
They labour; & when their Wheels are broken by scorn & malice
They mend them sorrowing with many tears & afflictions

William Blake, Jerusalem

I wander thro' each charter'd street,
Near where the charter'd Thames does flow
And mark in every face I meet
Marks of weakness, marks of woe.

In every cry of every Man,
In every Infants cry of fear,
In every voice; in every ban,
The mind-forg'd manacles I hear

How the Chimney-sweepers cry
Every blackning Church appalls,
And the hapless Soldiers sigh
Runs in blood down Palace walls

But most thro' midnight streets I hear
How the youthful Harlots curse
Blasts the new-born Infants tear
And blights with plagues the Marriage hearse

In the sixteen lines of his 1794 Song of Experience, *London*, Blake produces a nightmarish vision of London – both as a city and as a space of systemic modern oppression. It is precisely because Blake identifies London with more than its material and physical spatiality (its buildings, streets, etc.) that, in charting a space of systemic oppression, he is *also* able to chart the space of London as a material city with physical and tangible dimensions. The poem recognizes that London cannot be apprehended *except* in such figurative or symbolic terms. This is the poem's claim: that it can somehow represent all of London, if not by producing a vision of its tangible spatiality, then by producing a vision – a map – of what we may call its figurative or symbolic spatiality. Blake's attempt to produce a symbolic map of London amounts to something akin to what has been identified as the political aeshetic of cognitive mapping.[1] For London can only be comprehended in such totalized terms; and only in such totalized symbolic terms is it possible to relate the perceptual space of the individual subject to the social and world space that that subject inhabits.

The claim to totality is established partly through the hammering relentlessness of "every" – every face, every cry, every Man, every infant, every voice, every ban. The poem also moves incessantly through a range of registers, from the figurative to the literal, from the narrowly political to the economic, from the sexual to the religious, from the intangible to the material. Thus, the Harlot's curse is no sooner uttered than it condenses into physicality and blights the delicate materiality of the infant's dripping tear, as well as the machinic vehicle of institutionalized, commercialized, and commodifed love, the marriage "hearse."[2] The Chimney-sweeper's existential cry of weakness materially "appalls" (drapes) the Church, while the Soldier's intangible and aural "sigh" quickly condenses into the crude and awful materiality of a river of blood running down the all-too-material walls of another of the simultaneously and interactively material and intangible institutions of oppression (the State) that the poem maps in the space of London.

This is a text forever in the process of becoming. Blake's London is a practiced space: it exists as it is created through the multitudinous processes of experience, so that its realities are produced by the very people experiencing them. And yet the four institutions of oppression that Blake charts in the poem – the State; state religion and the Church; sexual oppression; and above all Trade and Commerce – also define London not merely as an imaginary landscape, but as a spatial force-field controlled and organized by their interactions and overlaps. Since virtually all daily experience is channeled through and structured around them, each of these institutions contributes towards the production of London's space by delimiting and controlling the experience of the city's population. That is, these institutions and the system of oppression that they define are coextensive with their victims' space of experience. In effect, the institutions produce the individual subjects who then experience them as oppression.[3]

If this vision of London differs from Wordsworth's, it does so not by virtue of the distinction (pointed out by E. P. Thompson) between Wordsworth's rendering of the city as a "theatre of discrete episodes" and Blake's vision of the city as a "unitary experience."[4] For the experience and vision of Blake's London is never unitary (indeed, vision and visuality are, according to Blake, always contingent).[5] The city exists as a spatial forcefield produced by, and consisting in, the interaction and mutual reinforcement of the forces and institutions of oppression and their human victims. That is, the institutions and system of oppression are coextensive with, on the one hand, the space that they define; and on the other, their victims' space of experience. Experience and vision here both determine and are determined by reality (as in *The Garden of Love*, that Song of Experience whose imaginary terrain is re-envisioned and rewritten by and through the changing experience, knowledge, and vision of the tortured narrator).[6]

Many critics have argued not only that this vision of London is diametrically opposed to that of Wordsworth, but that what is specifically un-Wordsworthian about it is, as David Punter suggests, "its rejection of meaninglessness, Blake's insistence that all these aspects of London life, puzzling as they are, must have roots somewhere, either in deficiencies of the State, or in psychological malaise, or both."[7] Yet these institutions (which will re-appear in *The Song of Los* as "Churches, Hospitals, Palaces / Like nets & gins & traps to catch the joys of Eternity"[8]) do not lie at the "root" of this *systemic* oppression, which is neither a question of psychological malaise nor of governmental deficiency. Nor does the oppression pre-exist the institutions. Stewart Crehan argues that Blake sees the city "imaginatively," perceiving "in its familiar landmarks, its streets, buildings, people and places not empirical facts, but *symbols*, a symbolic reality behind the surface appearance."[9] But this would suggest that the institutions merely represent something that somehow stands behind and precedes them – having ontological and epistemological priority over them – so that they can be symbols of it, "superstructural" signifiers for some "basic" signified referentiality.

Blake's *London* is not merely a comprehensive "condensation" of the poet's larger vision, as Michael Ferber argues during the course of his (otherwise compelling) attack on Harold Bloom's emptying-out of the poem's politics.[10] Nor does it simply offer a "blueprint" for the later prophetic books of *Vala*, *Milton*, and *Jerusalem*.[11] The *London* of the *Songs of Innocence and of Experience* does not restrict itself – nor should we restrict it

– to the city whose name it takes, so that, while one may agree with Max Dupperay that it marks the entry into the literary scene of the modern *city*, it also marks the arrival of the much broader processes of moderniz-ation itself.[12]

For, in mapping London, Blake is mapping the emerging space-time of modernization, of capital, of empire – in a word, the world-system that he would identify, in his own anti-history of modernization, with "Urizen," the governing principle and ruler of "the Universal Empire" in opposition to whom and to which Blake would situate himself and his own visions and prophecies. I am suggesting that we consider Blake's London no longer as solely the designation of "a city embodied in Time and Space," an urbal sprawl straddling the banks of the river Thames in southeastern England towards the end of the eighteenth century (though at a literal level it is that as well). To live and experience this modernization is to live and experience "London." In Blake's prophetic vision, the space of modernization has both a metaphor and a center in the city of London.

It is not merely in the eponymous poem that London is Blake's spatial figuration of modernization. The space of London is not limited to the city of London, even though it is anchored there, at the core of the commercial networks spanning the British empire. Carried through the sinews and tissues of those and other networks, the spatio-temporal experience, of London – of modernization – has spread out from the city of London, coextensively with the ever-increasing spread of what Blake calls the "Universal Empire," a spatial system of unequal and ex-ploitative relations and exchanges gradually overspreading the four continents and thirty-two nations of his world. This Universal Empire must, however, be distinguished from the institutional entity more narrowly defined and experienced as the *British* empire, which it en-compasses and exceeds. In Blake's geography, then, London is the spatial representation of the experience of the Universal Empire of modernizing capitalism; a process that was, in Blake's vision, gradually reterritorializing and transforming the globe.

The system of relations defining the Universal Empire is virtually planetary in scale, forming one interlocking network. Inside Britain and outside it, in America, Africa, Asia, and Europe, it is simultaneously a global network of production and exploitation and a political and military system, together forming an indissoluble whole. The relays that criss-cross and tie together the four great continents of Blake's world are, hence, both economic and political. Not only does Orc, the spirit of revolution, cross the oceans (as do the plagues of anti-democratic reaction) in *America*, but, as David Erdman argues, so do the networks of production, exploitation, and exchange linking colonial slavery in the Caribbean with textile factories in Britain (in the *Visions of the Daughters of Albion*).[13]

Blake's vision of London is both informed and sustained by its incorporation into – and interpenetration with – his larger vision of a global system. Notwithstanding this, Blake's London is invariably seen from within: his (constructed, rather than essential) narrative perspective is never that of the outsider or the tourist. Thus the urban scenery and blasted terrain of Blake's London stand in stark contrast to both Wordsworth's and Byron's visions of the city.[14] Blake's London is a working-class London, even if his vision is not entirely captured, defined, or restricted by his subject-position as a member of the rapidly-vanishing artisan class, whose constituents in his own lifetime were being absorbed into the new industrial working class. Blake's London establishes and provides a counter-narrative to the view of London as seen and narrated from the perspective of either the urban aristocrat, whether Whig or Tory (including Byron), or the visiting outsider (including Wordsworth).

Working-class London in the late eighteenth and early nineteenth centuries was not merely dismal and oppressive. One nineteenth-century observer writes:

The streets are generally unpaved, rough, dirty, filled with vegetable and animal refuse, without sewers or gutters, but supplied with foul, stagnant pools instead. Moreover, ventilation is impeded by the bad, confused method of building of the whole quarter, and since many human beings here live crowded into a small space, the atmosphere that prevails in these working-men's quarters may readily be imagined . . . The houses are occupied from cellar to garret, filthy within and without, and their appearance is such that no human being could possibly want to live in thtem. But all this is nothing in comparison to the dwellings in the narrow courts and alleys between the streets, entered by covered passages between the houses, in which the filth and tottering ruin surpass all description.[15]

Although, Jacob Bronowski writes, such districts "were, of course, unlawful," it is, as he says, not clear "that they were more unwholesome than the cottages of the country poor. They were riotous and dangerous, the home of the pimp and the pickpocket, the sharper, the footpad, and the gangster: even the highwayman was a London, not a country-pest."[16] Blake peoples his own distinctive version of the space of London with just such types. The people stumbling painfully about in his London – and indeed throughout his poetry and designs – are harlots and soldiers, chimney-sweepers and vagrants, blacksmiths and cobblers. They are, in other words, almost always either artisans or workers; they are the people who make up the "swarm" of the terrible crowd in Wordsworth's London, though they are seen in Blake's poetry from the perspective and standpoint of the crowd itself – from within and from underneath, and always in a spatial and visual field dominated by the institutions of oppression that are charted in the Song *London*: Urizen's "Looms & Mills & Prisons & Work-Houses."[17] For if, as David Erdman argues, Urizen is in Blake's universe the great Work-Master, then these are indeed his workers.[18]

"Cruel Works / Of many Wheels I view, wheel upon wheel, with cogs tyrannic, / Moving by compulsion each other."[19] One invariably hears these terrible and Satanic wheels grinding, churning and rumbling away in the "background" of Blake's poetry. For he was not merely "reporting," imitating, or representing the material realities of industrialization; rather, the machinic tyranny of the industrial revolution is transcoded in his works, and appears in his poetry as this complex of wheels and cogs, metaphors for both the material and the figurative processes and apparatuses of production, commerce, and domination in the Universal Empire.[20] The monstrous wheels are at once the wheels of Blake's "dark Satanic mills" and also the figurative ones of the institutions of oppression, already charted in *London*, against which Blake's writings situate themselves, in a literary counterpart to the various radical working-class movements of the time, from the shoemaker Thomas Hardy and his London Corresponding Society to the Gordon Rioters – at whose head Blake found himself when they stormed and burned London's infamous Newgate Prison[21] – to the mutineers of the "Floating Republic" at the Nore in 1797.

Blake's vision of the Universal Empire and of the Urizenic process of production is literally "prophetic" inasmuch as, in his time, the industrial factory system itself was still quite small, and almost entirely confined to the spinning-mills of the textile industry (even this was not fully mechanized).[22] Several late eighteenth-century technological inventions and adaptations in this industry – notably the spinning jenny and the water frame, as well as their combination in Crompton's "mule," to which steam power was soon applied – gave a powerful impetus to the widespread development of factory production. But the primary weaving itself was, well into the nineteenth century, still mostly or even entirely performed by men on physically-demanding hand-looms, and it was not until the successful application of a power-loom to the weaving process that the entire textile industry could be industrially revolutionized. When it was, in the period following the Napoleonic Wars, tens of thousands of England's weavers lost their jobs and either became factory operatives, or (more typically) starved to death, since power-looms could be operated as efficiently by underpaid and over-worked women and children as by men.

By the late 1830s, barely over 20 percent of textile factory workers were men.[23] And by then, as Blake had anticipated in *The Four Zoas* and elsewhere, not only were the Daughters of Albion – the women of England – working at (Enitharmon's) looms as weavers; children had been "sold to trades, / Of dire necessity, still labouring day & night till all / Their life extinct they took the spectre form in dark despair." Their suffering is here figuratively and materially connected to the misery of the "slaves in myriads, in ship loads," who "burden the hoarse sounding deep, / Rattling with clanking chains," and whose collective agony endows the Universal Empire with its own "groans." Indeed, the British textile industry, fed and sustained by the cotton produced on West Indian and American slave plantations (seen in *Visions of the Daughters* as well as *The Four Zoas*), was the first to industrialize, launched – as Hobsbawm puts it – "like a glider, by the pull of the colonial trade to which it was attached."[24]

"Trembling I sit day and night, my friends are astonish'd at me, / Yet they forgive my wanderings. I rest not from my great task!"[25] Blake's task – of which he writes so anxiously and feverishly, driven by an unrelenting sense of urgency and crisis – was, at least in part, to conceptualize the Universal Empire before it took full shape. His writings, so often compared to the insane ravings of a lunatic, are thus "prophecies" in the sense that they grasp at and try conceptually to map a complex and tendentially global system which has not yet fully materialized but whose constituent elements and conceptual discourses were already in place in his own time. The accompanying sense of urgency, then, may derive partly from his sense that this conceptualiz-ation or mapping had to be complete before the system itself was; but it also derives, I think, from Blake's sense (surely not simply paranoia in those days of terror and reaction) that he, as an individual, was in danger of captivity, and as a representative of a dying artisan class, was in imminent danger of destruction (like Britain's wretched weavers).

His task, in other words, is to produce a critical concept of something that (in his time) does not yet fully exist, both before it does exist and before he can be stopped by his enemies – real or imagined – or indeed by the Empire itself. Hence that astonishing excess of signification in Blake's poetry, especially in the prophetic books. This is an excess that defies the narrow and unilinear institutions and paradigms of modern rational thought, which, as Blake puts it in *The Marriage of Heaven & Hell*, "impose" on us, limit and restrain us, in our daily lives in this world of Urizenic Reason.

These "enemies" are presumably those who "mock at the Labourer's limbs: they mock at his starv'd Children: / They buy his Daughters that they may have the power to sell his Sons: / They Compell the Poor to live upon a crust of bread by soft mild arts: / They reduce the Man to want, then give with pomp & ceremony."[26] But why would Blake, an artisan-craftsman, align himself with the common labourer at an historical moment in which the differences between the one and the other were culturally and socially still very distinct? How does Blake transcend the institutionalized class distinction between artisan and common labourer – a distinction which strictly pertains to pre-capitalist social formations? For in capitalism these archaic distinctions would be substantially dissolved, not only by the commodification of labor-power, but above all by a rationalized hourly wage-system which no longer needed or heeded such differences.

At one level, Blake's prophetic works are the politically charged narratives of an emerging collective discourse that simultaneously challenges the hierarchy of labor within the archaic system while mobilizing the putative unalienated labor of that very system to critique the unfolding "Universal Empire" of modern capitalism. And here enters Blake's implicit use of the (mythic) figure of the Free-Born Englishman, a figure widely championed by the oppositional and radical movements of the romantic period. Stripped of his communal and "natural" rights by a brutal and machinic new order, robbed of his attachment to the land, the Free-Born Englishman paradoxically came into being as an "*ideologeme*"[27] at the very moment of his supposed extinction, which took place during the eradication of the archaic and agricultural mode of production with which he was identified as a spokesman for the commoner. Thus Blake's critique of the Universal Empire comes partly as a reflection on – though *not* an appeal to return to – the bygone days of a lost "innocence," days before the onset of industrialization and the reorganization and re-production of space into the modernity which we now "experience." Writing from this bitter standpoint, Blake equates this "fall" as a passage from one state to another, as though from life to death:

> And all the Arts of Life they chang'd into the Arts of Death in Albion.
> The hour-glass contemn'd because its simple workmanship
> Was like the workmanship of the plowman, & the water wheel
> That raises water into cisterns, broken & burn'd with fire
> Because its workmanship was like the workmanship of the shepherd;
> And in their stead, intricate wheels invented, wheel without wheel,
> To perplex youth in their outgoings & to bind to labours in Albion
> Of day & night the myriads of eternity: that they may grind
> And polish brass & iron hour after hour, laborious task,
> Kept ignorant of its use: that they might spend the days of wisdom
> In sorrowful drudgery to obtain a scanty pittance of bread,
> In ignorance to view a small portion & think that All,
> And call it Demonstration, blind to all the simple rules of life.[28]

The old moral economy is here typified not only by the organic and presumably unalienated *workmanship* – as opposed to the mere "labour" to which workers are now "bound" – of the plowman and the shepherd, but by the harmonic temporal framework of these bygone days. The transition from one social and economic order to another is thus registered at once as a shift from workmanship (evocative of artisanal labor) to alienated labor; and from the cyclical motions of the water-wheel as well as the constant re-beginning of time signified though not quite measured by the hourglass, to the relentless machinic diachrony of clock-time. Indeed the two are one and the same, marking the movement from certain harmonic temporalities and cycles of labor to the highly specific, punctuated and measurable temporality of the factory system and wage-labor under the Universal Empire. Modernity is given figurative form here in the terrible machinic and diabolical wheels upon wheels which grind the Free-born Englishman in his factory servitude.

In this vision, the Free-born Englishman not only summons up the "memories" of an old moral economy, which was then being eradicated ("broken and burned with fire") by a system starving weavers, enslaving children and rapidly reducing farmers and master artisans alike to the status of "hands" performing rigidly rationalized tasks ("bound to labour") in the new spatio-temporal environment of the factory. This figure also announces, proclaims, and demands the extension of the old and foresaken *rights* for the workers whom the new system was not only exploiting but daily consuming in the fire and heat of its mills, in the dismal shafts of its coal mines, in the holds of its ships, in the battles of its armies ("We were carried away in thousands from London & in tens / Of thousands from Westminster & Marybone, in ships clos'd up, / Chain'd hand & foot, compell'd to fight under the iron whips / Of our Captains, fearing our officers more than the enemy"[29]) and in the workhouses of its new industrial cities.[30] In opposing what was for him the "nightmare" of a rigidly enforced and uniformly measured clock-time, Blake claims some sort of continuity with a much deeper structure and concept of time – prophetic time – which still allows him to see or at least to believe in the "myriads of eternity."[31]

In looking at the Universal Empire, and at the symbolic and moral communities being destroyed by modernization, Blake was doing so from the vantage point not merely of its many victims, but from his position as a member of a dying profession, which was being displaced by the cheaper and more efficient graphics-reproduction processes developed during the Industrial Revolution. "Blake, whose own craft was dying as surely as the woodcomber's and the weaver's," Bronowski argues, "was writing in prophecy the story of his own life."[32] It is, indeed, hardly coincidental that so many of the radical and revolutionary movements of Blake's day were founded and run by other artisans (including the London Corresponding Society's Thomas Hardy, a shoemaker), who, though they were not affected any more directly by the onset of modernization and industrialization than the majority of casualty-workers and others, had at least the invaluable assets of an education and increasing amounts of free time. Blake, gradually forced to take on hackwork (anticipating later literary careers, for example, both that of *New Grub Street*'s Edwin Reardon and that of Gissing himself), and, despite his worsening financial situation, his involvement in the Gordon Riots, and later on his trial on a charge of treason, seems not to have been actively involved in any organized radical movements, and to have steadily withdrawn from the world, if not from his own (increasingly private) political commitments.[33]

If Reason restrains, imprisons, and shackles the inhabitants of Blake's London, the only possible lines of escape are opened up by Energy – Eternal Delight – which according to Blake opens up the possibility of breaking free from the restraints imposed by the "mind-forged man-acles" of modern thought. If generalized throughout the world, such an unleashing of Energy would amount to nothing less than the revolutionary and apocalyptic destruction of London and the Universal Empire;

to the replacement of the oppressive space of London by the redemptive
and liberatory space of Golgonooza. Golgonooza here signifies not just
art, but art unchained from the demands of commerce and of capital.

Spatially, the redemptive process is figured in Blake's prophetic works
not as a sudden flash, but as the slow and difficult work of building the
visionary city of Golgonooza in the space of London. Thus, Blake's hope
for revolution, transformation, and salvation – i.e., apocalypse – is
expressed in terms of a profound political and material intervention in
the very world from which he might seem otherwise to have withdrawn.
For the work of salvation in Blake's prophecies is at once abstract and
metaphorical and awfully and crudely material. The all-important prophetic figure of Los (who in certain of his incarnations stands for Blake
himself) is a blacksmith, and the feverish poundings of his hammer and
anvil boom continually in the background of *Jerusalem*. His prophetic
work is physical – exhaustingly so – as well as visionary:

> Yet ceas'd he not from labouring at the roarings of his Forge,
> With iron & brass Building Golgonooza in great contendings,
> Till his Sons & Daughters came forth from the Furnaces
> At the sublime Labours: for Los compell'd the invisible Spectre
> To labours mighty with vast strength, with his mighty chains,
> In pulsations of time, & extensions of space like Urns of Beulah,
> With great labour upon his anvils, & in his ladles the Ore
> He lifted, pouring it into the clay ground prepar'd with art,
> Striving with Systems to deliver Individuals from these Systems.[34]

In their struggle to free themselves, the sons and daughters of Los here
struggle not only materially to transform the environment in which they
are trapped, but to use the very tools to which they have been condemned to labor, freeing themselves from that very labor. The process of
liberation according to Blake thus not only centers on the purity of
labor, but on the purification that labor itself enables when discharged
in cataclysmic bursts. Moreover, in this process, that which is to be
overcome and overthrown has not only to be imitated to a certain
extent, but its very tools, apparatuses and discourses have to be used
against it – and in the process, the tools, apparatuses, discourses themselves will be annihilated. The creation of a new System thus involves
first of all a replication of those systems which are to be destroyed, and
then finally the destruction of all systems together. Robert Gleckner
observes here that Los's mission is to deliver all individuals from the
systems that bind them – including his own: thus, as Gleckner argues,
Blake's is necessarily an "antiallegorical allegory."[35] For as I suggested

in a previous chapter, Blake's revolutionary art was not founded on dialectical principles, but rather on the need to detonate the dialectic of modernity and anti-modernity.

In material terms, then, the redemptive operation in Blake's vision involves both revolting against the fetters of the relations of production in the Universal Empire, and at the same time turning the technical and material capacity of that Empire's forces of production against themselves – in order to destroy them forever, and with them the structures, concepts, and networks of time and of space that they reinforce, define, and delimit (the space of London). Moreover, according to Blake, this redemptive apocalypse must be undertaken not only by the workers of a nascent industrial Britain, but by the slaves and the others bound into this Urizenic system throught the conduits of the Universal Empire. In a prophetic note added to his engraving (which Rosetti erroneously entitled "Glad Day"), Blake writes of this apocalypse: "Albion rose from where he labour'd at the Mill with Slaves: giving himself for the Nations he danc'd the dance of Eternal Death."

Spatially, the redemptive process is figured in Blake's prophetic works not as a sudden flash, but as slow and difficult work – building the visionary city of Golgonooza in the space of London. The space of London in Blake's work is, as I've already noted, not strictly coextensive with the city of London. "I write in South Molton Street," he says in *Jerusalem* (plate 38), "what I both see and hear / In regions of Humanity, in London's opening streets." London's visionary streets here are not closed and self-referential, but "open" onto the rest of the world and the "regions of Humanity." For if, in Blake's prophetic vision, the space of London is the space of modernization, and if through the spatial networks of the Universal Empire this modernization is transforming other regions and spaces of the world (so that to experience modernity is to experience London, *anywhere in the world*), then the streets of the city of London spread out symbolically and become the streets of the world. Or in other words the "Exchanges of London," *both as material streets and as figurative centers of finance and trade*, are the exchanges of the world. In Blake's spatial dialectic, this means on the one hand that the space of London – i.e., modernity and the Universal Empire of capitalism – is spreading outwards over "the nations"; and on the other hand that the world itself, as well as the spatial relays of the colonial networks, can be seen and mapped in the space of London (and vice versa). Hence, finally, the space of London and Los's feverish work on the building of Golgonooza both take place on a simultaneously local and global scale:

From Golgonooza the Spiritual Four-fold London eternal,
In immense labours & sorrows, ever building, ever falling,
Thro' Albion's four Forests which overspread all the Earth
From London Stone to Blackheath east: to Hounslow west:
To Finchley north: to Norwood south: and the weights
Of Enitharmon's Loom play lulling cadences on the winds of Albion
From Caithness in the north to Lizard Point & Dover in the south.

Loud sounds the Hammer of Los & loud his Bellows is heard
Before London to Hampstead's breadths & Highgate's heights, to
Stratford & old Bow & across to the Gardens of Kensington
On Tyburn's Brook: loud groans Thames beneath the iron Forge
Of Rintrah & Palambaron, of Theotorm & Bromion, to forge the instruments
Of Harvest, the Plow & Harrow to pass over the Nations.
The Surrey hills glow like the clinkers of the furnace; Lambeth's Vale
Where Jerusalem's foundations began, where they were laid in ruins,
Where they were laid in ruins from every Nation & Oak Groves rooted,
Dark gleams before the Furnace-mouth a heap of burning ashes.
When shall Jerusalem return & overspread all the Nations?
Return, return to Lambeth's Vale, O building of human souls!
Thence stony Druid Temples overspread the Island white,
And thence from Jerusalem's ruins, from her walls of salvation
And praise, thro' the whole Earth were rear'd from Ireland
To Mexico & Peru west, & east to China & Japan[36]

The movement described here is a translation of Blake's mythic history,
from the fall to the apocalypse, into an imaginary map of London – a
map that expands outwards to encompass the rest of Britain and the
world through the colonization of spaces of "unfallenness," and their
incorporation into the Universal Empire of modernization. It traces,
first, the spread of the Urizenic system of exploitation and production,
and, second, the great movement for the redemption of humankind in
the great revolution against this system (through the building of a
universal Golgonooza, simultaneously in the city of London, in Britain,
and in the world). According to this and later versions of Blake's
imaginary map of the world in London and London in the world – since
by now London and the world are coextensive with one another – there
is a correspondence between the geographical spread of London's outer
limits (the suburbs of Hounslow, Finchley, Blackheath, and Norwood);
the British isles (here delimited by the triangulation Caithness–Lizard
Point–Dover, though it later appears more "neatly" as a fourfold map as
well: England, Wales, Ireland, and Scotland); and the rest of the world
(here defined by the east-west spread anchored by Ireland: Mexico and

Peru to China and Japan, though again it appears in laters versions as the quaternary Asia, Africa, Europe, America).

What these imaginary geographical "correspondences" establish is a simultaneously and inextricably multidimensional and inter-referential map of the world. In it, the relay from the eastern London suburb of Blackheath to the western suburb of Hounslow (where Heathrow airport is today) somehow corresponds, through a phantasmatic and incalculable calculus, to the relay from Dover (southeast England) to Lizard Point (in Cornwall, southwest England), or to the relay from China to Ireland, or Ireland to Peru. This is, in other words, not the sort of geographical correspondence proposed by Northrop Frye, who says that Blake establishes specific connections between English and Palestinian geography; rather, it is a series of simultaneous superimpositions, in which these "different" geographies no longer remain separable, but become interlocking and even indistinguishable.[37] Thus the individuality or distinctiveness of each once-isolated space becomes dissolved as it is absorbed into and then reordered in the geographical flux of modernity; spatial specificities are obliterated in the homogenizing spatial-temporal process of modernization.

In the more elaborate version of this map, which Blake produces in *Jerusalem*, the fourfold directional correspondences fit even more neatly, so that one can imagine a constellation in which the quaternary Hounslow (west) – Finchley (north) – Blackheath (east) – Norwood (south) can be endlessly extended or contracted, superimposing on and being superimposed upon by the quaternary Ireland (w) – Scotland (n) – England (e) – Wales (s); and also America (w) – Europe (n) – Asia (e) – Africa (s) (see figure on following page).

The center of this imaginary map is not exactly London itself, but the semi-mythical object called London Stone, originally a Roman milestone, and according to Damon apparently the central marker for the ancient road network of Britain. In Blake's mythology it also stands for a place of execution.[38] London itself becomes for Blake a virtually unmappable space, its own spatial particularities and specificities being mixed up with those of the other regions that are mapped in its space. Indeed, London "as such" fits into none of his quaternaries, and becomes conceptually distinct both from the rest of the world and from the rest of Britain, and even from England. The spaces within London – Kensington, Highgate, Hampstead – and even the spaces bounding London – the four suburbs – are "removable" from the map of England insofar as their space *corresponds* to that of Britain and the world.

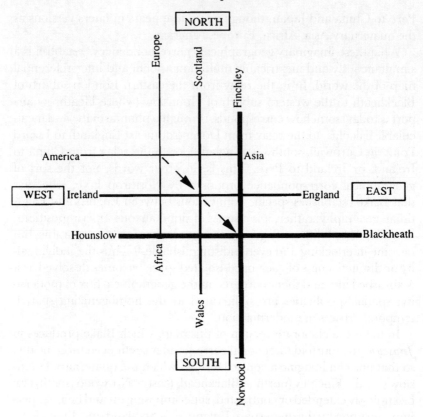

Thus, Blake produces a map of the world inscribed in his attempted cognitive map of London, just as Wordsworth sees the world in the space of London. Yet Blake's map is not always visible in the mundane physical landmarks of the city: to visualize it requires prophetic vision, the vision of the imagination and of poetic Genius. For, according to Blake, "Man's perceptions are not bounded by organs of perception; he perceives more than sense (tho' ever so acute) can discover."[39] Blake, as Northrop Frye argues, not only rejects the empiricist notion that vision and visuality are restricted and confined by the limits of sensory perception, but he insists that perception is not something done with the senses, but is a *creative* and productive act. Hence a visionary is someone who can create – precisely by "seeing" – not merely the mundane world of "Generation" but a world in which Generation's mundane and material "objects" of perception are transfigured.[40] To see Blake's map of the world in its superimposition on his map of London requires the transformation of the "normal" perception of London's space in its objectivity and materiality, and the perception instead of, at a different level, more complex spatial networks, assemblages, and relations. For Blake, as Northrop Frye eloquently argues,

The world outside us, or physical nature, is a blind and mechanical order, hence if we merely accept its conditions we find ourselves setting up blind and mechanical patterns of behaviour. The world outside is also a fiercely competitive world, and living under its conditions involves us in unending war and misery. Blake's lyrics contrast the vision of experience, the stupefied adult view that the evils of nature are built into human life and cannot be changed, with the view of innocence in the child, who assumes that the world is a pleasant place made for his benefit.[41]

In the larger prophecies, however, this view involves both seeing the "fallen" world of Jerusalem (the fleeting glimpses of a more "innocent" world-order) in the space of London (hence Blake can say that Jerusalem's foundations were laid in ruins in the London district of Lambeth); and it involves the capacity to imagine, to see, and prophetically and materially to transform the space of London into the redemptive space of Golgonooza. Thus in *Jerusalem* Blake maps onto the space of London both the memory-like glimpses (though *not* memories) of a time when "In the Exchanges of London every Nation walk'd, / And London walk'd in every Nation, mutual in love & harmony" and the prophetic glimpses of a future when this dream might be realized. For Blake's project – and Los's – was not to excavate the fallen Jerusalem in order to return to it, but rather to construct the redemptive space of a new Jerusalem out of the nightmare of the present-day "mind-forg'd manacles" in the space of London.

In other words, superimposed on Blake's fourfold symbolic or cognitive map of London, there are two other maps as well, both unfolding in London, a space that is never static but that is rather in an ongoing and perpetual process of production and reproduction ("in immense labours & sorrows, ever building, ever falling"). These are the maps of Jerusalem. When Los goes on visionary walks through the streets and districts of London ("Los search'd in vain; clos'd from the minutia, he walk'd difficult. / He came down from Highgate thro' Hackney & Holloway toward London/ Till he came to old Stratford, & thence to Stepney & the Isle / Of Leutha's Dogs, thence thro' the narrows of the River's side"[42]), he sees both the flashes of Jerusalem and the hope for

Golgonooza. For it is out of the space of London that Golgonooza must
be built, and "Los stands in London building Golgonooza":

> And they builded Golgonooza: terrible eternal labour!
> What are those golden builders doing? where was the burying place
> Of soft Ethinthus? near Tyburn's fatal Tree? is that
> Mild Zion's hill's most ancient promontory, near mournful
> Ever weeping Paddington? is that Calvary and Golgotha
> Becoming a building of pity and compassion? Lo!
> The stones are pity, and the bricks, well wrought affections
> Enamel'd with love & kindness, & the tiles engraven gold,
> Labour of merciful hands: the beams and rafters are forgiveness:
> The mortar & cement of the work, tears of honesty: the nails
> And the screws and iron braces are well wrought blandishments . . .[43]

In this ever-changing space, with its endless dialectic between the
material and the figurative, the physical landmarks of London are slowly
being built into the towers of the new Jerusalem, so that London districts
and buildings (Paddington, not yet a train station, or Tyburn gallows,
today marked by the Marble Arch) are superimposed on an imaginary
map of biblical Jerusalem (and vice versa); and at the same time there is
a continual shift from the very physical materials being used to build
Golgonooza – screws, nails, braces, beams, mortar, cement – and their
redemptive visionary transfiguration into tears, forgiveness, love, and
kindness. But if the terrible eternal labor through which Golgonooza is
being built is transforming London ("Here, on the banks of the Thames,
Los builded Golgonooza . . . In fears he builded it, in rage & in fury. It is
the Spiritual Fourfold / London continually building & continually
decaying desolate"[44]), it is necessarily simultaneously being built all over
the world – for even if Blake is mapping the production of Golgonooza
on the space of London, the space of London is always already for him
the space of the wider world, chained together through the groans of the
Universal Empire. For, as Frye argues, Blake's conception of this apocalyptic revolution involved the creation of another and better world,[45]
which had to be both spiritually and materially constructed out of the
physicality and spatiality of London. Los's hammers are not only heard
banging and booming in Asia and Africa and Europe and America as if
from the distance of London: Los and his symbolic children are at work
wherever the Universal Empire groans, for the world produced by the
brutal, oppressive and exploitative spatial networks of the Empire is
centered on London, so that, in the vision of the Apocalypse towards the
end of *Jerusalem*, all continents and nations and cities and peoples

... center in London & Golgonooza, from whence
They are Created continually, East & West & North & South,
And from them are Created all the Nations of the Earth,
Europe & Asia & Africa & America, in fury Fourfold.

And Thirty-two Nations to dwell in Jerusalem's Gates.
O Come ye Nations! Come ye People! Come up to Jerusalem!
Return, Jerusalem, & dwell together as of old! Return,
Return O Albion! Let Jerusalem overspread all Nations
As in the times of old! O Albion awake![46]

There is of course a considerable degree (to say the very least) of
anglocentrism here; an imperial and almost missionary-like conflation
of the destiny of various colonial peoples with those of England itself.
Indeed, one could easily produce a reading of this poem in terms of an
aggressive evangelical nationalism transcribed to the imperial stage – as
has often been done.

But instead of doing that, I would like to propose an alternative and
utopian reading of these lines, one that is consistent with the latter
reading but in fact transfigures and cancels it out. In order to free
themselves from their oppressors, the workers of Albion must use the
tools which have been their fetters. In order to be free of the "mind-
forg'd manacles" of London, London must be turned against itself, its
own bricks and mortar and screws and boards and braces and buildings
– *even as they serve* as the sinews of the dark Satanic factories and as the
tissues of the Looms & Mills & Prisons & Work-houses – used to
transform its space into the space of Golgonooza. Los, who says "I must
Create a System or be enslav'd by another Man's. / I will not Reason &
Compare: my business is to Create," has, according to the terms of what
Gleckner defines as an "antiallegorical allegory," to strive with systems
in order to deliver individuals from those systems – including his own.

The Universal Empire works by crushing its victims in its tyrannic
wheels, by enslaving women and children in Mills, by chaining men in
ships "clos'd up," by pillaging and looting the peoples of three continents, bringing its loot and its bounty home to London. But it is precisely
in the darkest and most terrifying visions of this cruel system that Blake
sees hope. By chaining the "nations" and peoples of humankind together, according to his vision, the Universal Empire has united them.
They can now turn that Empire's most powerful and oppressive features
against it in order to free themselves and each other; for Blake, then,
resistance to the Universal Empire must come not from its dialectical

"others," or in other words from various putative "outsides." Rather, the Universal Empire's destruction and overthrow – the apocalypse – will be made possible by the very strength and global unity of the Empire itself. This revolutionary vision (in which the greatest strength of the Universal Empire is shown to be its greatest weakness) is, finally, not only what Gleckner calls an antiallegorical allegory – it is a vision of an anti-imperial imperialism, for according to Blake it is only at the very height of Empire that the possibility for destroying it can be imagined.

And it is here in these closing pages that I want to return one last time to Blake's insight (intuitive, prophetic, or otherwise) that from its very beginnings the "Universal Empire" had to be understood on a planetary scale. For throughout Blake's prophecies and visions the struggle between Urizen and Los takes place globally, as they chase each other over the four continents of Blake's world (America, Europe, Asia, and Africa).[47] It is well known to Blake scholars (but seemingly not particularly significant in political terms) that Blake produced two prophetic books called *America* and *Europe*, but developed *Asia* and *Africa* as the two halves of *The Song of Los*. Thus, indeed, *The Song of Los* needs to be read against *America* and *Europe* as their simultaneous counterpart.[48] Urizen is after all the master of the global system; Los, even more than Orc, is the one who fights against him, also on a global scale.[49] It is in this context that it becomes important to see the anti- or perhaps negative-dialectical energy of Blake's prophecies; for in seeking to overcome the dialectical opposition-in-unity of Los and Urizen by the ultimate explosion of that unity – an explosion that would indeed destroy Los himself fully as much as it would vanquish Urizen – Blake was trying to imagine and hence to bring into being a genuinely post-imperial world. Blake thus writes feverishly for the apocalypse: for the day when we can finally proclaim, as he anticipates in *A Song of Liberty*:

EMPIRE IS NO MORE! AND NOW THE LION & WOLF SHALL CEASE.

CHAPTER 8

Conclusions

Decolonization is the meeting of two forces, opposed to each other
by their very nature, which in fact owe their originality to that sort
of substantification which results from and is nourished by the
situation in the colonies. Their first encounter was marked by
violence and their existence together – that is to say the exploitation of the native by the settler – was carried on by dint of a great
array of bayonets and cannons. The settler and the native are old
acquaintances. In fact, the settler is right when he speaks of knowing "them" well. For it is the settler who has brought the native into
existence and who perpetuates his existence.

Frantz Fanon, *The Wretched of the Earth*

As an overall cultural moment, the romantic period in Britain was
characterized by, on the one hand, a sense of suspension, transition,
disruption; and, on the other, by a vast and momentous acceleration, by
a sense of crisis and catastrophe, as though a sudden and permanent
break with the past were being experienced, and a whole new world of
hitherto unimaginable possibilities opened up on what would literally be
– for the first time – a planetary scale. We are now in a position to
evaluate some of the signal political and economic changes in terms of
the broader cultural development of modernization.

The revolutionary situation within Britain (and Ireland), as well as the
wars with France, helped to generate a feeling of a virtually suspended
transition – as though this was a period of change whose full ramifications would become clear only later. Whereas the American and
Haitian Revolutions in the West and the dramatic change in imperial
rule in India and the East (symbolized by the Warren Hastings crisis)
marked some of the key political beginnings of this moment of transition, the end of the Napoleonic Wars in 1815 marked another decisive
turning-point (as I have already argued in terms of romanticism itself).
By 1815, as Hobsbawm argues (even if he somewhat overstates the case),

Britain had "gained the most complete victory of any power in the entire history of the world, having emerged from the twenty years of war against France as the *only* industrialized economy, the *only* naval power – the British navy in 1840 had almost as many ships as all other navies put together – and virtually the only colonial power in the world."[1] After the immediate and immediately palpable threat of an internal revolution was put down by the ferocious reaction of the state (it would resurface later, of course, after the Peterloo massacre in 1819 and then in a different form in the 1830s and 1840s), and, above all, after Waterloo, things suddenly seemed very different, as though a climactic change had somehow been *realized*.

Britain in 1815 was not yet, properly speaking, an industrial economy. If anything, the concept that Richard Brown and others have termed "proto-industrialization" is more appropriate for understanding Britain in this period than that full-scale industrialization which would emerge around heavy industry later on in the nineteenth century. As late as the 1840s, over three-quarters of British manufacturing was in "diverse, dispersed and unspectacular industries – neither cotton nor iron and decidedly not steam-powered."[2] The struggle between the emergent forces of industrial capital and the more entrenched, though effectively residual, interests of mercantile capital (as well as the latter's landed aristocratic allies) would be fought on and off and in and out of Parliament and the marketplace right through the first decades of the nineteenth century.

This struggle was marked, despite the setback posed by the passage of the Corn Laws in 1812, by such significant victories gained by the industrialists as the ending of the East India Company monopoly on the India trade (1813); the modification of the Navigation Acts (1825); the ending of the East India Company's monopoly on the China trade (1830); the end of the sugar monopoly in the home market (1836); and the great culminating battle which ended with the abolition of the Corn Laws (1846) and of the Navigation Acts (1849); and finally, after the abortive Indian Revolution of 1857, the dissolution of the East India Company, more than two and a half centuries after its establishment (1858). Nevertheless, it is essential not to understate the importance of the textile industry, in which a new industrial manufacturing process and division of labor was already most visible, as the locus of industrialization much earlier in the century. This had as much to do with various premonitions of a new social order given expression by the early textile mills (as in Blake's "Dark Satanic Mills") as it did with the actual realization of that order in the textile industry (in any case, the textiles sector was arguably already the most important in Britain and in the world-economy as a whole).

In examining the romantic period, then, we are forced to contend with the gradual coming-into-being of the new social dynamics that constitute the culture of modernization. This emerging cultural formation would eventually rise to dominance not only within Britain, but in much (perhaps even all) of the world, after the crises of 1848 and especially during and after the huge expansion of colonial activity in the late nineteenth century, the "Age of Empire" by the end of which the European powers would control roughly 85 percent of the earth's surface as colonies, dominions, protectorates, and territories.[3] To say, however, that this period marks one of transition into a new moment – which would take firm hold beginning in the 1830s and definitively after 1848 – should not by any means minimize the enormous and cataclysmic changes experienced by those living through it.

It is also important to bear in mind that these changes were unfolding globally, rather than merely radiating outwards from some primary point or metropolitan center. This emergent "center" was as much in a process of definition as were the zones on its "peripheries," and it should not be granted any kind of ontological or epistemological priority in our account of modernization. Rather, the preceding discussion of romanticism should make it clear that this process of definition, which took place in cultural terms, was mutual. Romanticism, as I have been trying to suggest, can be understood as a cultural discourse defining the mutual constitution of the modern imperial metropolitan center and its anti-modern colonies and peripheries.

Thus, the significant changes in early nineteenth-century imperial practices pointed out by Edward Said in *Culture and Imperialism* should not distract us from the equally drastic changes taking place inside Britain itself.[4] For if, as Said argues, "imperialism" refers to "the practice, the theory, and the attitudes of a dominating metropolitan center ruling a distant territory,"[5] then one of the difficulties presented by Britain and by British imperialism in the romantic period is that this metropolitan center was itself being constituted, was itself coming into being, at the same time as it was constituting these distant territories as imperial possessions. Or, to be more precise, the metropolitan center was defining these imperial territories at the very same time as they were defining the metropolitan center itself (as I argued in chapter 2, the anxieties attendant upon this mutual cultural constitution pervade the

London book of *The Prelude*). It is important to bear in mind here that the imperialism examined by Said is specifically *modern* imperialism – whose emergence in embryonic form I am discussing here – which would take hold as an established metropolitan project only well into the nineteenth century.[6]

If in some meaningful sense metropolitan Britain had constructed or produced an imperial identity for itself by the late nineteenth century, this metropolitan identity was in the romantic period still in the process of emergence and definition as much as that of the territories being brought under imperial rule. Moreover, this metropolitan identity would henceforth not be understood or defined only in terms of imperial rule in the strict or narrow sense of that term, but above all in terms of modernization – as the very locus of the modern, albeit one also inhabited by its others (this is precisely the status of London in Wordsworth's account of it in *The Prelude*).

The anti-modern (henceforth pre-modern) peripheries produced through the process of imperial modernization were not only located outside of Britain, but inside it as well. Thus the shift in British conceptions of modernity must be located not only in the sites of anti-modernity beyond Britain's shorelines or in colonial spaces within the United Kingdom, but also in all the anti-modern sites of Britain itself. As I have argued, these internal sites include most prominently the colonial presence within Britain (of which the Scottish Highlands were to be the most radically and violently redefined in this period), but they also include zones of concentration of the emergent industrial working-class (the nightmarish cityscapes of Manchester, Birmingham, Sheffield, Glasgow).

In other words, we have also been discussing the formation of a properly bourgeois culture, whose others would be defined at one and the same time in terms of class and in terms of race and nationality, as Mary Poovey reminds us in her discussion of the intersections and overlaps of the discourses of class, race, and gender around the figure of Florence Nightingale.[7] In a very important sense, the emerging dominant attitude in this period towards the Highlanders of Scotland did not significantly differ from that towards the "Orientals" who were increasingly drawn under the sway of the British empire. The Highlands and the colonial realm outside of Britain were all in this period redefined in terms of a scalar opposition to modernity, an opposition that overrides the differences between their own unique characteristics and structures of feeling.

The project entailed by modernization does not imply the actual obliteration of cultural difference and the proliferation of homogeneity as such. It implies the production of a seemingly endless range of hybridities. Modernization does, however, involve the production of a formal or structural homogeneity, ultimately on a global scale.[8] (In much the same way, the global spread of capital does not and cannot imply a true homogeneity, but rather the emergence of a global system that articulates unevenness and dislocation; for uneven development is one of the most fundamental aspects of capitalism.)[9] This implies a rewriting of cultural differences in terms of the discourse of moderniz-ation. The latter thus defines not only the relationship between the modern and the pre-modern, but also the relationship between various pre-modern zones themselves, as the distinctions between the latter seem to fade in the face of its overarching sameness; James Mill's explicit leveling of the differences between Indians and Scottish Highlanders (see chapter 5, above) is a perfect example of this.

Modernization implies a temporal project by which, in principle, all places and cultures become comparable by being reducible to the same set of temporal terms. This necessitates the production of a uniform and tendentially global temporality that can designate the relative status of different spaces according to a certain "scale" of development. In his book *Time and the Other*, Johannes Fabian has termed this project the naturalization and subsequent rehistoricization of time, which he says takes place during the nineteenth century.[10] As a result of this process, according to Fabian, dispersal in space would reflect movement along a certain sequence in time, with an increasing spatial distance from some predefined "center" marking a temporal distance as well, one that reflects a move back "down" one or more successive "stages" of devel-opment. Fabian argues that this involved the production of a scheme "in terms of which not only past cultures, but all living societies, were irrevocably placed on a temporal slope, a stream of Time – some upstream, others downstream. Civilization, evolution, development, acculturation, modernization (and their cousins, industrialization, ur-banization) are all terms whose conceptual content derives, in ways that can be specified, from evolutionary Time."[11]

Fabian suggests that such a project implies what he terms the "denial of coevalness," so that different societies may be seen to inhabit different moments or "stages" along the stream of evolutionary or developmental time. Thus, rather than allowing the incorporation of difference, he says, this project to the contrary necessitates the literally endless maintenance of a rigid distance based on spatio-temporal dispersion. "Evolutionary sequences and their concomitant political practice of colonialism and imperialism," Fabian argues, "may *look* incorporative; after all, they create a universal frame of reference able to accommodate all societies. But being based on the episteme of natural history, they are founded on distancing and separation."[12] The denial of coevalness in Fabian's terms amounts to an assertion of the synchronism of the non-synchronous, to use Ernst Bloch's famous phrase.

However, the denial of coevalness in and of itself is not necessarily a temporalized process. Earlier conceptions of difference, for example, could easily assert the lack of temporal synchronicity between the posessors of a certain "modernity" and various "other" barbarians and primitives (noble or otherwise), just as pre-evolutionary European understandings of biological hierarchy could conceive of a "great chain of being," with white human beings at the top. The great innovation of evolutionism, as Stephen Jay Gould argues, involves the temporalization of this chain, by which it is turned into a sequential ladder that could be ascended, a scale of development that could be climbed.[13]

While I agree with Fabian that there is an implicit denial of coevalness in the conceptualization of modern evolutionary time, and while this denial clearly implies a spatially defined temporal separation, an understanding of the project of modernization becomes even more crucial here. The "pre-modern" may still be totally different from the modern, but by virtue of being understood in terms of the modern, it is identified as tendentially modern, and hence no longer as forever different. Whereas *anti*-modernity implies perpetual difference, the possibility of a perpetual synchronism of the non-synchronous, *pre*-modernity (the operative term in the discourse of modernization) implies the principle of absorption into the spatio-temporal logic of the modern – so that pre-modern difference is revealed to be only a question of time. Modernization must therefore be understood as a process, not as a permanent status or attribute (as "modernity" once was in various European pre-romantic configurations going back at least to 1492).

Modernization appears to separate and distinguish, but in practice it unites, even if it does so by discursively separating. For the "inside" and "outside," "modern" and "pre-modern," even the "historical" and "non-historical" distinguished in the process of modernization are actually the products of a division that it has itself produced. Enclaves of cultural otherness, of the pre-modern or the natural, are defined by the discourse of modernization as its outsides. Here the limit between the modern and its supposed other, for example Nature, in fact helps to constitute that which is on the far side (Nature) as in fact fully a part of what lies on the near side of the limit (the social, the modern, the historical), "internally" reconstituting it by virtue of "externally" defining it.[14] Nature should be understood as an historically produced space, and not, as it has sometimes been understood by some romantic environmentalists, including Jonathan Bate, as real and actual, that is, an ahistorical something that has been there all along (see chapter 3, above).[15]

The modernizing logic of relating by separating would appear in colonialism in full force – as seen in British India in the 1880s, in French Algeria in the 1950s, in Israeli Jerusalem in the 1990s. It is worth reminding ourselves here of Frantz Fanon's dictum that "the colonial world is a world cut in two." For Fanon, the profound dividing line is spatial, expressed for instance in the violent division of the colonial city (of which French-occupied Algiers is his prime example, though allegorically it can be readily extended to other contexts):

> . . . The zone where the natives live is not complementary to the zone inhabited by the settlers. The two zones are opposed, but not in the service of a higher unity. Obedient to the rules of pure Aristotelian logic, they both follow the principles of reciprocal exclusivity. No conciliation is possible, for of the two terms, one is superfluous. The settlers' town is a strongly built town, all made of stone and steel. It is a brightly lit town; the streets are covered with asphalt, and the garbage cans swallow all the leavings, unseen, unknown and hardly thought about . . . The settlers' town is a well-fed town, an easygoing town; its belly is always full of good things. The settlers' town is a town of white people, of foreigners.
>
> The town belonging to the colonized people, or at least the native town, the Negro village, the medina, the reservation, is a place of ill fame, peopled by men of ill repute. They are born there, it matters little where or how; they die there, it matters not where, nor how. It is a world without spaciousness; men live on top of each other, and their huts are built one on top of the other. The native town is a hungry town, starved of bread, of meat, of shoes, of coal, of light, a town on its knees, a town wallowing in the mire. It is a town of niggers and dirty Arabs.[16]

The native town, no matter how segregated from the settlers' town, is not any less the product of the very same colonial system that produced the settlers' town. And yet modernizing colonialism seems at times to posit its own limits, so that the town of "niggers and dirty Arabs" seems to be "outside" it, not a part of it, even though the colonized are defined as colonized by the colonial system itself, even though colonialism consists on the ground of nothing but the dialectical unity of *both* colonizer and colonized. As Fanon reminds us, "the settler and the native are old acquaintances. In fact, the settler is right when he speaks of knowing 'them' well. For it is the settler who has brought the native into existence and who perpetuates his existence."

Indeed, the cultural logic of modern imperialism is that of modernization itself. This relationship, often forgotten or elided in contemporary analyses of imperialism, many of which focus on imperialism in isolation from the broader process of modernization, or even other (often but not always related) aspects of that process, including the development of capitalism, must now be examined in greater detail.

The process of modernization produces a new sense of space, one that is defined by the limits and confines of modern secular time. In the extension of the spatio-temporal process of modernization, alternative conceptions of space and time are covered over and done away with, to be replaced by modern space and above all modern time. Modern time is measured not only in specific and indeed mechanically reproducible units, but above all in very precise units (seconds, minutes, hours) that are really only mechanically measurable at all. Henceforth, people would have to turn to clocks and watches, or listen for bells and buzzers, to judge the passage of time, according to the rules of this new temporality that relies upon units too small and finally too abstractly regular to be discerned by human perception. The dependency on mechanical time takes the place of the temporal categories of previous or alternative modes of cultural organization. The latter categories are generally not quantifiable into strict and precise units whose ultimate horizon – the one unit of time that endlessly renews itself, the unit in terms of which all other units of time become merely denominators or multiples – would no longer be the year or even the season, but the working day.

The significance of the temporal structure of modernity is, not coincidentally, clearest when it comes to the measurement and regulation of work time. The development of the culture of industrial capitalism was characterized not only by various spatial innovations in the sites of production and circulation and other spaces whose significance Michel Foucault and others have elaborated (workhouses and factories, but also banks, schools, hospitals, prisons, and so forth, in addition to the newly re-organized countryside, once it had been enclosed, drained, reordered, cleared). It was also, as E. P. Thompson argues, characterized by temporal innovations, including "a greater sense of time-thrift among the improving capitalist employers."[7] Indeed, Thompson's insistence that the shift into industrial capitalism be thought of as a large-scale cultural transformation, rather than merely as a material intensification of production techniques, becomes particularly pressing and evident in his consideration of the new temporality of modern capitalist society. For, lest we either abstract the clock from its historical and cultural context, or, worse, fall into some kind of technological determinism, what matters here is not so much the innovation of clock-time or of the clock itself, but rather the application of that innovation to the working day and to all cultural time. For in modern capitalist societies, time becomes the very form in which value is created and circulated.

Thus the temporality of modernization must be taken to denote not only the time of the work-place, but of all life, the time of culture understood, to borrow Raymond Williams's phrase, as "a whole way of life." Just as the spatial project undertaken in modernization would encounter resistance (and would have to constantly reinvent itself according to the pressures of that resistance), the temporality of modernization would as well. Thompson reminds us that, in England as much as anywhere else, it took decades of struggle before the new categories of temporality were adapted by the whole culture. Ultimately, however, modern temporality *was* adopted and, "by the division of labour; the supervision of labour; fines; bells and clocks; money incentives; preachings and schoolings; the suppression of fairs and sports," new labor habits were formed, and a new time-discipline was imposed across the whole culture.[18] Thus, the "abstract" space of the modern corresponds not only to abstract labor, but to abstract time, to a *homogeneous* modern temporality in which, as Perry Anderson argues (via Benjamin), "each moment is perpetually different from every other moment by virtue of being *next*, but – by the same token – each moment is eternally the *same* as an interchangeable unit in a process of infinite recurrence."[19] Recalled now in this light, Wordsworth's spot of time seems even clearer as a potential form of resistance to the domination of this new abstract space-time.[20]

The culture of modernization thus takes the form of political and economic discourses; but the latter are put into practice only through struggle. Modernization is in other words not an absolute, not a blanket homogeneous culture, but rather a hegemonic project that is always in a process of redefinition. It is constantly expanding, changing, developing, reinventing itself; but also being limited, constrained, resisted, challenged, altered. Modernization always exists as process and practice *along with* its others. Its space-time is by definition never homogenous but rather always a space of contradiction, combination, differentiation, resistance: at once smooth and striated, at once abstract and differential – but always with the potential of some ultimate apocalyptic purification into the homogeneous, the abstract.

Modernization can in this sense be understood as the purest form of imperialism. It occurs at once in large-scale sweeps and bursts, but also in terms of the micrological, the quotidian; at once in the historic sense of reorientation towards and through the structures of Braudelian world-time and Millian world-history, and in the minute changes in daily life brought about by its intense and totalitarian "abstraction," for instance in the recomposition of daily life in terms of abstract clock-time ("the hours of folly are measured by the clock; but of wisdom no clock can measure"). This recomposition takes place not only in the work-place but in all zones and forms and areas of life. It enables our very understanding of culture, both synchronically and diachronically, in the broadest sense of the term.[21] Yet the discourses of modernization not only tolerate resistance: they require and demand it at an absolutely fundamental level, which is why modernization always implies a certain (greater or lesser) degree of hybridization and of unevenness. In effect, the project of modernization begins at the very moment a new territory is defined as pre-modern. From that moment on, the only question that will remain is the degree or extent to which it has already been modern-ized – that is, reproduced as a hybrid space, as a modernizing space, as a modern space.

Imperialism in the romantic period not only implies the sort of geopolitical and national-imperial project discussed by Said. Such a project would take off later in the nineteenth century only with the relative consolidation of the metropolitan center itself. Rather, in the romantic period this amorphous and even effectively non-existent "cen-ter" was itself precisely subject to the very same modernizing pressures as Britain's more distant colonies in Africa or Asia would be later in the century; and as certain of its colonial territories (principally India) already were to a certain extent. As one of the key constitutive discourses and processes of modernization, "imperialism" here need not be restric-ted to "the practice, the theory, and the attitudes of a dominating metropolitan center ruling a distant territory," as Said has put it; though, to be sure, it means that as well, and perhaps above all.

Within Britain, then, "imperialism" might be taken to mean, simply, modernization, or at any rate the development of a certain stage of the process of modernization. For it was only with a certain level of capitalist modernization complete in the metropolitan center itself – i.e., only with a certain degree of the metropolitan center's definition or constitution *as a center* – that the processes of imperialism and capitalism would converge once again and with redoubled energy on the more distant overseas territories in the form of the properly modern imperialism discussed by Said. In historically specific terms, this involves the period of imperialism that took off into the 1840s, and accelerated dramatically in the 1870s and 1880s. This is not to suggest merely that, for example, the Highlands of Scotland served after Culloden as a practice stage for a dress-rehearsal of the "real" imperialism of the late nineteenth century (though in a sense they did). Rather, the "real" imperialism of the later nineteenth century fundamentally – i.e., ideologically and epistemologically – required some sense of mission outwards, away from a relatively secure domestic center (though a center still involved in a continuous process of definition, principally in terms of the developing ideologies of "domesticity," which have been elaborated in recent materialist feminist theory[22]) and into the many hearts of darkness "out there."

This also implies some fundamental continuity between the process of modernization within the metropolitan center and outside it (a continuity that Blake – as I argued in chapter 7 – would figure through *Jerusalem*'s complex and interreferential map of the world, in which the quaternary England–Ireland–Scotland–Wales corresponds to the quaternary Asia–America–Europe–Africa precisely in terms of the planetary spread of the Universal Empire of modernization[23]). And it is in this sense that the discourses of imperialism and capitalism converge in Britain – with modernization – and become virtually or effectively, operatively, indistinguishable. How, for instance, could one possibly describe the late eighteenth-century modernization of the Scottish Highlands in terms that did not ultimately refer to imperialism? And how, other than in the vaguest of metaphysical or sentimental ways, could one describe the romantic transformation of Nature in terms that did not ultimately refer to capitalism?

Imperialism during the romantic period may thus be understood as the principal process – simultaneously discursive and material, imaginary and real – of modernization. Projected outwards later in the nineteenth century, especially after the transfer of India to the Crown with the demise of the East India Company in 1858, it would become more readily identifiable in national terms as "British" imperialism. But the full force of what I am arguing here becomes evident only when one considers the process of modernization within Britain not as "outside imperialism's" parallel or complementary "internal imperialism," but as contiguous and even coextensive with British imperialism as such; for the very dualism of "inside" and "outside" was produced as a result of this process – there having previously been no "metropolitan center" in any meaningful sense of that term as we use it today.[24]

The cultural project of modern British imperialism in the romantic period must be seen as a continuous *spatial* process, operating both "inside" and "outside" Britain, mediating – indeed defining – the limit and the nature of the limit between that "inside" and "outside" through the production of modern space-time, both within and without Britain. What would signal the (tentative) end of this period is not so much the actual completion of that project (which would require several more decades), but rather the attainment of a certain consolidation of a new, modern, metropolitan identity; an identity that, increasingly, would no longer locate anti-modern otherness within the metropolitan center but would have to seek that otherness beyond its shores (i.e., in the Empire). To be sure, the anti-modern other would continue to recur within the metropolitan center, but increasingly it would take the form of hang-overs, nightmares, and hauntings – like the colonial madwoman in the attic of *Jane Eyre* – nightmares plaguing the political consciousness (and indeed constituting the political unconscious) of an increasingly pacified and modernized United Kingdom of Great Britain and Ireland. But these recurrences must inhabit some other political moment (identified in literary history as the moment of Victorian realism). For what we are dealing with in the romantic period are not so much the dying vestiges of the archaic and the pre- or anti-modern, but rather their full force, at the very moment at which they are about to be vanquished, tamed, domesticated, and defused: modernized.

Romanticism marks the symbolic terrain of a rupture between one cultural moment and another. It marks the nexus or conjuncture be-tween radically opposed paths and trajectories of Europe's relations with its cultural others, roads historically taken and not taken since that rupture. Perhaps what makes a text like *Childe Harold* or *Waverley* roman-tic is its uneasy combination of a fascinated attraction to a space of otherness (like the Orient or the Scottish Highlands) with a dawning realization that such spaces are inevitably doomed by the encroaching world of modernization whose central "will" would be to draw every-thing into itself, to destroy the many synchronous worlds and histories, and incorporate them into the one unilinear, universal, diachronic, and tyrannical world history so thoroughly exemplified by Mill's *History of British India*. But then the unfulfilled and unfulfillable utopian moment of such a text would be an unspoken desire to avoid this incorporation, to allow the persistence and the expansion of the non-identical and the anti-modern in the face of the historical forces first announced by Mill and triumphantly celebrated by others in later decades and up to our own time. Maybe it is this that lies at the heart of romanticism's uneasiness: at once seeing what the world would become, and hoping without hope that it might be different.

Notes

I INTRODUCTION: UNIVERSAL EMPIRE

1 James Mill, *The History of British India* (1836; University of Chicago Press, 1975), pp. 33–34.

2 It is important to distinguish modern (industrial) capitalism from other modes of capitalist development, including money capital and mercantile capital; the latter can coexist with other modes of social and economic organization indefinitely, whereas, at least in the long run, the former *tends* to reorganize all forms of socio-economic activity according to its own principles and priorities. In his history of modern capitalism, for example, Marx writes, "It can be understood, therefore, why, in our analysis of the primary form of capital, *the form in which it determines the economic organization of modern society*, we have entirely left out of consideration its well-known and so to speak antediluvian forms, merchants' capital and usurers' capital." Mercantile capital and money capital are here placed alongside modern capital (i.e., industrial capital, capital as a mode of *production*, which is the form of capital that primarily concerns Marx, insofar as it forms the dominant economic mode of modern society) as its historic pre-conditions and at the same time as crucial elements in the modern existence of capital. See Karl Marx, *Capital*, vol. I, trans. Ben Fowkes (1867; New York: Vintage, 1977), p. 266. My emphasis.

3 Modernization is at once *tendentially* global and *tendentially* homogenizing, internally and conceptually "driven" to rewrite or erase difference in the name of identity. "If capitalism is the universal truth," as Gilles Deleuze and Félix Guattari argue, "it is so in the sense that makes capitalism *the negative* of all social formations." If this system has a will to "create a world in its own image," it does so by absorbing – colonizing – other worlds, worlds of cultural difference, dissidence, otherness, and resistance, by overriding their unique characteristics and social-cultural codes, and rewriting them in terms of a universal *potential* (i.e., modernity) which, even if only initially, it claims uniquely for itself. See Gilles Deleuze and Félix Guattari, *Anti-Oedipus: Capitalism and Schizophrenia*, trans. Robert Hurley, Mark Seem, and Helen Lane (Minneapolis: University of Minnesota Press, 1983), p. 153.

186

4 It is very important not to see modernization or capitalism as processes that radiate outwards from a predefined center. Modern capitalism developed at once in Europe and outside of Europe; this conjuncture was not even unilaterally determined by Europe or by Europeans. To consider capitalism as a European-born phenomenon that then radiated outwards to impose itself on other parts of the world is merely to reiterate the claim of modernization itself; it is to claim, like James Mill (and more recently Francis Fukuyama) that world history begins and ends with the history of Europe. To do so is, moreover, also to reiterate worn-out claims regarding some sort of European "miracle," which supposedly led to the industrial revolution and to the development of various theories predicated on what J. M. Blaut refers to as the historical "tunnel vision" of Eurocentric diffusionism; namely, that capitalism, freedom, democracy, the pursuit of happiness, etc., were essentially *European* phenomena that then expanded outwards, the generous "gifts" of the European empires, to encompass non-Europeans and "free" them from their despotisms, their inertia, and the shackles of their traditional ways of life (Percy Shelley, of all people, is particularly passionate on this point, as I will argue in a later chapter). See J. M. Blaut, *The Colonizer's Model of the World: Geographical Diffusion and Eurocentric History* (New York: Guilford Press, 1993).

5 "The tendency to create a world market" is "directly given in the concept of capital itself," Marx argues in the *Grundrisse*. For while "capital must on one side strive to tear down every spatial barrier to intercourse, i.e., to exchange, and conquer the whole earth for its market, it strives on the other side to annihilate this space with time, i.e., to reduce to a minimum the time spent in motion from one place to another. The more developed the capital, therefore, the more extensive the market over which it circulates . . . the more does it strive simultaneously for an even greater extension of the market *and for greater annihilation of space by time*." See Karl Marx, *Grundrisse*, trans. Martin Nicolaus (1857; Harmondsworth: Pelican, 1973), pp. 408–09, 459. My emphasis.

6 William Blake, *A Descriptive Catalogue*, in *The Complete Poetry and Prose of William Blake*, ed. David Erdman (New York: Archer Books, 1988), p. 543. All subsequent Blake references are to Erdman's edition, hereafter abbreviated to E.

7 One of the clearest recent examples of world history as the history of modernization itself can be found in Immanuel Wallerstein's *Historical Capitalism* (London: Verso, 1989).

8 See Fernand Braudel, *The Perspective of the World: Civilization and Capitalism, 15th–18th Century*, vol. III, trans. Siân Reynolds (New York: Harper & Row, 1986), pp. 21–88, esp. pp. 24–45.

9 See Johannes Fabian, *Time and the Other: How Anthropology makes its Object* (New York: Columbia University Press, 1983). Also see Eric Wolf, *Europe and the People Without History* (Berkeley: University of California Press, 1982).

10 See, for example, E. P. Thompson, "Custom, Law and Common Right," in

his *Customs in Common: Studies in Traditional Popular Culture* (New York: New Press, 1993), pp. 97–184.

11 See, for example, Peter Laslett, *The World we have lost: England Before the Industrial Age* (New York: Scribners, 1971).

12 See, for example, Eric Hobsbawm, *Industry and Empire* (Harmondsworth: Pelican, 1969); E. P. Thompson, *The Making of the English Working Class* (New York: Vintage, 1966).

13 See, for example, Peter Linebaugh, *The London Hanged: Crime and Society in the Eighteenth Century* (Cambridge University Press, 1994).

14 See, for example, E. P. Thompson, "Time, Work-Discipline and Industrial Capitalism," in his *Customs in Common*, pp. 352–403; Peter Bowler, *The Invention of Progress: The Victorians and the Past* (Oxford: Blackwell, 1989); Stephen Jay Gould, *Time's Arrow, Time's Cycle: Myth and Metaphor in the Discovery of Geological Time* (Cambridge, MA: Harvard University Press, 1987).

15 See, for example, Harold Perkin, *Origins of Modern English Society* (New York: Routledge, 1991).

16 See, for example, Jacob Bronowski, *William Blake and the Age of Revolution* (New York: Harper & Row, 1965); Phyllis Deane, *The First Industrial Revolution* (Cambridge University Press, 1990).

17 See, for example, "Marxism, Communism and History: A Reintroduction," in Saree Makdisi, Cesare Casarino, and Rebecca Karl, eds., *Marxism Beyond Marxism* (London: Routledge, 1996), pp. 1–13.

18 As one index of this transition, the proto-industrialization of the textiles industry as early as the late eighteenth and early nineteenth centuries constituted an explosion in the growth of production as well as trade. British cotton imports rose from 11 million lb in 1784 to 283 million lb in 1832. At the same time, Britain's exports of cotton manufactures experienced a huge expansion: exports of printed cloth from the UK grew from 20 million yards in 1796 to 347 million yards in 1830; having exceeded £1 million in 1785, textile exports increased by a factor of over 3,000 percent by 1830, to £31 million. Cotton products in the decades after Waterloo accounted for approximately one half of the value of all British exports, just as raw cotton, by the 1830s, amounted to roughly 20 percent of total net imports into the UK – at a moment when the UK alone accounted for about one third of all world trade. What distinguished this new era from the mercantile era was the paramount fact that trade was no longer at the service of individual or household consumers – no longer an end in itself – but rather a moment of production. See Richard Brown, *Society and Economy in Modern Britain, 1700–1850* (London: Routledge, 1991), pp. 160–82; Eric Williams, *Capitalism and Slavery* (London: André Deutsch, 1993), pp. 120–28; Hobsbawm, *Industry and Empire*, p. 69.

19 Far from being autonomously determined by British imperial policy, this shift in the geographical location of intense imperial activity was partly the result of the American and Haitian revolutions in the West and partly the

result of internal crises and changes in the eastern empires. See C. L. R. James, *The Black Jacobins, Toussaint L'Ouverture and the San Domingo Revolution* (New York: Vintage, 1963); Ramkrishna Mukherjee, *The Rise and Fall of the East India Company* (New York: Monthly Review Press, 1974); Arthur Waley, *The Opium War Through Chinese Eyes* (Stanford University Press, 1958); Philip Curtin, *Cross-Cultural Trade in World History* (Cambridge University Press, 1984); Robin Blackburn, *The Overthrow of Colonial Slavery* (London: Verso, 1988); C. A. Bayly, *Imperial Meridian* (London: Longman, 1988).

20 Here I am taking issue with some of the arguments put forward by Marshall Berman in *All that is Solid melts into Air: The Experience of Modernity* (Harmondsworth: Penguin, 1988) and by Perry Anderson in "Modernity and Revolution," in Cary Nelson and Lawrence Grossberg, eds., *Marxism and the Interpretation of Culture* (Urbana: University of Illinois Press, 1988).

21 See Marilyn Butler, *Romantics, Rebels and Reactionaries* (Oxford University Press, 1981), esp. pp. 178–87.

22 *Ibid.* p. 184.

23 I consider some of the consequences of this for the Arab world in "'Post-Colonial' Literature in a Neo-Colonial World: Modern Arabic Culture and the End of Modernity," in *Boundary 2* (Spring 1995), pp. 85–115.

24 James Chandler argues this point comprehensively in *England in 1819: The Politics of Literary Culture and the Case of Romantic Historicism* (University of Chicago Press, 1997).

25 See Edward Said, *Culture and Imperialism* (New York: Knopf, 1993), p. 58.

26 *Ibid.*, p. 71. Fredric Jameson makes what I would suggest is a parallel argument concerning the relationship of the realist novel and structures of feeling in bourgeois society; see *The Political Unconscious* (Ithaca: Cornell University Press, 1981), pp. 103–50.

27 See Said, *Culture and Imperialism*, pp. 186–90. Also see Jameson's important essay "Beyond the Cave: Demystifying the Ideology of Modernism," in *The Ideologies of Theory: Essays 1971–1986*, vol. II (Minneapolis: University of Minnesota Press, 1988), pp. 115–32.

28 See Said, *Culture and Imperialism*, p. 186.

29 I would argue that this is so even though the modernists themselves (most clearly in the case of T. S. Eliot) often denounced romanticism as an aberration.

30 This is the understanding of modernism elaborated in Fredric Jameson's *Postmodernism; Or, the Cultural Logic of Late Capitalism* (Durham: Duke University Press, 1991), pp. 302–13. What I am proposing here partly involves tracing Jameson's argument backwards to areas that he does not, for the most part, discuss.

31 See chapter 5, below.

32 Joseph Conrad, *Heart of Darkness* (1899; New York: Norton, 1988), p. 9.

33 Indeed, as Neil Smith and others have argued, there has always been a contradiction at the heart of capitalism between "geographic differentiation" and "the universalizing tendency of capital." See Neil Smith, *Uneven*

Development: Nature, Capital, and the Production of Space (London: Blackwell, 1990), p. 152. See also Henri Lefebvre, *The Production of Space*, trans. Donald Nicholson-Smith (Oxford: Blackwell, 1991).

34 See William Wordsworth, "Preface to the Second Edition of *Lyrical Ballads*," 1800. See also "Great Men Have Been Among us" (1802).

35 Jean Baudrillard argues that "modernity imposes itself throughout the world as a homogeneous unity, irradiating from the Occident." (See Baudrillard, "Modernity," in *Canadian Journal of Political and Social Theory*, 9:3 (1987), p. 63.) However, modernity can never exist in pure form or "as such," but rather in relation to an anti-modern; the process of modernization involves the production of a practically infinite range of cultural hybridities, rather than merely the imposition of a standard homogeneity: for there can be no such thing as the modern unless there is an anti-modern against which it can be dialectically defined. While earlier, pre-romantic, conceptions of modernity defined it as a property or an attribute, by the end of the eighteenth century, modernization could be seen as a process that is always in a state of *becoming*; or, rather, a process of becoming whose condition of possibility is the continual positing of its own limits – limits that it needs to transcend and then rediscover, re-posit, in other forms, or at greater distances. I discuss some implications of these questions for the contemporary world, particularly the third world, in, "'Post-Colonial' Literature in a Neo-Colonial World: Modern Arabic Culture and the End of Modernity," in *Boundary* 2 (Spring 1995), pp. 85–115. Deleuze and Guattari suggest that we can see such deterritorialization in terms of the production of an isomorphic, rather than a strictly homogeneous, world-system. See Deleuze and Guattari, *A Thousand Plateaus: Capitalism and Schizophrenia*, trans. Brian Massumi (Minneapolis: University of Minnesota Press, 1988), pp. 434–37. Finally, with the eradication of the anti-modern, modernity itself is transfigured. Hence the concept of postmodernism elaborated by Fredric Jameson, according to whom the postmodern develops out of a situation of completed modernization. See Jameson, *Postmodernism*.

36 See James Chandler, "Representative Men, Spirits of the Age, and Other Romantic Types," in Kenneth Johnston et al., eds., *Romantic Revolutions: Criticism and Theory* (Bloomington: Indiana University Press, 1990), p. 108.

37 Indeed, the heterotopic spot of time should not be seen as entirely devoid of oppositional potential. In his work on the nineteenth-century sea novel, Cesare Casarino explores the radical possibilities of the ship as a heterotopic zone (almost a floating "spot of time"), which exemplifies and embodies the spatio-temporal logic and socio-political structures of capitalist modernity – sometimes at their most extreme – and, at the same time, allows for the possibility of imagining and even enacting alternative forms of desire and community within that space: forms of desire and community that are antithetical to the social, cultural, and political rules and regulations of modern capitalism. See Cesare Casarino, "Gomorrahs of the Deep; or, Melville, Foucault, and the Question of Heterotopia" in *Arizona Quarter-*

ly, 51: 4 (Winter 1995), pp. 1–25; and "The Sublime of the Closet; or Joseph Conrad's Secret Sharing" in *Boundary 2*, 24: 2, (Summer 1997).

38 For example, to take the most important of these spots of time, the fact that Wordsworth's appeal to the permanence of Nature implies a construction of Nature rather than a return to an actually-existing transhistorical and universal ("natural") given seems to have been lost on certain critics, including Jonathan Bate. Pointing to the demise of Eastern European "communism" and what he sees as the concomitant "death of Marxism," Bate argues that the time has come to rejuvenate "the Romantic tradition" as a locus of "green," rather than "red," opposition to materialism and capitalism. The driving force of Bate's book seems to be his insistence that one can either criticize a poet like Wordsworth for his suppression of certain socio-political realities, or one can join Wordsworth in an attempt to defy the world of industrialization and pollution by clinging to the threatened "permanence" of Nature. Thus, in response to critics such as Jerome McGann, Marjorie Levinson, Annabel Patterson, Marilyn Butler, and Alan Liu, Bate seems to insist that there is indeed something called Nature that still defies commodification and private property. And hence, Bate argues, we can either side with the romantics and defend this Nature from the predatory ruinations brought about by capitalism and Marxism, or, like the "red" critics he despises, we can criticize the romantics and hence perpetuate the depradations of capitalism and a Marxism that is supposed to have died but still has not. See Jonathan Bate, *Romantic Ecology: Wordsworth and the Environmental Tradition* (London: Routledge, 1991), esp. pp. 8–10, 15–19, 33–34, 46, 56–57.

39 I plan to elaborate the more complicated version of this argument in a separate book-length project on Blake's art and poetry of the 1790s.

40 Blake, *Annotations to Wordsworth* [E665].

41 Blake, *Marriage* [E37].

42 Blake, *Song of Los* [E68].

43 Blake, *Song of Los* [E67].

44 See the discussion of James Mill, above.

45 Blake, *Four Zoas* [E314].

46 *Ibid.* [E328].

47 Though the Universal Empire itself is also anthropomorphized; in one of the most memorable passages of the *Four Zoas*, groans of anguish are heard to come not from its victims, but from the empire itself.

48 Blake, *Four Zoas* [E355].

2 HOME IMPERIAL: WORDSWORTH'S LONDON AND THE SPOT OF TIME

1 See lines 121–42.

2 See John Barrell, *The Idea of Landscape and the Sense of Place* (Cambridge University Press, 1972).

3 For a discussion of cognitive mapping, see Jameson, *Postmodernism*, pp. 45–54.

4 See Max Byrd, *London Transformed: Images of the City in the Eighteenth Century* (New Haven: Yale University Press, 1978), p. 139.

5 Friedrich Engels, *The Condition of the Working Class in England* (1844; Moscow: Progress Publishers, 1973), p. 63.

6 This is, in other words, the history of the social production of what Lefebvre calls the "abstract" space of commodities and of capital. See Henri Lefebvre, *The Production of Space*, trans. Donald Nicholson-Smith (Oxford: Blackwell, 1991), pp. 48–55, 229–91. Lefebvre ties the production of abstract space not merely to capitalism but specifically to urban space.

7 *The Prelude* (1805), VIII, 746–51.

8 Thus the failure here is not one of vision, but rather of subjectivity.

9 T. C. Barker discusses the gigantic growth in traffic in and out of London to the rest of Britain during this period, in "Transport: The Survival of the Old beside the New," in Peter Mathias and John Davis, eds., *The First Industrial Revolutions* (Oxford: Blackwell, 1989), pp. 86–100, esp. pp. 94–95.

10 Eric Hobsbawm, *Industry and Empire* (Harmondsworth: Pelican, 1969), p. 28.

11 See Phyllis Deane, *The First Industrial Revolution* (Cambridge University Press, 1990), pp. 32–36.

12 "From its general hue of greenish coffee-colour, the [Thames] river water deepened to the colour and density of black treacle near the outfalls, and a viscous scum covered the mud banks exposed at low tide. When there was a rainy season the sewage might be diluted and its stench diminished; a southerly wind might bring relief to Vauxhall or a westerly one to Chelsea, but the inescapable fact remained: this was the water that Londoners had to drink, and eighty-two million gallons were taken daily from the Thames for London's needs." R. J. Mitchell and M. D. R. Leys, *A History of London Life* (Harmondsworth: Penguin, 1958), p. 271. Significant steps were taken to improve these infrastructural conditions beginning only in the 1830s; see Gordon Cherry, "Public Policy and the Morphology of Western Cities," in Richard Lawton, ed., *The Rise and Fall of Great Cities* (London: Bellhaven, 1992), pp. 32–43.

13 See Roy Porter's excellent *London: A Social History* (Cambridge: Harvard University Press, 1995); also see George Rudé, *Hanoverian London* (Berkeley: University of California Press, 1971); Andrew Saint, "The Building Art of the First Industrial Metropolis," in Celina Fox, ed., *London: World City, 1800–1840* (New Haven: Yale University Press, 1992), pp. 51–76; and Peter Linebaugh, *The London Hanged: Crime and Civil Society in the Eighteenth Century* (Cambridge University Press, 1993), esp. pp. 402–41.

14 Braudel, *Perspective of the World*, p. 365. He argues that not only imports and exports, but commercial exchanges taking place between internal markets wholly outside of the city were increasingly relayed through the central clearing-house of London: "whether bound inland or abroad, everything had to pass through London." Thus, one former prisoner during the war

with France concluded that "if all the interests of England are concentrated in the city of London, which is today the meeting place of all business, one can also say that London is present in the rest of England." Quoted p. 367.

15 See Steen Eiler Rasmussen, *London: The Unique City* (Cambridge: MIT Press, 1934), pp. 129–30. Over 600 stage coaches were licensed to run between London and towns within 20 miles, carrying some 70,000 passengers from London's 123 stations every day on this inner network alone. Rasmussen says that London was "not only the junction of a series of main roads but it protected them as they crossed the broad river Thames. Its possibilities as a commercial center were unique. It was at the same time a great seaport and the main junction of all the roads of the interior."

16   Oh, blank confusion! and a type not false
        Of what the mighty City is itself
        To all except a straggler here and there,
        To the whole swarm of its inhabitants;
        An undistinguishable world to men,
        The slaves unrespited of low pursuits,
        Living amid the same perpetual flow
        Of trivial objects, melted and reduced
        To one identity, by differences
        That have no law, no meaning, and no end.
            (*The Prelude* (1805), VII, 695–704)

17 See *The Country and the City* (Oxford University Press, 1983).
18 Thompson, *English Working Class*, pp. 264–65.
19 See Porter, *London*, p. 180.
20 Lines 186–87 and 205–08; see also lines 215–32.
21 Mary Jacobus, "The Art of Managing Books: Romantic Prose and the Writing of the Past," in Arden Reed, ed., *Romanticism and Language* (Ithaca: Cornell University Press, 1984), p. 227.
22 De Quincey writes in his *Confessions*: "I used often, on Saturday nights, after I had taken opium, to wander forth, without much regarding the direction or the distance, to all the markets, and other parts of London, whither the poor resort on a Saturday night for laying out their wages. Many a family party, consisting of a man, his wife, and sometimes one or two of their children, have I listened to, as they stood consulting on their ways and means, or the strength of their exchequer, or the price of household articles . . . Whenever I saw occasion, or could do it without appearing to be intrusive, I joined their parties, and gave my opinion upon the matter in discussion, which, if not always judicious, was always received indulgently." See *Confessions of an English Opium-Eater* (New York: A. L. Burt, 1856), p. 168.
23 See Byrd, *London Transformed*, p. 143.
24 See George Rudé, *Hanoverian London*, pp. 228–55.
25 See George Rudé, *Wilkes and Liberty* (Oxford University Press, 1962), p. 173–81. He goes on to say that these were the people who "demonstrated in St. George's Fields, at Hyde Park Corner, at the Mansion House, in

Parliament Square and at St. James's Palace; who shouted, or chalked up, 'Wilkes and Liberty' in the streets of the City, Westminster and Southwark; who pelted Sheriff Harley and the common hangman at the Royal Exchange when they attempted to burn No. 45 of *The North Briton*; who smashed the windows of Lords Bute and Egremont and daubed the boots of the Austrian Ambassador; who paraded the Boot and the Petticoat in the City streets, and burned Colonel Luttrell and Lords Sandwich and Barrington in effigy outside the Tower of London. These are the elements whom contemporaries and later historians have – either from indolence, prejudice or lack of more certain knowledge – called 'the mob.'"

26 Marilyn Butler has argued that from the late 1790s onwards, Wordsworth "ceases to see others as social pheonomena; they are objects for contemplation, images of apparent alienation which the poet's imagination translates into private emblems of his troubled communion with nature." Butler, *Romantics, Rebels and Reactionaries*, p. 67.

27 William Blake, "London," see chapter 7, below.

28 Lines 657, 645–48.

29 Line 185.

30 He is referred to in the 1850 *Prelude* as "Genius of Burke!" See James Chandler, *Wordsworth's Second Nature: A Study of the Poetry and Politics* (University of Chicago Press, 1984), esp. pp. 40–61.

31 See Geoffrey Hartman, *Wordsworth's Poetry, 1787–1814* (Cambridge: Harvard University Press, 1971), p. 239. Also see Book VII of the 1850 *Prelude*, lines 512–43. In the general panic which gripped the propertied classes in the 1790s, Burke referred to the working class not only as the "swinish multitude," but as "objects of eternal vigilance," the more dangerous elements of which had to be excised from the body politic through "the critical terrors of the cautery and the knife." Quoted in Thompson, *English Working Class*, 137.

32 See Victor Kiernan, *Poets, Politics and the People* (London: Verso, 1989), pp. 96–123; he argues (p. 118) that "Wordsworth's retreat from London was in one way an instinctive flight" from the demands of the radical movement of the time.

33 Lines 615–16.

34 Lines 233–51.

35 See James, *The Black Jacobins*, p. 200.

36 See David Simpson, *Wordsworth and the Figuring of the Real* (Atlantic Highlands, NJ: Humanities Press, 1982), p. 54.

37 See Brown, *Society and Economy*, pp. 160–83.

38 Eric Hobsbawm, *The Age of Revolution, 1789–1848* (New York: Mentor, 1962), p. 35.

39 See Martin Daunton, "London and the World," in Celina Fox, ed., *London: World City, 1800–1840* (New Haven: Yale University Press), pp. 21–38; also see Curtin, *Cross-Cultural Trade*, pp. 230–34.

40 See Harold Perkin, *Origins of Modern English Society* (London: Routledge,

1991), pp. 160–75.

41 Asa Briggs, *Victorian Cities* (New York: Harper & Row, 1970), p. 92.

42 See Rudé, *Hanoverian London*, p. 235.

43 Braudel, *The Structures of Everyday Life: Civilization and Capitalism, 15th–18th Century*, vol. I, trans. Siân Reynolds (New York: Harper & Row, 1979), p. 365. It is important to try to recognize the staggering scale of this trade: Braudel writes elsewhere that 13,444 ships cleared the port of London in 1798 alone (see *ibid.*, p. 548). Rudé indicates that the volume of ships entering the port of London increased from 14,000 in 1794 to well over 20,000 by 1822 (see Rudé, *Hanoverian London*, p. 230). This is partly why the 1797 mutiny in the Royal Navy's North Sea Fleet, based at the Nore (in the Thames Estuary, east of London), was an event of such major significance; for not only did the mutineers of the so-called "Floating Republic" refuse to fight in the war agaist France: they commenced a blockade of the port of London, thereby disrupting the entire British economy at one stroke. See G. E. Manwaring and Bonamy Dobrée, *Mutiny: The Floating Republic* (London: The Cresset Library, 1987), pp. 187–88.

44 Engels, *Condition of the Working Class*, p. 63.

45 Quoted in Sidney Mintz, *Sweetness and Power: The Place of Sugar in Modern History* (Harmondsworth: Penguin, 1986), p. 116.

46 *Ibid.*, pp. 116, 119. Fredric Jameson has argued this point in more strictly phenomenological terms. He says that, at a certain point in the development of capitalism, "the phenomenological experience of the individual subject . . . becomes limited to a tiny corner of the social world, a fixed-camera view of a certain section of London or the countryside or whatever. But the truth of that experience no longer coincides with the place in which it takes place. The truth of that limited daily experience of London lies, rather, in India or Jamaica or Hong Kong; it is bound up with the whole colonial system of the British Empire that determines the very quality of the individual's subjective terms." See Fredric Jameson, "Cognitive Mapping," in Cary Nelson and Lawrence Grossberg, eds., *Marxism and the Interpretation of Culture*, (Urbana: University of Illinois Press, 1988), p. 349.

47 See the discussion of Bartholomew Fair and other festivals in Roy Porter, *London: A Social History*, p. 172.

48 Lines 655–91.

49 See, for example, the famous passage in the *Confessions* in which De Quincey is overwhelmed by an avalanche of dehistoricized, detemporalized, and despatialized Oriental images: "I was stared at, hooted at, by monkeys, by paroquets, by cockatoos. I ran into pagodas, and was fixed for centuries at the summit, or in secret rooms; I was the idol; I was the priest; I was worshipped; I was sacrificed. I fled from the wrath of Brahma through all the forests of Asia; Vishnu hated me; Seeva lay in wait for me. I came suddenly upon Isis and Osiris: I had done a deed, they said, which the ibis and the crocodile trembled at. Thousands of years I lived and was buried in stone coffins, with mummies and sphinxes, in narrow chambers at the heart

of eternal pyramids. I was kissed, with cancerous kisses, by crocodiles, and was laid, confounded with all unutterable abortions, among reeds and Nilotic mud." This striking passage actualizes the degeneration from sublimity to terror, which is coextensive with the degeneration of the narrator's own subjectivity. Quite apart from the usual attributes of European racism and Orientalism, etc., the result is a bizarre and contradictory combination of simultaneous paranoia and loss of subjectivity: the narrator takes on multiple identities (at once idol and priest, at once an object of worship and sacrifice, etc.) but still somehow remains *the* center of attention (everyone from cockatoos to gods is chasing *him* around this miasmic Orient, as though they had nothing better to do). The terror and the loss of identity are one and the same; and also the loss of identity and the loss of stable spatio-temporal coordinates are identical: the one signifies the other. What I would like to suggest is that a similar process takes place for Wordsworth in Book VII of the *Prelude*, though he is considerably more resistant than De Quincey to the loss of paramount subjectivity and in the end turns to Nature to reestablish the parameters of both a stable spatio-temporal existence and a concomitant unitary subjectivity. See chapter 1 for the relationship between subjectivity and phenomenological spatio-temporal coordinates. See *Confessions of an Opium-Eater*, pp. 216–17.

50 *The Prelude* (1805), VII, 695–706.
51 See Wordsworth, ["The Sublime and the Beautiful"] in *William Wordsworth: Selected Prose*, ed. John Hayden (Harmondsworth: Penguin, 1988), pp. 263–74.
52 "To talk of an object as being sublime or beautiful in itself, without references to some subject by whom the sublimity is perceived, is absurd," Wordsworth argues in the essay on the sublime. It is important to keep in mind here the all-important operative distinction, "the mighty difference," as Wordsworth puts it, between "seeing" as mere sensory input, and "perceiving," as an act of the will.
53 Burke is careful to distinguish terror from sublimity: he writes, "when danger or pain press too nearly, they are incapable of giving any delight, and are simply terrible; but at certain distances, and with certain modifications, they may be, and they are delightful." Thus he argues that the sublime emerges (among other considerations) from a situation in which the sensation of fear occurs simultaneously with the knowledge of actual safety. See Edmund Burke, *A Philosophical Enquiry into the Origin of our Ideas of the Sublime and Beautiful* (1757; repr. Notre Dame: University of Notre Dame Press, 1968).
54 *The Prelude* (1805), VII, 609–42.
55 Wordsworth writes in the essay on the sublime, "the capability of perceiving these qualities, and the degree in which they are perceived, will of course depend upon the state or condition of the mind, with respect to habits, knowledge, and powers, which is brought within the reach of their influence." This is why when it comes to the question of extending a rail

line into the Lake District Wordsworth writes with such outrage that "a vivid perception of romantic scenery is neither inherent in mankind, nor a necessary consequence of even a comprehensive education." Thus a "taste" beyond the most basic ability to perceive a natural scene as pretty, "is not to be implanted at once; it must be gradually developed both in nations and in individuals. Rocks and mountains, torrents and wide-spread waters, and all those features of nature which go to the composition of such scenes as this part of England is distinguished for, cannot, in their finer relations to the human mind, be comprehended, or even very imperfectly conceived, without process of culture or opportunities of observation in some degree habitual." See Wordsworth's article on the Kendal and Windermere Railway in *Selected Prose*, ed. Hayden, pp. 76–94.

56 Here the spot of time functions not as a magnet for personal memories, but instead as a socially (rather than personally) constituted refuge that retains a "renovating virtue," as Wordsworth puts it in the famous passage in *The Prelude* (1850, xii, 208–18). I will return to the spot of time in a fuller discussion in the next chapter.

3   WORDSWORTH AND THE IMAGE OF NATURE

1 See "Essay on the Sublime and the Beautiful," in *William Wordsworth: Selected Prose*, ed. John Hayden (Harmondsworth: Penguin, 1988), p. 265.

2 ". . . The precipitous sides of the mountain, and the neighbouring summits, may be seen with effect under any atmosphere which allows them to be seen at all; but *he* is the most fortunate adventurer, who chances to be involved in vapours which open and let in an extent of country partially, or, dispersing suddenly, reveal the whole region from centre to circumference." See the *Guide to the Lakes*, in *Selected Prose*, ed. Hayden, p. 65.

3 Daniel Defoe, *A Tour through the Whole Island of Great Britain* (Harmondsworth: Penguin, 1978), pp. 549–50.

4 *Ibid.*, p. 551.

5 See Anthony Easthope, *Wordsworth Now and Then* (Buckingham: Open University Press, 1993), p. 1.

6 See Adam Smith, *The Wealth of Nations* (1776; repr. Harmondsworth: Penguin, 1982), pp. 486–90.

7 *Guide to the Lakes*, in *Selected Prose*, ed. Hayden, p. 433. Emphasis in original.

8 Elizabeth Helsinger, "Turner and the Representation of England," in W. J. T. Mitchell, ed., *Landscape and Power* (University of Chicago Press, 1994), pp. 103–25. Also see Helsinger's *Rural Scenes and National Representation: Britain, 1815–1850* (Princeton University Press, 1996).

9 See Marjorie Levinson, *Wordsworth's Great Period Poems* (Cambridge University Press, 1986), pp. 24–39.

10 See William Cobbett, *Rural Rides* (1830; London: J. M. Dent, 1957).

11 Alan Liu, *Wordsworth: The Sense of History* (Stanford University Press, 1989), p. 10.

12 See Cobbett's *Rural Rides*. Also see Raymond Williams, *The Country and the City* (Oxford University Press, 1983), pp. 108–12.

13 See chapter 4, below.

14 See *The Ordnance Survey Atlas of Great Britain* (Southampton: Ordnance Survey, 1985), p. 154.

15 Raymond Williams insists on seeing enclosure as a factor within a "complex of change, but not a single isolated cause." It is necessary, he writes, "to see the essential continuity of this appropriation, both with earlier and with later phases . . . Indeed in history it is continuous from the long process of conquest and seizure: the land gained by killing, by repression, by political bargains." See *The Country and the City*, pp. 96–107. Similarly, Eric Hobsbawm notes that "the fundamental structure of landownership and farming was already established by the mid eighteenth century, and certainly by the early decades of the Industrial Revolution. England was a country of mainly large landlords [who held by then at least 75 per cent of the land], cultivated by tenant farmers working the land with hired labourers." See Hobsbawm, *Industry and Empire*, pp. 98–99.

16 "Everything was different: hardly a landmark of the old parish would have remained. Perhaps here and there the old man would have found some evidences of the former world: the windmill of his younger days still standing in the corner of a new field, though now derelict and forlorn, or the traces of the former strips in the ridge-and-furrow of the new pastures, but not much else." Hoskins, *The Making of the English Landscape* (Harmondsworth: Pelican, 1987), p. 179.

17 That this proverb of hell and its correlate ("The hours of folly are measur'd by the clock, but of wisdom no clock can measure") constitute a critique of modern capitalism is an indication of the fundamental role space and time play as means of production in capital; a role that Blake clearly already identified. See *Marriage of Heaven & Hell* [E36–37].

18 Barrell, *Landscape*, pp. 94–95.

19 Hobsbawm, *Industry and Empire*, p. 99.

20 Geoffrey Hartman, *The Unremarkable Wordsworth* (Minneapolis: University of Minnesota Press, 1987), p. 169.

21 Hartman, *Wordsworth's Poetry*, p. 212.

22 One of the most comprehensive treatments of this turning-point in Wordsworth's life is Marjorie Levinson's celebrated essay on *Tintern Abbey* (see Levinson, *Wordsworth's Great Period Poems*, pp. 14–57). Also see the discussion of *Tintern Abbey* in Carol Jacobs's *Telling Time* (Baltimore: Johns Hopkins University Press, 1993), pp. 159–87. For a discussion of the broader political crisis of the early 1790s, see Butler's *Romantics, Rebels and Reactionaries*, pp. 11–68. There is some evidence that Wordsworth started drafting what would become *An Evening Walk* as early as 1788–89, but he carried out very extensive revisions before publishing the first edition, together with *Descriptive Sketches*, in 1793; many more drastic revisions as well as additions that almost doubled the poem's length appeared in the 1794 version. See Harriet

Jump, "'That Other Eye,' Wordsworth's 1794 Revisions of *An Evening Walk*," in *The Wordsworth Circle*, 17:3 (Summer 1986), pp. 156–63.

23 Alan Richardson suggests that we can see already see the spot of time in the 1799 *Prelude*; see "Wordsworth at the Crossroads: 'Spots of Time' in his 'Two-Part Prelude,'" in *The Wordsworth Circle*, 19:1 (Winter 1988), pp. 15–19. What I want to propose is not just, as Ashton Nichols has argued, that we can trace the development of the 1805/50 *Prelude's* spots of time back to *An Evening Walk*, but rather that the spot of time is already fully functional in the earlier poem; see Ashton Nichols, "Towards 'Spots of Time': 'Visionary Dreariness' in 'An Evening Walk,'" in *The Wordsworth Circle*, 14:4 (Autumn 1983), pp. 233–37.

24 I quote lines 37–52 from the 1849–50 version of the poem, in John Hayden, ed., *William Wordsworth: The Poems* (New Haven: Yale University Press, 1977), vol. II. I will make extensive references to two earlier versions of the poem, of 1793 and 1836; these are found in James Averill, ed., *An Evening Walk* (Ithaca: Cornell University Press, 1984).

25 Parliamentary enclosure stipulated that allotments had to be thus fenced off within twelve months of the relevant act, though in some areas of Britain rock walls, rather than hedges, are used to mark off enclosures. See Hoskins, *English Landscape*, pp. 187–199.

26 See Wordsworth's "Lines Composed a Few Miles Above Tintern Abbey, on Revisiting the Banks of the Wye During a Tour, July 13, 1798," lines 15–16.

27 See E. P. Thompson, *Whigs and Hunters: The Origin of the Black Act* (New York: Pantheon, 1975). Also see Hobsbawm, *Industry and Empire*, p. 81.

28 Williams, *The Country and the City*, p. 121. Theodor Adorno makes a strikingly similar point; Natural beauty, he says, "focusses exclusively on nature as appearance, never on nature as the stuff of work and material reproduction of life, let alone as a substratum of science. Nature is perceived as appearance of the beautiful and not as an object to be acted upon." Theodor Adorno, *Aesthetic Theory*, trans. C. Lenhardt (London: Routledge & Kegan Paul, 1984), p. 97.

29 See Annabel Patterson, "Hard Pastoral: Frost, Wordsworth, and Modernist Poetics," in *Criticism*, 23:1 (Winter 87), p. 83. Also see John Barrell, *The Dark Side of the Landscape: The Rural Poor in English Painting, 1730–1840* (Cambridge University Press, 1980); and John Murdoch, "The Landscape of Labour: Transformations of the Georgic," in Kenneth Johnston et al., eds., *Romantic Revolutions* (Bloomington: Indiana University Press, 1990), pp. 176–93.

30 *An Evening Walk*, lines 124–27.

31 In the 1836 version, the barge is depicted actually coasting, since "The sails are dropped." (125). In the 1849–50 version, the barge is driven by oars, so that human labor has been reinserted, even though it is effectively negated.

32 *An Evening Walk*, lines 128–41. Emphasis in original.

33 *Ibid.*, lines 156–67.

34 Hartman, *Wordsworth's Poetry*, p. 90. Also see Hartman, *Unremarkable Words-*

worth, p. 40; and Stephen Parrish, "Wordsworth as Satirist of His Age," in Kenneth Johnston and Gene Ruoff, eds., *The Age of William Wordsworth* (New Brunswick, NJ: Rutgers University Press, 1987), p. 24.

35 A following section will investigate what the term "natural" might mean under these circumstances.

36 *An Evening Walk*, 1849–50, lines 53–71. My italics.

37 The 1793 passage reads:

> Then Quiet led me up the huddling rill,
> Bright'ning with water-breaks the sombrous gill;
> To where, while thick above the branches close,
> In dark brown bason its wild waves repose,
> Inverted shrubs, and moss of darkest green,
> Cling from the rocks, with pale wood-weeds between;
> Save that, atop, the subtle sunbeams shine,
> On wither'd briars that o'er the crags recline;
> Sole light admitted here, a small cascade,
> Illumes with sparkling foam the twilight shade.

The 1836 passage is almost identical to that of 1849–50 (though it reads "sombrous ghyll" as opposed to "hollow ghyll") until the last few lines, which read:

> . . . Cling from the rocks, with pale wood-weeds between;
> Save that aloft the subtle sunbeams shine
> On withered briars that o'er the crags recline;
> Sole light admitted here, a small cascade,
> Illumes with sparkling foam the impervious shade.

38 I am using the term "world-economy" in the sense developed by Fernand Braudel, to indicate "an economically autonomous section of the planet able to provide most of its needs, a section to which its internal links and exchanges give a certain organic unity." This does not necessarily mean *the* world-economy. See Braudel, *Perspective of the World*, p. 22.

39 With Ireland as a colony, rather than an integral part of the nation, despite the formal act of Union in 1801. Wales and Scotland had to be subdued, of course, the former in the sixteenth century, and the latter following the failure of the final Jacobite Rebellion in 1745. I will discuss this question in more detail in the next chapter.

40 See Lefebvre, *Production of Space*, p. 85.

41 For the development of Britain's transport network in the late eighteenth and early nineteenth centuries, see Deane, *First Industrial Revolution*, pp. 72–86; also see Paul Knox and John Agnew, *The Geography of the World Economy* (London: Edward Arnold, 1994), pp. 172–73; and Brown, *Society and Economy*, pp. 126–59.

42 Rasmussen, *Unique City*, p. 128.

43 See Barker, "Transport," pp. 86–100.

44 See *ibid.*, pp. 94–99.

45 Hobsbawm, *Age of Revolution*, p. 24.

46 The Survey was founded in 1791. Its first maps, produced in the following years, were designed for military purposes during the war with France.
47 Barrell, *Landscape*, p. 86.
48 *Ibid.*, p. 86.
49 See chapter 6; also see Braudel, *Structures of Everyday Life*, pp. 365–75; Rasmussen, *Unique City*, pp. 51–62; Hobsbawm, *Industry and Empire*, p. 151, John Langton and R. J. Morris, eds., *Atlas of Industrializing Britain, 1790, 14* (London: Methuen, 1986) pp. 80–93.
50 Braudel, *Perspective of the World*, pp. 42–45.
51 *Ibid.*, p. 42.
52 Though this is not at all to say that all such neutral zones come to be considered "natural."
53 I have elsewhere tried to address this question from the perspective of a colonized society; see "The Empire Re-narrated: *Season of Migration to the North* and the Re-invention of the Present," in *Critical Inquiry*, 18 (Summer 1992), pp. 804–20.
54 Here, once again, it is useful to bear in mind the distinction between "alternative" and "oppositional"; the hidden bower exists as an alternative site, rather than as a locus of opposition to the existing social/political order: the "resistance" that it offers is, by definition, limited to its own space.
55 This may provide some insight into the periodization of romanticism, especially in it relation to modernism. Fredric Jameson has argued that modernism "drew its possibilities from being a backwater and an archaic holdover, within a modernizing economy: it glorified, celebrated, and dramatized older forms of individual production, which the new mode of production was elsewhere on the point of displacing and blotting out." (*Postmodernism*, p. 307). Thus if modernism arises out of a situation of incomplete modernization, in which the last residues of the pre-modern are on the verge of eradication, romanticism can be placed at the other end of the experience of modernity: at a time when pre-modern enclaves (not least Nature and the colonies) still appeared to be capable of withstanding its processes. That is, they may have been felt to be surrounded and endangered, but they still survived and could be transformed into sites of supposed alternatives or opposition.
56 Karl Marx and Friedrich Engels, *The German Ideology*, trans. W. Lough et al. (New York: International Publishers, 1988), p. 62.
57 "For the first time, nature becomes purely an object for humankind, rather than a matter of utility; ceases to be recognized as a power for itself; and the theoretical discovery of its autonomous laws appears merely as a ruse so as to subjugate it under human needs, whether as an object of consumption or as a means of production." Marx, *Grundrisse*, p. 410. Also see: Williams, *Country and City*, p. 38; Adorno, *Aesthetic Theory*, pp. 96–101; Adorno and Horkheimer, *Dialectic of Enlightenment*, trans. John Cumming (New York: Continuum, 1988), pp. 3–9; Sigmund Freud, *Civilization and its Discontents*,

trans. J. Strachey (New York: Norton, 1961), pp. 40–44, Aldous Huxley, "Wordsworth in the Tropics," in *Rotunda: A Selection from the Works of Aldous Huxley* (London: Chatto & Windus, 1932), pp. 873–74.

58 "The more purely nature is preserved and transplanted by civilization, the more implacably it is dominated. We can now afford to encompass ever larger natural units, and leave them apparently intact within our grasp, whereas previously the selecting and taming of particular items bore witness to the difficulty we still had in coping with nature." Theodor Adorno, *Minima Moralia*, trans. E. F. N. Jephcott (London: Verso, 1987), pp. 115–16.

59 Olive Cook, *The English Country House* (New York: Thames & Hudson, 1974), p. 208. It is extremely interesting for the purposes of my project that this represented only one kind of house-and-garden fashionable during the romantic period – the other was planned out in the "Oriental" style! (A good example of the latter is the Royal Pavilion at Brighton.) Such houses and gardens can be clearly contrasted with earlier (seventeenth and eighteenth century) styles, and their associated literary forms, including such prospect poems as Marvell's "Upon Appleton House." Marvell's poem, which I take to be paradigmatic of at least one aspect of that earlier phase of the prospect poem (and specifically the country-house poem), stresses the scalar relationship of world to garden, so that the garden, far from being "Natural," is a closely controlled miniature version of the outside world ("a lesser world"), rather than an opposite of the outside. And yet, as in Marvell's "The Garden," this "lesser world" can *also* be a site in which one can seek solace, a space into which one can escape from the pressures of the outside world that produced it. For Wordsworth, the Natural is still a site of solace and escape, but it is increasingly defined as a non-produced space, rather than as a miniature and hence carefully controlled version of the outside realm of the social.

60 Barrell, *Landscape*, pp. 78–79. It is certainly the case that the places of Britain which Defoe describes as beautiful are those which are productive: see his *Tour*.

61 Williams, *Country and City*, p. 128. Such tours obviously take on a class meaning; they could never be undertaken by those who so often serve as aestheticized objects in the background of a landscape!

62 Wordsworth, *Guide to the Lakes*, p. 1.

63 Wordsworth, "Letter to the Editor of the Morning Post," 9 December 1844, quoted in *Selected Prose*, ed. Hayden.

64 "Not Italy is offered, but evidence that it exists." Adorno and Horkheimer, *Dialectic of Enlightenment*, p. 148.

65 This approach to controlling through visuality would reach a kind of climax in our own postmodern era, in which the spectacle itself becomes the ultimate commodity as well as the key to understanding possession. See Fredric Jameson, *Signatures of the Visible* (New York: Columbia University Press, 1995).

4 *WAVERLEY* AND THE CULTURAL POLITICS OF DISPOSSESSION

1 As, for instance, its concerns with revolution have to do not only with the Jacobite Rebellion of 1745, but also the revolutionary situation in Britain in the early nineteenth century.

2 Sir Walter Scott, *Waverley* (1814; Harmondsworth: Penguin, 1983), p. 492.

3 See Benedict Anderson, *Imagined Communities: Reflections on the Origin and Spread of Nationalism* (London: Verso, 1983).

4 Good colonial examples of this is are the Thames and the Congo in Conrad's *Heart of Darkness*; a good postcolonial instance of writing this theme "back to the empire" is the river Nile in al-Tayyeb Saleh's *Season of Migration to the North*, which is in some ways a counter-narrative of the European voyage of exploration into the unknown.

5 Fabian, *Time and the Other*, p. 17.

6 See Hugh Trevor-Roper, "The Invention of Tradition: The Highland Tradition of Scotland," in Eric Hobsbawm and Terence Ranger, eds., *The Invention of Tradition* (Cambridge: Cambridge University Press, 1983), p. 16.

7 A similar occurrence took place in Wales at about the same time, with the reinvention of the bardic meeting or *eisteddfod*, Druidism, and so forth. See Prys Morgan, "From a Death to a View: The Hunt for the Welsh Past in the Romantic Period," in *The Invention of Tradition*, pp. 43–100. But if Wales and Scotland had been colonized by England and annexed into a Union with it long before the romantic period (1536 and 1707, respectively), Ireland was still facing the process of this incorporation, for its Act of Union with England was only legislated in 1800.

8 Lukács, *The Historical Novel*, trans. Hannah and Stanley Mitchell (Lincoln: University of Nebraska Press, 1962), p. 55.

9 Much of the post-45 legislation explicitly used the language of colonialism, calling, for instance, for "the better civilizing and improving the Highlands of Scotland, so preventing disorders there in future." Quoted in Eric Richards, "Scotland and the Uses of the Atlantic Empire," in Bernard Bailyn and Philip, eds., *Strangers Within the Realm: Cultural Margins of the First British Empire*, Morgan (Chapel Hill: University of North Carolina Press, 1991), p. 111.

10 See the previous chapter. Also see J. D. Mackie, *A History of Scotland* (Harmondsworth: Pelican, 1978), pp. 266–315.

11 Quoted in Richards, "Scotland," pp. 80–81.

12 See Trevor-Roper, "Highland Tradition," p. 22. Indeed, earlier legislation to pacify the Highlands, after the Fifteen, had proscribed the Irish longshirt which had originally been worn by the inhabitants. The kilt was invented by Thomas Rawlinson, an Englishman.

13 See Eric Wolf, *Europe and the People Without History* (Berkeley: University of California Press, 1982), pp. 239–52; J. D. Mackie, *A History of Scotland* (Harmondsworth: Penguin, 1978) pp. 280–81; Marx, *Capital*, pp. 877–96. The French did precisely the same thing in Algeria later in the 19th century, destroying the old Berber and Arab family-property system and replacing it with the private ownership of land.

14 John Prebble, *The Highland Clearances* (Harmondsworth: Penguin, 1963), p. 14.
15 Compare this to the Dutch murder or eviction of the inhabitants of various East Indian islands, such as Banda, to make room for spice plantations worked by a few natives and supervised by even fewer Europeans. See Wolf, *People with History*, pp. 237–39.
16 See Prebble, *Highland Clearances*, pp. 139–44; also see Christopher Harvie, "Scott and the Image of Scotland," in Raphael Samuel, ed., *Patriotism: The Making and Unmaking of British Identity*, edited by Raphael Samuel (London: Routledge, 1989), p. 189.
17 Prebble, *Highland Clearances*, p. 67.
18 *Ibid.*, p. 79.
19 Marx, *Capital*, p. 891. Also see Prebble, *Highland Clearances* pp. 49–115; Mackie, *History of Scotland*, pp. 289–91. After her clan's outcries against their eviction, the Duchess, then in London, wrote to a friend: "I hope to be in Scotland this summer, but I am uneasy about a sort of mutiny that has broken out in one part of Sutherland, in consequences [*sic*] of our new plans having made it necessary to transplant some of the inhabitants to the sea-coast from other parts of the estate. The people who are refractory on this occasion are part of Clan Gun, so often mentioned by Sir Robert Gordon, who live by distilling whisky and are unwilling to quit that occupation for a life of industry of a different sort which was proposed to them. London is more full and gay, if possible, than usual. A great many foreigners from Russia, etc., *parlant bon anglais-russe.*" Quoted in Prebble, *Highland Clearances*, p. 65.
20 See Homi Bhabha, "The Other Question: Difference, Discrimination and the Discourse of Colonialism," in Francis Barker et al., eds., *Literature, Politics and Theory* (London: Methuen, 1986), pp. 148–72.
21 Quoted in Richards, "Scotland," p. 106.
22 Trevor-Roper, "Highland Tradition," p. 15. The invention of the Highland "tradition," he goes on, had not only to do with the retrospective invention of cultural forms and their presentation to the Lowlands, but also with a cultural revolt against Ireland, a usurpation of Irish culture.
23 See Robert Gleckner, *Blake and Spenser* (Baltimore: Johns Hopkins University Press, 1985), pp. 311–18.
24 *Waverley* can be read as a narrative of the colonization of Ireland, in addition to being a "map" of the colonization of the Highlands and of the suppression of insurgency in Britain. There are several – hardly surprising – connections between the 1745 Jacobite Rebellion and the doomed 1798 revolution in Ireland (although the Forty-Five arose out of the 1707 Union of Scotland and England, and the 1798 rebellion *led to* the 1800 Union of England and Ireland, as a better means of controlling the Irish). There are strong connections between the United Irishmen, one of the movements involved in the 1798 rebellion, and Jacobitism in general (partly through the UI's articulation of Defenderism, which is itself caught up with Irish

Catholicism and Jacobitism). But there are also striking connections between the revolutionary situations in Scotland (1745), Ireland (1798), and *Waverley*'s Britain (1805–14), not least in that French involvement, and ultimately the involvement of the French Revolution, was an underlying British fear in all three contexts (as it was during the American Revolution). Also the United Irishmen had strong connections to an English revolutionary organization (not surprisingly called the United Englishmen), who were actively involved in the 1797 Mutiny in the Royal Navy's Channel and North Sea Fleets at Spithead and the Nore.

25 Quoted in Prebble, *Highland Clearances*, pp. 107–07.
26 Michael Hechter, *Internal Colonialism: The Celtic Fringe in British National Development, 1536–1966* (Berkeley: University of California Press, 1975), p. 65. Hence his use of the term "internal colonialism."
27 In relentlessly using the same language of nationalism and national development as Scott uses in *Waverley*, Georg Lukács not only overlooks the colonial – rather than national – incorporation of the Highlands into the United Kingdom: he ruthlessly consigns the novel to English (not even British) literature, arguing in the course of his discussion of "English reality" and "English development," that "it is no accident that this new type of novel arose in England" (*The Historical Novel*, pp. 31, 54). It seems to me, on the contrary, that it is no coincidence that the historical novel arose not at all in England, but in Scotland (with Walter Scott) and Ireland (with Maria Edgeworth).
28 Scott, *Waverley*, p. 73.
29 *Ibid.*, p. 74.
30 *Ibid.*, pp. 144–45.
31 James Kerr, *Fiction Against History: Scott as Storyteller* (Cambridge University Press, 1989), p. 24. Tourism is *never* politically innocent, so that this is, I think, a difference of degree rather than of kind.
32 Scott, *Waverley*, p. 75. My italics.
33 Just as workers and landscape are reduced to aestheticized background objects in other kinds of tours: see Barrell, *Dark Side of the Landscape*.
34 "The bagpipers, three in number, screamed, during the whole time of dinner, a tremendous war-tune; and the echoing of the vaulted roof, and clang of the Celtic tongue, produced such a Babel of noises, that Waverley dreaded his ears would never recover from it" (p. 164).
35 Scott, *Waverley*, p. 138.
36 See, for example, pp. 56, 63, 91, 83, 139, 174 and 324.
37 Scott, *Waverley*, p. 63.
38 See *ibid.*, p. 174.
39 One result of this arrangement in an Oriental tale is the sense that the exoticism of the Orient cannot be approached simply by reading what is supposed to be an Arabic or Turkish (or Indian, or Chinese) text. Rather, the Orient fundamentally requires the mediation of the Orientalist, who alone is capable of understanding all of its complexities and dangers, and of

communicating his or her understanding to other Europeans. This is precisely the effect of the enormous weight of the notes at the end of William Beckford's *Vathek* and each of Byron's Turkish tales, for these notes do not convey useful information about this or that detail of Oriental culture as much as they convey a sense of the "vast complexity" of the Orient to the sheltered European reader. Because each noted reference in the main body of an Oriental tale necessarily brings up a dozen other references, the overall effect of the notes is not to clarify things, but rather to make them more obscure – and hence to reinforce the need for the intervention of the knowledgeable or informed authority figure (the Orientalist).

40 See Trevor-Roper, "Highland Tradition." He says that "the whole concept of a Highland culture and tradition is a retrospective invention," developed after the 1707 Union with England, against which it was a protest. Also see the Introduction to Bernard Bailyn and Philip Morgan, eds., *Strangers Within the Realm: Cultural Margins of the First British Empire* (Chapel Hill: University of North Carolina Press, 1991), p. 27.

41 James Reed, *Sir Walter Scott: Landscape and Locality* (London: Athlone Press, 1980), p. 6.

42 Hence the novel contrasts the ahistorical essences of the Highlands with the historically constructed identity of the Lowlands.

43 Though, as I will discuss more fully later on, the Highlands are the spatialized past that cannot enter or become the future. They remain immutably past.

44 This is one way in which the novel uses characters to embody social or historical positions. See Lukács, *Historical Novel*, pp. 33–39.

45 Scott, *Waverley*, p. 424

46 "The character of Colonel Talbot dawned upon Edward by degrees" (p. 366); indeed, Edward's appreciation of the Colonel is in a mutually-determining relationship with his own gradual maturation and development. The other proper English gentlemen (and officers) in the novel – notably Melville, Morton, and Gardiner (given Scott's benediction in the Notes as "a good Christian and gallant man") – hold the same "correct" attitudes as Talbot. As characters, they are virtually indistinguishable from one another, since their propriety, justice, warmth, loyalty, and generosity fade into and blend with one another, just as the selfishness, crudeness, and fanaticism of some the Highlanders – principally Evan Dhu, Callum Beg, and Fergus in his "Highlander" mode – make each also indistinguishable from the others.

47 See, for instance, pp. 366, 387, 424, and especially p. 463, where Talbot pronounces judgment on Fergus's fate: "Justice . . . which demanded some penalty of those who had wrapped the whole nation in fear and in mourning, could not perhaps have selected a fitter victim. He came to the field with the fullest light upon the nature of his attempt. He had studied and understood the subject. His father's fate could not intimidate him; the lenity

of the laws which had restored to him [after the 1715 Jacobite revolt] his father's property and rights could not melt him. That he was brave, generous, and possessed many good qualities, only rendered him the more dangerous; that he was enlightened and accomplished made his crime the less excusable; that he was an enthusiast in the wrong cause only made him the more fit to be its martyr. Above all, he had been the means of bringing many hundreds of men into the field who, without him, would never have broken the peace of the country." Talbot's assessment and the historical assessment of the narrator in the opening and closing chapters of the novel are not only exactly the same, they even *sound* the same in tone, phrasing, and emphasis. From the Unionist/Hanoverian standpoint, Talbot is historically "correct" to point to the "lenity" of the laws following the 1715 revolt; and indeed after the Forty-Five, the Highland chiefs were stripped of their hereditary jurisdictions (and hence of their ability to bring fighters into the field), and ultimately transformed into landlords in the capitalist sense: a process which led to the great Clearances, whose full ramifications were being felt in Scott's own time.

48 Scott, *Waverley*, p. 153.

49 *Ibid.*, p. 157.

50 *Ibid.*, p. 170.

51 See Hayden White, *Metahistory: The Historical Imagination in Nineteenth-Century Europe* (Baltimore: Johns Hopkins University Press, 1974), pp. 7–11. Emplotment, he says, "is the way by which a sequence of events fashioned into a story is gradually revealed to be a story of a particular kind."

52 Prince Charles had, with French assistance, attempted a proper invasion in 1744, but a violent storm scattered his fleet and ended that attempt. Having financed his own operation, he returned to western Scotland on 25 July 1745, in a small boat with seven men (of whom three were Irish, and one more a Macdonald from Ulster), to begin his attempt to topple the British government in the name of his father (James VIII of Scotland/III of England) and the House of Stuart. For more on the Jacobites, see Mackie, *History of Scotland*, pp. 221–82; Christopher Haigh, ed., *The Cambridge Historical Encyclopedia of Great Britain and Ireland* (Cambridge University Press, 1990), pp. 197–222; and Christopher Hill, *Reformation to Industrial Revolution* (Harmondsworth: Penguin, 1969), pp. 213–38.

53 The battle of Culloden (16 April 1746) marked the end of the Forty-Five rebellion, and the final collapse of Jacobitism. Charles was spirited away by Flora Macdonald to the Isle of Skye, and thence to France, where he died in exile. His followers at Culloden suffered heavily; over a thousand were killed in the battle; a further 120 were executed afterwards; 1,000 were transported; and 700 others disappeared.

54 Thus the novel exaggerates the identification between Highlands and Jacobitism, since the latter stood for much more than the former. Indeed, this identification is merely the result of the defeat of the House of Stuart during and after 1688 in all of Britain, the Highlands merely being one of

their last areas of support. But the novel collapses Jacobitism into the
Highlands, so that the one becomes the other. It also collapses anti-
Unionism into Jacobitism.

55 "Unaccustomed to the address and manners of a polished court, in which
Charles was eminently skilful, his words and his kindness penetrated the
heart of our hero, and easily outweighed all prudential motives. To be thus
personally solicited for assistance by a Prince, whose form and manners, as
well as the spirit which he displayed in this singular enterprise, answered his
ideas of a hero of romance; to be courted by him in the ancient halls of his
paternal palace, recovered by the sword which he was already bending
towards other conquests, gave Edward, in his own eyes, the dignity and
importance which he had ceased to consider as his attributes." Scott,
Waverley, p. 295.

56 *Ibid.*, pp. 355–56.

57 When Waverley "had surmounted a small craggy eminence, called St
Leonard's Hill, the King's Park, or the hollow between the mountain of
Arthur's Seat, and the rising ground on which the southern part of Edinburgh is now built, lay beneath him, and displayed a singular and animat-
ing prospect. It was occupied by the army of the Highlanders, now in the
act of preparing for their march . . ." (*Ibid.*, p. 321).

58 *Ibid.*, p. 324.

59 *Ibid.*, p. 332. Gladsmuir is the Highlanders' name for the battle on 21
September 1745, which the English called Prestonpans, after the nearby
town (southeast of Edinburgh).

60 *Ibid.*, p. 340.

61 Peter Watkins's 1965 documentary film *Culloden* provides a harsh and
unromantic representation of the battle and its aftermath as well as the
Highland clan system and the Jacobite leadership.

62 Jameson, *Political Unconscious*, pp. 81–82.

63 *Waverley*, pp. 484, 487.

64 Thus, defending Edward from charges of treason, one of the novel's
spokesmen for the rational present (Morton) says that "He whom ambition,
or hope of personal advantage [i.e., Fergus], has led to disturb the peace of
a well-ordered government, let him fall a victim to the laws; but surely
youth [i.e., Edward], misled by the wild visions of chivalry and imaginary
loyalty [i.e., Prince Charles], may plea for pardon." *Waverley*, p. 252.

65 *Ibid.*, p. 222.

66 At the same time, *Waverley* chronicles not only the growth and maturity of
its hero, but the growth and maturity of the British nation away from
what it posits as the irrationality of its "past." The 1707 Act of Union was
a necessary and beneficial act, in the novel's view. The Highlands and
their people pay the price for being the "immature" area away from
which the nation had to develop, or, put differently, the space that had to
be sacrificed in order to achieve the unity of the nation. The novel, as
Lukács suggests, uses personal feelings and attractions to express political

attachments. Waverley's homoerotic attraction to Fergus, a supplement to his attraction to Flora, thus expresses his attachment to the Jacobites. His drift away from Flora and Fergus and his growing fondness of Rose express his gradual move away from Jacobitism. The homoerotic supplement to his attraction to Rose is Talbot himself, Waverley's "true" father-figure (since his own has had little to with him). The novel's politicized sexual dynamics lead Waverley toward an Oedipal "crisis" which it suppresses.

67 Lukács *The Historical Novel*, p. 53.

68 Scott, *Waverley*, p. 489.

69 "Unreserved alienation is thus unreserved representation. It wrenches presence absolutely from itself and absolutely re-presents it to itself." Jacques Derrida, *Of Grammatology*, trans. G. C. Spivak (Baltimore: Johns Hopkins University Press, 1976), p. 296.

70 It is precisely in these terms that the invention of a Highland (or any other) tradition does not necessarily lose its "authority" and "authenticity" for being a forgery. On the contrary, it becomes a powerful political reference and referent.

71 Gleckner, *Blake and Spencer*, p. 312.

72 Quoted in Hechter, *Internal Colonialism*, p. 76.

5 DOMESTICATING EXOTICISM: TRANSFORMATIONS OF BRITAIN'S ORIENT, 1785–1835

1 Edmund Burke, "Speech Opening the Impeachment, first day, Friday, February 15, 1788," at the Trial in Parliament of Warren Hastings, esquire, late Governor-General of Bengal, for High Crimes and Misdemeanors, pp. 378–79. My emphasis.

2 Hastings was Governor of Bengal from 1772 to 1774; and, following the expansion of his post, Governor-General from 1774 to 1786.

3 Said's influential book *Orientalism* makes what I take to be a fundamentally important distinction between modern Orientalism (which, Said argues, emerged in the late eighteenth century) and earlier forms of Orientalism. However, in certain passages in his book Said glosses over this distinction, and stresses instead the continuity of Orientalism across or between different historical moments. See Edward Said, *Orientalism* (New York: Pantheon, 1977); also see below for more on Said.

4 See Fabian, *Time and the Other*.

5 "When the Company acquired that high office in India, an English corporation became an integral part of the Mogul empire. When Great Britain virtually assented to that grant of office, and afterwards took advantage of it, Great Britain guaranteed [*sic*] the performance of all its duties. Great Britain entered into a virtual act of union with that country, by which we bound ourselves as securities to preserve the people in all the rights, laws, and liberties which their natural, original sovereign was bound to support, if

he had been in condition to support them. By the disposition of events [!], the two duties, flowing from two different sources, are now unified in one. The people of India, therefore, come in the name of the Commons of Great Britain, but in their own right, to the bar of this House, before the supreme royal justice of this kingdom, from whence originally all the powers under which they have suffered were derived." Burke, Trial of Warren Hastings, Day One, p. 347.

6 *Ibid.*, p. 330.

7 Quoted in Thompson, *English Working Class*, p. 137. The great difference between Indians and England's own "swinish multitude," of course, was that the Indians were reasonably far off; the working class, on the other hand, was an enemy within, which could disease the body politic and thus require the "critical terrors of the cautery and the knife." At one level, this points to the difference between Burke's notion of Terror as opposed to the reassuringly distant Sublime.

8 Burke, Trial of Warren Hastings, Day One, p. 382.

9 Burke, "Speech on Mr. Fox's East India Bill," 1 December 1783, pp. 444–45.

10 Indeed many of the late eighteenth-century advocates of polygeny were irrevocably opposed to the notion of evolution. Charles White, for instance, "railed against the idea that climate might produce racial differences, arguing that such ideas might lead, by extension, to the 'degrading notion' of evolution between species." See Stephen Jay Gould, *The Mismeasure of Man* (New York: Norton, 1981), pp. 41–42.

11 Hence Burke's "message" to the working poor during the terrible famine year of 1795: "Patience, labour, sobriety, frugality and religion, should be recommended to them; all the rest is downright fraud." Quoted in Thompson, *English Working Class*, p. 56.

12 Burke, "Speech on Mr Fox's East India Bill," p. 448.

13 This is not by any means to suggest that the concepts of polygenesis and preformationism necessarily lead to cultural relativism; only that, perhaps ironically, certain versions of relativism can be derived from the notion of a fixed and untranscendable cultural/racial hierarchy, in which each culture or race has "its proper place." Or, as Renan put it, "The regeneration of the inferior or degenerate races is part of the providential order of things for humanity"; thus he argues that "Nature has made a race of workers, the Chinese," and "a race of tillers of the soil, the Negro," and finally "a race of masters and soldiers, the European race . . . Let each one do what he is made for, and all will be well." [Quoted in Aimé Césaire, *Discourse on Colonialism*, trans. Joan Pinkham (New York: Monthly Review Press, 1955), p. 16]. In other words, cultural relativism "as such" is *not* incompatible with certain paradigms of racism. Stephen Jay Gould writes that "throughout the egalitarian tradition of the European Enlightenment and the American revolution, I cannot identify any popular position remotely like the 'cultural relativism' that prevails (at least by lip-service) in

liberal circles today. The nearest approach is a common argument that black inferiority is purely cultural and that it can be completely eradidcated by education to a Caucasian standard." (See Gould, *Mismeasure of Man*, pp. 30–72). Now I would suggest that Burke's position is indeed some sort of cultural relativism, if not quite like the ones that are paid lip-service in liberal circles today; though it would be interesting to compare Burke's position on Indian cultural autonomy (within the framework provided by a benevolent British imperialism, of course) with today's debates on "multiculturalism" in the American academy, especially to the extent that "respect" for other cultures can indeed be based (or premised) on a notion of racial superiority.

14 This position is closer to that of Cuvier (held later by Richard Owen) than that of Larmarck or even Saint-Hilaire, let alone the much later views of Charles Darwin and Alfred Russel Wallace, which marked the final departure in scientific discourse from a belief in fixed types. This notion of permanent hierarchy was also applied to the various levels of social class, to which I will return presently.

15 See Stephen Jay Gould, *Ontogeny and Phylogeny* (Cambridge, MA: Harvard University Press, 1977). Indeed, certain pre-evolutionary scientific theories, for example, that of von Baer, did away with the hierarchy of higher and lower, so that different groups of species were simply different, and not necessarily "more" or "less" developed. Without a concept of phylogenetic transformation, a theory of recapitulation (a fundamental basis of racist doctrines), in which an individual organism, in the course of its development, "recapitulates" features of older and less developed species (e.g., human embryos have gills), is also inconceivable. With later theories of Orientalism and views of the colonial project, which were inextricably intertwined with the logic and discourse of an emergent evolutionary theory, this no longer obtained.

16 See Fabian, *Time and the Other*.

17 Maxime Rodinson, *Europe and the Mystique of Islam*, trans. Roger Veinus (Seattle: University of Washington Press, 1991), p. 65.

18 See *ibid.*, pp. 60–65. Thus Rodinson contrasts what he describes as the "pre-critical *naïvité*" of the eighteenth century with the unabashed Eurocentrism of the nineteenth.

19 Sara Suleri, *The Rhetoric of British India* (University of Chicago Press, 1992), p. 28.

20 *Ibid.*, p. 31.

21 Sir William Jones, "A Discourse on the Institution of a Society, for Enquiring into the History, Civil and Natural, the Antiquities, Arts, Sciences, Literature, of Asia, By the President." (1784). In *The Works of Sir William Jones in Thirteen Volumes* (Delhi: Agam Prakashan, 1977), vol. III, p. 2

22 Javed Majeed, *Ungoverned Imaginings: James Mill's* The History of British India *and Orientalism* (Oxford: Clarendon Press, 1992), p. 20.

23 Gauri Viswanathan, *Masks of Conquest: Literary Study and British Rule in India*

(New York: Columbia University Press, 1989), p. 28. Jones took this so far as to compose hymns for the various Indian gods and goddesses.

24 Majeed, *Ungoverned Imaginings*, p. 38.

25 Sir William Jones, "An Essay on the Poetry of the Eastern Nations," in *The Works of Sir William Jones in Thirteen Volumes*, vol. x (Delhi: Agam Prakashan, 1799), pp. 359–60.

26 Raymond Schwab, *The Oriental Renaissance: Europe's Rediscovery of India and the East, 1680–1880*, trans. by G. Patterson-Black and V. Reinking (New York: Columbia University Press, 1984), p. 23.

27 See Michael Adas, *Machines as the Measure of Men: Science, Technology, and Ideologies of Western Dominance* (Ithaca: Cornell University Press, 1989), pp. 103–25; and S. N. Mukherjee, *Sir William Jones: A Study in Eighteenth-Century British Attitudes to India* (Hyderabad: Orient Longman, 1987).

28 Ramkrishna Mukherjee, *The Rise and Fall of the East India Company* (New York: Monthly Review Press, 1974), pp. 300–01.

29 These royal chartered companies included: the Levant Company (1592), the East India Company (1600), the Virginia Company (1606), the English Amazon Company (1623), the Massachusetts Bay Company (1629), and the Royal African Company (1660, originally called the Royal Adventurers in Africa!). See Wolf, *People Without History*, p. 122

30 Thus the Dutch VOC, having secured a monopoly over the produce from what was for them merely a "spice island," would sometimes depopulate the island, massacring or expelling the inhabitants, in order to intensify spice production there. This they did, for instance, to the people of the island of Banda in 1621. See Wolf, *People Without History*, pp. 232–61. Also see C. R. Boxer, *The Dutch Seaborne Empire* (Harmondsworth: Penguin, 1988), pp. 209–72. NB: those who spoke out most loudly about the preservation of Highland traditions were the ones who had played the most active role in destroying Highland culture. See chapter 4, above.

31 "The 'territory' of a trading post or company headquarters proceeded from a concession by local authorities, difficult to obtain and never granted without something in return. Taken as a whole, the system was another form of colonization – of a purely commercial nature: the Europeans settled within easy reach of the points of production and the markets, at the intersections of trade routes, using networks in existence before their arrival, thus saving themselves the trouble of creating infrastructures, and leaving to local communities the tasks of transporting the goods to the ports, organizing and financing production and handling elementary exchange." Braudel, *Perspective of the World*, p. 495.

32 Hobsbawm, *Age of Revolution*, p. 135.

33 There were, for instance, only about 31,000 English in India as late as 1805. Thomas Roe, Ambassador of the East India Company to the Mogul court, adivsed his company in the 17th century: "Keep to this rule if you look for profit: seek it out on the seas and in peaceful trading; for there is no doubt that it would be an error to maintain garrisons and to fight in India on

land." See Braudel, *Perspective of the World*, pp. 488–93.

34 I will take up the consequences of this shift as well as its implications for constructions of a universal world history of modernity and capitalism in the next chapter ("Beyond the Realm of Dreams: Byron, Shelley, and the East").

35 See Hobsbawm, *Age of Revolution*, pp. 337–38; Majeed, *Ungoverned Imaginings*, p. 15; also see Stephen Jay Gould, *The Panda's Thumb: More Reflections in Natural History* (New York: Norton, 1980), pp. 27–34. Gould quotes an indicative passage from Darwin: "Rudimentary organs may be compared with the letters in a word, still retained in the spelling, but become useless in the pronunciation, but which serve as a clue in seeking for its derivation." Quoted p. 27.

36 Indeed, it is well known that, while tracing the connections of Sanskrit to Greek and Latin (or former the derivation of the rather from the latter), Jones stressed the superiority of the older language over the more "modern" and European ones. In an address in 1786, for instance, he argues that "The Sanskrit language, whatever be its antiquity, is of a wonderful structure; more perfect than the Greek, more copious than the Latin, and more exquisitely refined than either, yet bearing to both of them a stronger affinity, both in the roots of the verbs and in the forms of the grammar, than could possibly have been produced by accident; so strong, indeed, that no philologer could examine them all three, without believing them to have sprung from some common source, which, perhaps, no longer exists." Sir William Jones, Third Anniversary Discourse, Vol. III, p. 34. The identification of evolution with progress came, well after Darwin himself (who did not share in the enthusiasm over progress), in the late nineteenth century, most prominently perhaps with the writings of Herbert Spencer. As Eric Leed and others have observed, even Alfred Russel Wallace (the "co-discoverer" of evolution) "insisted upon the superiority of uncivilized beings and preindustrial society." See Eric Leed, *The Mind of the Traveler: From Gilgamesh to Global Tourism* (New York: Basic Books, 1991), p. 209.

37 See chapter 1, above.

38 See chapter 6, above.

39 Thomas B. Macaulay, "Minute on Indian Education" (1835). Compare this to Jones's assessment of the richness and vitality of the various Asiatic literatures (see above).

40 See Robert Young, *Darwin's Metaphor: Nature's Place in Victorian Culture* (Cambridge University Press, 1985), esp. pp. 23–55.

41 See David Musselwhite, "The trial of Warren Hastings," in Francis Barker et al., eds., *Literature, Politics and Theory*, (London: Methuen, 1986), pp. 77–103; and Sara Suleri, *The Rhetoric of British India* (University of Chicago Press, 1992), pp. 49–74.

42 Suleri (*Rhetoric*, p. 52) argues that "the lie of the impeachment proceedings is thus its failure to admit that Hastings's misdeeds were merely synecdochical of the colonial operation, that to assume such government could take a

more palatable form was to allow Burke to have his cake of astonishment and eat it, too."

43 See Wolf, *People Without History*, p. 247. This resulted in increasing poverty for the people, as well as several major famines. (Also see chapter 4, "*Waverley* and the Cultural Politics of Dispossession," above).

44 Viswanathan, *Masks of Conquest*, p. 27.

45 *Ibid.*, p. 30. Pointing out James Mill's Utilitarian criticisms of England and of English society and law and manners, Javed Majeed adds a third term to Viswanathan's opposition between Anglicists and Orientalists, namely vernacularists (like James Mill) who sought not so much to replicate English society in India, but to create what for them was a Utopian society based on the principles of Utilitarianism. See Majeed, *Ungoverned Imaginings*, p. 141. However, I would argue that Majeed seeks too strongly to distinguish Mill's position from the more explicitly Eurocentric position of the Anglicists; for since when has the sort of universalism proposed by Mill not been Eurocentric – just because it substitutes claims of universal applicability for peculiarly English or European ones?

46 Hobsbawm, *Age of Revolution*, p. 134.

47 See Albert Hourani, *A History of the Arab Peoples* (New York: Warner, 1991), pp. 263–78. Also see chapter 6, below.

48 "Victory may be inconstant to our arms. But there are triumphs which are followed by no reverse. There is an empire exempt from all natural causes of decay. Those triumphs are the pacific triumphs of reason over barbarism; that empire is the imperishable empire of our arts and our morals, our literature and our laws." Thomas Macaulay, quoted in Patrick Brantlinger, *Rule of Darkness: British Literature and Imperialism, 1830–1914* (Ithaca: Cornell University Press, 1988), p. 30.

49 See Fabian, *Time and the Other*, p. 17.

50 James Mill, *The History of British India*, abridged by William Thomas (University of Chicago Press, 1975), pp. 232–33, 226.

51 *Ibid.*, p. 567.

52 For that matter, the real or imaginary links between Celtic society and the East would be put forward by way of *opposition* to British imperialism; this, for example, is how Javed Majeed nicely reads parts of Moore's *Lalla Rookh* (set in the Orient) as allegories of the British domination of Ireland. Moore also argued for the Eastern (specifically Phoenician) origins of Irish culture; hence, Majeed argues, "the vanquished Celts are placed in this tradition of cultures whose civilization was elevated over the military efficiency of the younger upstart cultures who suppressed this alternative tradition." (See Majeed, *Ungoverned Imaginings*, pp. 86–95.)

53 Of course, imperial projects involve not only the construction of colonized others, but also the continuous construction of a colonized "self." What Mill does in this passage and elsewhere is to posit some sort of ideal (and unattainable) colonizing self; he is, indeed, as interested in the aspects of this self as he is in the colonized other.

54 Mill, *History of British India*, p. 574.

55 See Richard Burton's "Terminal Essay" to his 1888 translation of the *Thousand and One Nights*, pp. 3748–82. Burton's Sotadic zone extends from Southwestern Asia (the Turks, he says, are "a race of born pederasts") to Japan and China (" . . . the Chinese, as far as we know them in the great cities, are omnivorous and omnifutuentes: they are the chosen people of debauchery, and their systematic bestiality with ducks, goats, and other animals is equalled only by their pederasty").

56 Mary Poovey, *Uneven Developments: The Ideological Work of Gender in Mid-Victorian England* (University of Chicago Press, 1988), pp. 194–97. I will return to Poovey's suggestive argument a little later on.

57 As discussed by Gauri Viswanathan and Javed Majeed, among others.

58 "The bourgeois class poses itself as an organism in continuous movement, capable of absorbing the entire society, assimilating it to its own cultural and economic level." Antonio Gramsci, *Selections from the Prison Notebooks*, trans. by Quintin Hoare and Geoffey Nowell-Smith (New York: International Publishers, 1971), p. 160. Compare this ideological construction of the bourgeois age with Burke's infinitely rigid pronouncements on class. On shifts in gender paradigms during the romantic period, see Nancy Armstrong, *Desire and Domestic Fiction: A Political History of the Novel* (Oxford University Press, 1989); Anne Mellor, *Romanticism and Gender* (London: Routledge, 1993); Mary Poovey, *The Proper Lady and the Woman Writer: Ideology as Style in the Works of Mary Wollestonecraft, Mary Shelley, and Jane Austen* (University of Chicago Press, 1984); Mary Poovey, *Uneven Developments*; Eve Kosofsky Sedgwick, *Between Men: English Literature and Male Homosocial Desire* (New York: Columbia University Press, 1985). I will return to some of these a little later on: see below.

59 More specifically, Said argues that it is the combination and interaction of Orientalist knowledge with the facts of imperial conquest and domination (sustained by Orientalism) that produces the Orient; "from the days of Sir William Jones," he writes (*Orientalism*, p. 215), "the Orient had been both what Britain ruled and what Britain knew about it."

60 Certain fundamental pre-conditions lay the ground and prepare the way for what Said categorizes as a specifically *modern* Orientalism. These elements, which accumulated through the late eighteenth century, include both the work of previous generations and formations of Orientalism (and it is on this basis that Said argues for some sort of continuity of Orientalism reaching back to pre-modern times), as well as historical events such as Napoleon's invasion of Egypt in 1798, "on whose presence the specific intellectual and institutional structures of *modern* Orientalism depend." (Said, *Orientalism*, p. 120, my emphasis).

61 See Said, *Orientalism*, pp. 52, 58, 67. Here Said's argument that the Orient had to be "Orientalized" is particularly debilitating for his larger and more powerful point: namely, that there is no Orient with ontogenetic priority to Orientalism. Claims about distortions of Oriental realities are similarly

troubling; which is not to say that Orientalists don't misrepresent, but rather that what they do represent as *Oriental* truths can't be misrepresentations, since there is no such thing as an Orient that spans and encompasses hundreds of millions of people scattered across hundreds of societies, speaking hundreds of different languages, living in different classes and gender identities, across thousands of years of history.

62 See Said, *Orientalism*, pp. 42, 50, 72.

63 See *ibid.*, p. 69.

64 In his book, *White Mythologies*, Robert Young points out what many critics have seen as a "major theoretical problem" in *Orientalism*. He asks how it can be that, on the one hand, Said "suggests that Orientalism merely consists of a representation that has nothing to do with the real Orient . . , while on the other hand, he argues that its knowledge was put to the service of colonial conquest, occupation, and administration." For according to Young, "this means that at a certain moment Orientalism as representation did have to encounter the 'actual' conditions of what was there, and that it showed itself at a material level as a form of power and control." However, this is only a problem if one sticks to the dualisms of text and context or representation and reality – dualisms to which *Orientalism* poses a very powerful challenge. For if one accepts Said's thesis that texts participate in the production of "contextual" realities, then one cannot cling to the notion of an uncomplicated and prior "raw" reality that exists independently of human, social, historical and political agency and contingency.

Javed Majeed has made a similar argument against the "circularity" of *Orientalism*: "Said's argument is self-reinforcing in so far as it does not make clear whether a sound undertaking of another culture is possible, and what such an understanding would consist of if it were possible." Thus, Majeed goes on to say, "Said aims to unmask and dispel illusion, and yet he does not specify what to replace this illusion with." If by "sound understanding" Majeed means "objective" knowledge without reference to contingency, then clearly he is right: Said does not provide any such possibility: such "sound understanding," is, according to *Orientalism*, simply not possible (though knowledge and understanding are subject to the contingencies of colonialism in ways that may or may not obtain following decolonization). Moreover, what Said does in *Orientalism* is *not* to unmask and dispel "illusion," but rather – and to the contrary – to specify the constructedness of *reality*. In other words, Orientalism, according to Said, is an intervention into historical, material and political realities by way of "illusion." That Said offers nothing with which to replace the "illusion" is precisely the point of his book.

What is a problem, however, is *Orientalism*'s occasional slippage into ahistorical and essentialist claims. Pointing out Said's "rather monolithic and ahistorical conception of Orientalism," for instance, Majeed argues that "if there was a dominant concern of British rule in this period [the late eighteenth and early nineteenth centuries], it was to appropriate and legitimize itself through indigenous idioms. This does not seem to fit into Said's rather monolithic conception of the irresistibility of imperial power." Even if Said does not insist on the irresistibility of imperial power (most of his career, both academic and extra-curricular, has been devoted to resistance against imperialism, above all in the case of Palestine), Majeed's point is an important one. See Robert Young, *White Mythologies: Writing History and the West* (London: Routledge, 1990), p. 129; and Majeed, *Ungoverned Imaginings*, pp. 197–98.

65 For what seem to be at least in part polemical reasons, Said largely discounts the importance of industrial capitalism (and indeed the shift away from mercantile capitalism) in the elaboration of this dominant.

66 Homi Bhabha, while critical of Said, recapitulates some of his ahistorical claims. Thus, Bhabha writes that what he calls the discourse of colonialism "seeks authorization for its strategies by the production of knowledge of colonizer and colonized which are stereotypical but antithetically evaluated. The objective of colonial discourse is to construe the colonized as a population of degenerate types on the basis of racial origin, in order to justify conquest and to establish systems of administration and instruction." (Bhabha, "The Other Question," p. 154.) Bhabha also argues in that essay that "colonial power produces the colonized as a fixed reality which is at once an 'other' and yet entirely knowable and visible." Much of what I am arguing in this chapter and the next attempts to show that the colonial other was never a fixed reality.

67 Billie Melman, *Women's Orients: English Women and the Middle East, 1718–1918* (Ann Arbor: University of Michigan Press, 1992), p. 2.

68 *Ibid.*, p. 7. Later on she writes that "these women's Orient is a *locus* that is markedly different from that of orientalists. Women travellers and ethnographers domesticated the exotic or, put slightly differently, these women normalized and humanized the harem" (p. 62). She adds, however, that "curiously it is feminists like Harriet Martineau and Amelia Edwards, who present the most glaring examples of racism and cultural narcissism" (p. 63).

69 On Lady Mary Wortley Montagu's *Turkish Letters*, for instance, Melman (*Women's Orients*, p. 78) writes (to distinguish Montagu from the "male" Orientalist tradition): "Lady Montagu's work represents a wider consciousness of the comparativeness of 'morality' (her own term, designating sexual morals) and the relativeness of Western European values. Last, but not least, the Letters exude an aura of broad-mindedness and tolerance towards the Ottomans, indeed towards Europe's religious and cultural 'other' as such. Lady Montagu's letters, in short, may be appropriately designated a key text, the corner-stone in the new, alternative [female] discourse that developed in the West on the Middle East." The trouble that I have with her argument here, that is, with her insistence on constituting this discourse as a peculiarly female one, is that this could as easily be said of Jones, of Burke, and of Byron, though for different reasons and at different historical moments.

70 Melman, *Women's Orients*, p. 316.
71 See Armstrong, *Desire and Domestic Friction*, esp. pp. 3–27.
72 Macaulay, quoted in Brantlinger, *Rule of Darkness*, p. 30.
73 Poovey, *Uneven Developments*, p. 196. She goes on to say that "Nightingale's discourse could be so appropriated by apologists for the empire because of the way the twin compromises she represented and forged mobilized and deployed gender" (p. 197).
74 *Ibid.*, p. 197.
75 See Leslie Marchand, ed., *Lord Byron: Selected Letters and Journals* (Cambridge, MA: Harvard University Press, 1982), p. 358.
76 See Mellor, *Romanticism and Gender*.
77 See Homi Bhabha, "Signs Taken for Wonders: Questions of Ambivalence and Authority under a Tree outside Delhi, May 1817," in Francis Barker, et al., eds., *Europe and its others*, (Colchester: University of Essex Press, 1984), p. 97.

6 BEYOND THE REALM OF DREAMS: BYRON, SHELLEY, AND THE EAST

1 Mill, *History of British India*, Preface, p. 13.
2 Frantz Fanon, *The Wretched of the Earth*, trans. Constance Farrington (New York: Grove Press, 1991), p. 36.
3 See Said, *Orientalism*.
4 See, for example, Shelley's *The Revolt of Islam* (1818) and *Hellas* (1822).
5 See Victor Kiernan, *The Lords of Human Kind* (New York: Columbia University Press, 1986), p. 13.
6 Byron, *Childe Harold's Pilgrimage*, canto II, stanza XLIII.
7 Bernard Blackstone, "'The Loops of Time': Spatio-Temporal Patterns in 'Childe Harold'." *Ariel*, 2:4 (October 1971), p. 5.
8 Fabian, *Time and the Other*, p. 6.
9 See Stephen Jay Gould, *Ever Since Darwin: Reflections in Natural History* (New York: Norton, 1977), pp. 147–52; also see Fabian, *Time and the Other*, pp. 6–12.
10 See Robert Gleckner, *Byron and the Ruins of Paradise* (Baltimore: Johns Hopkins University Press, 1967), esp. pp. 69–90.
11 *Childe Harold*, canto II, stanza III.
12 Indeed, Britain did not invade Egypt again until 1882; elsewhere in the Arab world, it made various "arrangements," for example, with the emirs of the Gulf – mostly concerning the overland and maritime approaches to India. Thus it is not a coincidence that the first two major conquests of Arab countries were by the French, in Egypt (1798) and Algeria (1830), while Britain intervened in the Mediterranean region mostly in response to French or Russian advances. See Hourani, *History of the Arab Peoples*, pp. 265–314.
13 As Bernard Blackstone puts it. See Bernard Blackstone, *Byron: A Survey* (London: Longman, 1975), pp. 88–89. The significance of such latter-day

"Orientalizing" among romanticists (Blackstone is by no means alone in this regard) cannot be overestimated.

14 According to Hourani, there was, for instance, little or no direct merchant traffic between the Levant and Britain before 1815; following the Wars, and especially in the 1830s, shipping lines connected the ports of the southern and eastern Mediterranean with London, Liverpool, and Marseille – and, while exports of Egyptian cotton to Lancashire increased dramatically following the Wars (tenfold from 1800 to 1850), British exports to the Levant increased by some 800 percent in value between 1815 and 1850. At the same time, the Ottoman sultans (notably Selim III and Murad II) and their governors – once again, especially Muhammad Ali of Egypt – began undertaking "westernizing" reforms, and European cultural production had a direct and enduring impact on the region. See Hourani's *History of the Arab Peoples*, and also his important book *Arabic Thought in the Liberal Age: 1798–1939* (Cambridge University Press, 1988).

15 See Blackstone, *Byron: A Survey*, p. 93; and Jerome McGann, *The Beauty of Inflections* (Oxford University Press, 1989), pp. 255–62.

16 "To withdraw myself from myself (oh that cursed selfishness!) has ever been my sole, my entire, my sincere motive in scribbling at all." Journal entry, 27 November 1813. See Marchand, ed., *Selected Letters*, p. 360. Also see *Childe Harold*, canto II, stanzas XXV–XXVII:

> But midst the crowd, the hum, the shock of men,
> To hear, to see, to feel, and to possess,
> And roam along, the world's tired denizen,
> With none who bless us, none whom we can bless;
> Minions of splendour shrinking from distress!
> None that, with kindred consciousness endued,
> If we were not, would seem to smile the less,
> Of all that flatter'd, follow'd, sought, and sued;
> This is to be alone; this, this is solitude!"

17 See chapter 4, above.
18 See Said, *Orientalism*.
19 See Timothy Mitchell, *Colonising Egypt* (Berkeley: University of California Press, 1991).
20 Gleckner, *Ruins of Paradise*, p. 81.
21 Here I would qualify Marilyn Butler's observation that "Orientalism is a major theme of English Romanticism," a statement that limits Orientalism to the status of a narrowly considered "theme." See Marilyn Butler, "The Orientalism of Byron's Giaour," in Bernard Beatty and Vincent Newey, eds., *Byron and the Limits of Fiction* (New York: Barnes & Noble, 1989), p. 78.
22 Patrick Brantlinger argues, for instance, that *Childe Harold* and the Turkish Tales "seem to celebrate a barbarism identified not only with Oriental despotism but with the desire for personal liberty and national independence from empire." See Brantlinger, *Rule of Darkness*, p. 140–41. McGann makes a similar point; see *The Beauty of Inflections* (Oxford University Press, 1989), p. 200.

23 Butler, "Byron's Giaour," p. 85. Note, however, that Butler elsewhere contrasts Byron's Orientalism with that of Shelley, whose works, she says, "display a kind of Orientalism with more complex potential than Byron's." See Marilyn Butler, *Romantics, Rebels and Reactionaries* (New York: Oxford University Press, 1980), p. 121.

24 Marilyn Butler, "Plotting the Revolution: The Political Narratives of Romantic Poetry and Criticism," Kenneth Johnston et al., eds., in *Romantic Revolutions: Criticism and Theory* (Bloomington: Indiana University Press, 1990), p. 142.

25 See, for example, Butler's essay on *The Giaour*, where she observes that Southey was one of the first writers of the time who believed that evangelical missions ought to be sent to India: a position that she contrasts with Byron's.

26 See Brantlinger, *Rule of Darkness*, p. 141–45.

27 Indeed, in his *Hebrew Melodies* (1815), Byron is evocative of a premature Zionism, one which predates the colonialist project of the mature Zionism developed by Theodor Herzl and others from the 1890s onwards (a project formally launched in 1897 and formally given the support of the British Empire in the Balfour Declaration of 1917).

28 Byron, *The Giaour*.

29 Mary Louise Pratt, "Scratches on the Face of the Country; or, What Mr. Barrow Saw in the Land of the Bushmen," in Henry Gates Jr., ed., *"Race," Writing, and Difference* (University of Chicago Press, 1986), p. 140.

30 Joseph-Marie Degérando, *The Observation of Savage Peoples* (1800). Quoted in Fabian, *Time and the Other*, p. 7.

31 *Alastor*, lines 387–93. My italics.

32 *Alastor*, lines 106–28.

33 The sphinx was damaged by Napoleon's artillery in 1798.

34 Not the Thebes in Greece, but the Thebes in Upper (i.e., Southern) Egypt, which was the Greek name for the capital of Upper Egypt, Luxor.

35 *Alastor*, lines 129–39.

36 Byron, *Childe Harold*, canto II, stanza x.

37 Shelley, "A Philosophical View of Reform."

38 *Ibid*. My emphasis.

39 See Fabian, *Time and the Other*, pp. 1–35.

40 Frantz Fanon, *The Wretched of the Earth*, p. 38. See chapter 8 for further reflections on Fanon's dictum.

41 Fabian, *Time and the Other*, p. 30.

42 To use one of Said's terms. See Said, *Orientalism*, pp. 49–72.

43 Sentiments which are echoed in a more elaborate form by Marx in *Capital*, vol. 1, where he says that capitalism will finally provide the key to the "riddle of the unchangeability of Asiatic societies." See Marx, *Capital*, vol. 1, p. 479.

44 Shelley, *Hellas*, line 1059.

45 *Ibid.*, lines 1060–65.

46 As my distinction between Byron and Shelley suggests, the relationship between different versions of philhellenism and imperialism needs to be examined much more closely. On the one hand, I am uneasy with Jerome McGann's proposition that Shelley's ideals, as expressed in his proclamation that "we" are all Greeks, are "typical philhellenist illusions, and, as such, were open to political exploitation by Europe's imperialist powers, as well as by poetical exploitation by writers like Shelley and Byron." On the other hand, I have grave disagreements, some already outlined above, with Mark Kipperman's reductive assertion that, in the context of the eastern Mediterranean in the 1820s, "philhellenism could be seen as nothing less than a challenge to the global order of empires negotiated in 1815." Kipperman goes on to say that, "Within its own forms and the real historical context it evokes, Shelley's idealism in *Hellas* does reflect the constitutionalist, nationalist, and essentially anti-imperialist progressivism of his time." I believe that Shelley represents a much more aggressive form of colonialism than Byron, precisely because his imperial world view is fired by progressivism, whereas Byron's is sustained by some sort of respect for the inalterable otherness of other cultures, a respect that, at least in his 1812 *Childe Harold*, tempered his philhellenism. But the point is not that Shelley was imperialist and Byron was anti-imperialist; as I have tried to suggest, their different approaches to and versions of philhellenism and Orientalism correspond to different moments or phases of imperial development. See Jerome McGann, *The Romantic Ideology* (University of Chicago Press, 1983), p. 125; and Mark Kipperman, "Macropolitics of Utopia: Shelley's *Hellas* in Context," in Jonathan Arac, ed., *The Macropolitics of Nineteenth Century Literature* (Philadelphia: University of Pennsylvania Press, 1991), p. 92.

47 See Martin Bernal, *Black Athena: The Afroasiatic Roots of Classical Civilization* (New Brunswick: Rutgers University Press, 1985), pp. 189–245.

48 See Earl Wasserman, *Shelley: A Critical Reading* (Baltimore: Johns Hopkins University Press, 1971), pp. 3–46.

49 See Martyn Crucefix, "Wordsworth, Superstition, and Shelley's Alastor," *Essays in Criticism*, April 1983 (1983); Christopher Heppner, "Alastor: The Poet and the Narrator Reconsidered," *Keats-Shelley Journal* (1988); Frederick Kirchhoff, "Shelley's Alastor: The Poet Who Refuses to Write Language," *Keats-Shelley Journal* (1983); John Rieder, "Description of a Struggle: Shelley's Radicalism on Wordsworth's Terrain," *Boundary 2* (1985); Edward Strickland, "Transfigured Night: The Visionary Inversions of *Alastor*," *Keats-Shelley Journal* (1984).

50 Harold Bloom, *The Visionary Company: A Reading of English Romantic Poetry* (Ithaca: Cornell University Press, 1971), p. 289.

7 WILLIAM BLAKE AND THE UNIVERSAL EMPIRE

1 See Jameson, *Postmodernism*, esp. pp. 51–54. Jameson proposes this as an extension beyond the old Althusserian schema of ideology as the Imaginary

representation of the individual's relationship to the Real by reinserting the Lacanian category of the Symbolic.

2 Harold Bloom and others have suggested that this is a reference to the very material blindness associated with the "plague" of venereal disease. See Harold Bloom, *Blake's Apocalypse: A Study in Poetic Argument* (Ithaca: Cornell University Press, 1963), p. 141.

3 This social order generates the constitution of individual subjectivity but at the same time negates the very potentials of that individuality. Blake's insistence on the dialectical necessity of linking true individuality and liberty to collective action anticipates in some important ways Oscar Wilde's views on Socialism at the other end of the nineteenth century. Wilde identified Socialism with Individualism; "The recognition of private property," he writes, "has really harmed Invidualism, and obscured it, by confusing a man with what he possesses. . . . Private property has crushed true Individualism, and set up an Individualism that is false. It has debarred one part of the community from being individual by starving them. It has debarred the other part of the community from being individual by putting them on the wrong road and encumbering them." Thus, he argues, "The chief advantage that would result from the establishment of Socialism is, undoubtedly, the fact that Socialism would relieve us from that sordid necessity of living for others which, in the present condition of things, presses so hard upon almost everybody. In fact, scarcely anyone at all escapes." See Oscar Wilde, "The Soul of Man under Socialism" (1891), in Oscar Wilde, *De Profundis and Other Writings* (Harmondsworth: Penguin, 1987), pp. 19–53.

4 See E. P. Thompson, "London," in Michael Phillips, ed., *Interpreting Blake* (Cambridge University Press, 1978), p. 21. Also see chapter 2, above.

5 Vision in each of the *Songs of Innocence and of Experience*, as Robert Gleckner has cautioned, is specifically contingent upon the poem's context, i.e., the Blakean state that it reproduces. See Gleckner, *The Piper and the Bard* (Detroit: Wayne State University Press, 1959), p. 63. This part of Gleckner's larger argument appears in a slightly different form in his essay, "Point of View and Context in Blake's Songs," in M. H. Abrams, ed., *English Romantic Poets* (Oxford: Oxford University Press, 1975), pp. 90–97.

6 "I went to the Garden of Love. / And saw what I never had seen:" in rediscovering this space, the narrator of the poem is not simply noticing something new about it. What he never had seen may or may not have been there before (indeed, the most terrifying possibility is that these things whose existence he has just registered had been there all along, silent and invisible effective forces). What matters is that, simultaneously with the narrator's new awareness, the spatial structures of the place have been reorganized, its physical dimensions have been altered, and what had been absent or invisible before now literally materialize and claim the narrator's attention and emotions. Thus corresponding to a new (heightened?) aware- ness and consciousness, is a new vision of the space of the Garden of Love:

And I saw that it was filled with graves,
And tomb-stones where flowers should be:
And Priests in black gowns, were walking their rounds,
And binding with briars, my joys and desires.

For it is not necessarily the case that the narrator has returned to the Garden to find new circumstances (graves, priests, briars); on the contrary, it is as though he were returning to a place and realizing, visualizing, what had been there all along–what is thrown into doubt, then, is not the new terrifying vision of oppression and confinement, but the old vision of flowers and greens: did that (past) ever exist as it is now remembered? Or was it always like this?

7　David Punter, "Blake and the Shapes of London." *Criticism*, 23:1 (Winter 1981), p. 9.
8　William Blake, *The Song of Los*, plate 4 (1795) [E67].
9　Stewart Crehan, *Blake in Context* (Dublin, NY: Gill & Macmillan, 1984), p. 76.
10　Michael Ferber, "London' and its Politics." *ELH*, 48 (1981), p. 314.
11　See Karl Kiralis, "London' in the Light of *Jerusalem*." *Blake Studies*, 1:1 (Fall 1968), pp. 5–14. Kiralis points out that the old man and the boy seen in the graphic print of *London* re-appear in plate 84 of *Jerusalem*, though heading in the opposite direction, and from the shadows into the light.
12　See Max Dupperay, "A la source de la ville fantastique: 'London' de William Blake." *Etudes Anglaises*, 28:4 (1975). He adds that "avec 'London' la ville des Romantiques est née, la fourmilière de Quincey, l'enfer de Shelley . . . le Londres oppressant de Wordsworth."
13　See David Erdman, "Blake's Vision of Slavery." *Journal of the Warburg and Courtauld Institutes*, 15:3–4 (1952); and David Erdman, *Blake: Prophet Against Empire* (Princeton University Press, 1969), pp. 226–42. The *Visions of the Daughters* is a byproduct of one of Blake's professional engraving commissions, for a book by John Stedman: *Narrative of a Five Years Expedition agains the Revolted Slaves of Surinam* (1790; Baltimore: Johns Hopkins University Press, 1988).
14　For Byron, London "is a damned place – to be sure – but the only one in the world – (at least in the English world) for fun – though I have seen parts of the Globe that I like better." Byron, letter to James Hogg, 1 March 1816, in Marchand, ed., *Lord Byron: Selected Letters*, 1982), p. 335.
15　Engels, pp. 66–67. For a much more thorough discussion of London, see chapter 2, above.
16　Jacob Bronowski, *William Blake and the Age of Revolution* (New York: Harper & Row, 1965), p. 51.
17　Blake, *Jerusalem*, plate 13 [E155].
18　Erdman, *Blake*, p. 329.
19　Blake, *Jerusalem*, plate 15 [E159].
20　Hence "the same dull round, even of a universe, would soon become a mill with complicated wheels." (*There is No Natural Religion*, Second Series.)

21 See Thompson, *English Working Class*; Butler, *Romantics, Rebels and Reactionaries*, pp. 44–51; James King, *William Blake: His Life* (New York: St. Martin's Press, 1991), pp. 70–92; and Bronowski, *Blake and Age of Revolution*, pp. 22–96.
22 For a fuller discussion of Blake's status as "prophet," see chapter 1, above.
23 Hobsbawm, *Industry and Empire*, p. 70. Also see Thompson *English Working Class*, pp. 269–313.
24 Hobsbawm, *Age of Revolution*, p. 52. Also see C. L. R. James, *Black Jacobins*, pp. 27–61.
25 Blake, *Jerusalem*, plate 5 [E147].
26 Blake, *Jerusalem*, plate 30 [E176–77].
27 See Jameson, *Political Unconscious*, p. 76. Jameson argues that a Marxist politics of interpretation takes place within three concentric frameworks: political history in the narrowest sense, society and class tensions, and history "in its vastest sense of the sequence of modes of production and the succession and destiny of the various human social formations." When we pass into the second of these phases, he argues, and "find that the semantic horizon within which we grasp a cultural object has widened to include the social order, we will find that the very object of our analysis has itself been thereby dialectically transformed, and that it is no longer construed as an individual 'text' or work in the narrow sense, but has been reconstituted in the form of the great collective and class discourses of which a text is little more than a *parole* or utterance. Within this new horizon then, our smallest object of study will prove to be the *ideologeme*, that is, the smallest intelligible unit of the essentially antagonistic collective discourses of social classes."
28 Blake, *Jerusalem*, plate 65 [E216].
29 *Ibid.*, plate 65 [E216–17].
30 See Hobsbawm, *Industry and Empire*, pp. 91–92; and Thompson *English Working Class*, p. 104. Thompson writes: "Not only the weavers and labourers of Wapping and Spitalfields, whose colourful and rowdy demonstrations had often come out in support of Wilkes, but working men in villages and towns all over the country [were] claiming *general* rights for themselves. It was this – and not the French Terror – that threw the propertied classes into panic."
31 See Northrop Frye, *Fearful Symmetry: A Study of William Blake* (Princeton University Press, 1969), p. 46.
32 Bronowski, *Blake and Age of Revolution*, p. 128.
33 See King, *Blake*. Marilyn Butler (*Romantics, Rebels and Reactionaries*, p. 51) writes that "Blake alienated one kind of potential patron with his 'enthusiasm,' another with his bleak and bitter popular humour, a third with his obscurity, and by mid-decade almost all the world with his radicalism."
34 Blake, *Jerusalem*, plates 10 and 11 [E154]. Bronowski (*Blake and the Age of Revolution*, p. 121) writes: "Although Blake's knowledge of industry was uncertain, his vision of it was not. It is an astonishing vision. The reader must turn the pages of the last prophetic books himself, at random: and find everywhere the same sooty imagery, the air belched by industry. Men of

letters, whom the machine keeps clean, have gone through this sulphurous rhetoric for the names tidily listed in the books of myth."

35 Gleckner, *Blake and Spenser*, p. 111.

36 Blake, *Milton*, plate 6 [E99–100].

37 See Frye, *Fearful Symmetry*, pp. 372–73.

38 See S. Foster Damon, *A Blake Dictionary: The Ideas and Symbols of William Blake* (New York: E. P. Dutton, 1971), p. 245.

39 *There is No Natural Religion*, second series (1788) [E2].

40 See Frye, *Fearful Symmetry*, p. 8. Frye goes on to say that for Blake "the acquiring of the power to visualize independently of sense experience was a painful and laborious effort, to be achieved only by relentless discipline," *ibid.*, 24. This has also to do with Blake's fourfold levels of vision and visuality (Ulro, or single vision; Generation, or double vision, which is vision of this mundane world; Beulah, or threefold vision; and finally Eden, the integrative fourfold vision), which both Frye and Gleckner have discussed; see Frye, pp. 48–49, and Gleckner, *Piper and Bard*, p. 50.

41 Northrop Frye, *Fables of Identity: Studies in Poetic Mythology* (New York: Harcourt, Brace & World, 1963), p. 164.

42 Blake, *Jerusalem*, plate 31 [E194].

43 *Ibid.*, plate 12 [E155]. Also see plates 10 and 11.

44 *Ibid.*, plate 53 [E203].

45 Frye, *Fearful Symmetry*, p. 69.

46 Blake, *Jerusalem*, plate 72 [E227].

47 See *The Song of Los* [E68].

48 Note, for example, that certain lines in *The Song of Los* also appear in *America*, most famously "The Guardian Prince of Albion burned in his nightly tent." If it were not already clear, these texts (each of which is non-identical to itself in any case) must be configured in overlapping and simultaneous terms, each enabling the multifarious "meanings" of the others.

49 See *The Book of Urizen*. Orc usually appears in an American or European context ("Orc raging in European darkness / Arose like a pillar of fire above the Alps / Like a serpent of fiery flame"); whereas Los tends to work against Urizen in the other continents as well as in Europe and America. There is some sense in which Orc, who is Los's son, figures precisely as the spirit of revolution, who appears to be particularly active in Europe and America in Blake's time (or so it might have seemed to Blake himself), a spirit which, like fire, cannot sustain itself for long but instead erupts in fiery bursts – whereas Los works against Urizen in simultaneously material and prophetic terms in a more sustained process of resistance, and his work takes place all over the world. It is significant in this context that *The Song of Los* begins and seems to end in "heart-formed Africa."

8 CONCLUSIONS

1 Hobsbawm, *Age of Revolution*, p. 134.

2 Brown, *Society and Economy*, p. 109.
3 Said, *Culture and Imperialism*, p. 8.
4 *Ibid.*, p. 58.
5 See *ibid.*, p. 9.
6 In the opening pages of *Culture and Imperialism*, for instance, Said writes, "my exclusive focus here is on the modern Western empires of the nineteenth and twentieth centuries" (p. xii). This is not to say that Said does not at times lose sight of the rigorously developed historical specificity of his project (as happens also in *Orientalism*), for, despite his insistence in that book that he is dealing with specifically modern Orientalist discourse, there are several passages that slip into ahistorical and timeless claims. And yet the interesting thing is not that Said's work should embody such contradictions, but rather that Said's work on imperialism and Orientalism has, generally, been taken for granted as something that has been "proven" and that hence requires little further effort; thus, whereas it was intended all along as a provocation and an intervention, a beginning, *Orientalism* has more often than not been taken as an ending. It is this taking for granted that has, I think, defused much of the potential, especially the political potential, of Said's project, through no fault of his own; for he has in effect been Orientalized by the academy.
7 See Poovey, *Uneven Developments*.
8 See Deleuze and Guattari, *A Thousand Plateaus*, pp. 424–73, esp. pp. 435–66.
9 Amin argues that "Modern history has, over five centuries, been shot through by a standing contradiction, always renewed and never surmounted, between the pressures exercised by worldwide capitalist expansion on all the societies of the planet, with a tendency to subject their entire evolution to the exclusive logic of its expansion, and the renewed revolts against this submission, notably from the peripheralized regions, revolts that have reached the pitch of a rupture with, and quasi-autarkic escape from, the system." See *Delinking*, trans. Michael Wolfers (London: Zed Press, 1990), p. 10.
10 See Fabian, *Time and the Other*, pp. 11–21. Darwin's theory of natural selection actually flies in the face of such assertions, which instead require the recombination of Darwin and above all the systematic highlighting of certain theoretical and epistemological elements underlying Darwin's theory – especially Malthus and Lyell. Much of what we today associate with Darwin we derive in fact from Spencer, who overcoded Darwin's theory of natural selection with the progressivist valence that it connotes today especially in cultural, political, economic and social terms where it has been wielded to considerable effect.
11 Fabian, *Time and the Other*, p. 17.
12 *Ibid.*, p. 26.
13 See Gould, *Ontogeny and Phylogeny*, p. 34. According to preformationist conceptions of the Great Chain of Being – which developed a concept of stratification without progress or development – Gould writes, "the chain

marked a complete sequence of increasing perfection," but one that was entirely static: "it had been created all at once, and its constituent links could not be transformed one into the other." *Ibid.*, p. 23.

14 Nature is no longer outside the social, but rather becomes (arbitrarily) defined as that part of the social which is "outside the social." For, as Marx and Engels remind us in their discussion of Feuerbach's romanticism, "nature, the nature that preceded human history, is not by any means the nature in which Feuerbach lives, it is nature which today no longer exists anywhere (except perhaps on a few Australian coral-islands of recent origin)." See Marx and Engels, *The German Ideology* (1847; New York: International Publishers, 1988), p. 63.

15 Modernization is a discourse that inhabits the interstices and the limits between itself and its erstwhile others, defining those limits and thus in effect capturing its others in that process. As Deleuze and Guattari argue in *A Thousand Plateaus*, "the problem of diffusion, or of diffusionism, is badly formulated if one assumes a center at which the diffusion would begin." Instead, as they suggest, diffusion "occurs only through the placing in communication of potentials of very different orders: all diffusion happens in the in-between, goes between, like everything that 'grows' of the rhizome type." Modernization is however preeminently an arborescent rather than merely a rhizomatic discourse (or rather it is at once rhizomatic and arborescent). If it develops in the in-between, at the limit between nodes of simulteneity (societies, spaces, cultures), it also reorders those nodes in terms of an overbearing arborescent lineage that denotes the various "stages" of its own completion or in other words the scale of modernization and development with which we are all familiar. See Deleuze and Guattari, *A Thousand Plateaus*, p. 435; for more on the distinction (but not opposition) between the arborescent and the rhizomatic, see *ibid.*, pp. 3–25.

16 Fanon, *Wretched of the Earth*, pp. 38–9.

17 See E. P. Thompson, "Time, Work-Discipline and Industrial Capitalism," in his *Customs in Common*, p. 380.

18 Thompson, "Time," p. 394.

19 Perry Anderson, "Modernity and Revolution," in Cary Nelson and Lawrence Grossberg, eds., in *Marxism and the Interpretation of Culture* (Urbana: University of Illinois Press, 1988), p. 321.

20 See chapters 2 and 3, above.

21 See Jameson, *Political Unconscious*, p. 97, where Jameson argues that "the overtly 'transitional' moments of cultural revolution are themselves but the passage to the surface of a permanent process in human societies, of a permanent struggle between the various coexisting modes of production. The triumphant moment in which a new systemic dominant gains ascendancy is therefore only the diachronic manifestation of a constant struggle for the perpetuation and reproduction of its dominance, a struggle which must continue throughout its life course, accompanied at all moments by the systemic or structural antagonism of those older and newer modes of

production that resist assimilation or seek deliverance from it." Thus, "culture" involves in Jameson's terms nothing less than a perpetual – though of course historical – cultural revolution.

22 See Poovey, *Uneven Developments*, and Armstrong, *Desire and Domestic Fiction*.

23 See chapter 7, above.

24 Except, possibly for the City of London; but "metropolitan" in imperial terms implies much more than a narrow identifaction as the urban; though there are interesting connections here, especially with regard to London itself (see chapter 2, above).

Bibliography

Abrams, M. H., "The Correspondent Breeze: A Romantic Metaphor," in M. H. Abrams, ed., *English Romantic Poets* (Oxford University Press, 1975).
"On Political Readings of Lyrical Ballads," in Kenneth Johnston et al., eds., *Romantic Revolutions: Criticism and Theory* (Bloomington: Indiana University Press, 1990).
Adas, Michael, *Machines as the Measure of Men: Science, Technology, and Ideologies of Western Dominance* (Ithaca: Cornell University Press, 1989).
Adorno, Theodor, *Aesthetic Theory*, trans. C. Lenhardt (London: Routledge & Kegan Paul, 1984).
Minima Moralia, trans. E. F. N. Jephcott (London: Verso, 1987).
Negative Dialectics, trans. E. Ashton (New York: Continuum, 1987).
Adorno, Theodor and Max Horkheimer, *Dialectic of Enlightenment*, trans. John Cumming (New York: Continuum, 1988).
Althusser, Louis, *Lenin and Philosophy*, trans. Ben Brewster (New York: Monthly Review Press, 1971).
Ahmad, Aijaz, *In Theory: Classes, Nationas, Literatures* (London: Verso, 1992).
Amin, Samir, *Eurocentrism*, trans. Russell Moore (New York: Monthly Review Press, 1989).
Delinking, trans. Michael Wolfers (London: Zed Press, 1990).
Anderson, Benedict, *Imagined Communities: Reflections on the Origin and Spread of Nationalism* (London: Verso, 1983).
Anderson, James, *Sir Walter Scott and History* (Edinburgh: The Edina Press, 1981).
Anderson, Perry, "Modernity and Revolution", in Cary Nelson and Lawrence Grossberg, eds., *Marxism and the Interpretation of Culture* (Urbana: University of Illinois Press, 1988).
Arac, Jonathan, *Critical Genealogies* (New York: Columbia University Press, 1989).
Armstrong, Nancy, *Desire and Domestic Fiction* (Oxford University Press, 1987).
Babington, Anthony, *Military Intervention in Britain* (London: Routledge, 1990).
Bahti, Timothy, "Wordsworth's Rhetorical Theft," in Arden Reed, ed., *Romanticism and Language* (Ithaca: Cornell University Press, 1984).
Bailyn, Bernard and Philip Morgan, eds., *Strangers Within the Realm: Cultural Margins of the First British Empire* (Chapel Hill, University of North Carolina Press, 1991).

Francis Barker et al., eds., *Europe and its Others* (Colchester: University of Essex Press, 1984).

Barker, T. C., "Transport: The Survival of the Old beside the New," in Peter Mathias and John Davis, eds., *The First Industrial Revolutions* (Oxford: Blackwell, 1989).

Barrell, John, *The Idea of Landscape and the Sense of Place* (Cambridge University Press, 1972).

    The Dark Side of the Landscape: The Rural Poor in English Painting, 1730–1840 (Cambridge University Press, 1980).

    The Infection of Thomas De Quincey: A Psychopathology of Imperialism (New Haven: Yale University Press, 1991).

Bate, Jonathan, *Romantic Ecology: Wordsworth and the Environmental Tradition* (London: Routledge, 1991).

Baudrillard, Jean, "Modernity." *Canadian Journal of Political and Social Theory*, 11:3 (1987).

Bayly, C. A., *Imperial Meridian* (London: Longman, 1988).

Beatty, Bernard, "Fiction's Limit and Eden's Door," in Bernard Beatty and Vincent Newey, eds., *Byron and the Limits of Fiction* (1989: Barnes & Noble, 1989).

Beatty, Bernard and Vincent Newey, *Byron and the Limits of Fiction* (New York: Barnes & Noble, 1989).

Behrendt, Stephen, "History, Mythmaking, and the Romantic Artist," in Stephen Behrendt, ed., *History and Myth* (Detroit: Wayne State University Press, 1990).

Belsey, Catherine, "The Romantic Construction of the Unconscious," in Francis Barker et al., eds., *Literature, Politics and Theory* (London: Methuen, 1986).

Benjamin, Walter, *Illuminations*, trans. Harry Zohn (New York: Schocken, 1985).

Berger, John, *Ways of Seeing* (Harmondsworth: Penguin, 1977).

Berman, Marshall, *All that is Solid melts into Air: The Experience of Modernity* (Harmondsworth: Penguin, 1988).

Bernal, Martin, *Black Athena: The Afroasiatic Roots of Classical Civilization* (New Brunswick: Rutgers University Press, 1985).

Bhabha, Homi, "The Other Question: difference, discrimination, and the discourse of colonialism," in Francis Barket et al., eds., *Literature, Politics and Theory* (London: Methuen, 1986).

Bialostosky, Don, "Wordsworth, New Literary Histories, and the Constitution of Literature," in Kenneth Johnston et al., eds., *Romantic Revolutions: Criticism and Theory* (Bloomington: Indiana University Press, 1990).

Blackburn, Robin, *The Overthrow of Colonial Slavery: 1776–1848* (London: Verso, 1988).

Blackstone, Bernard, *Byron: A Survey* (London: Longman, 1975).

    "'The Loops of Time': Spatio-Temporal Patterns in 'Childe Harold'." *Ariel*, 2:4 (October 1971).

Blaut, J. M., *The Colonizer's Model of the World: Geographical Diffusion and Eurocentric History* (New York: Guilford Press, 1993).

Bloom, Harold, *Blake's Apocalypse: A Study in Poetic Argument* (Ithaca: Cornell University Press, 1963).

"'The Internalization of Quest-Romance," in Harold Bloom, ed., *Romanticism and Consciousness* (New York: Norton, 1970).

The Visionary Company: A Reading of English Romantic Poetry (Ithaca: Cornell University Press, 1971).

Bone, J. Drummond, "Byron, Scott and Scottish Nostalgia," in Angus Calder, ed., *Byron and Scotland* (Totowa, NJ: Barnes & Noble, 1989).

Borst, William, *Lord Byron's First Pilgrimage* (New Haven: Archon Books, 1969).

Bowler, Peter, *The Invention of Progress: The Victorians and the Past* (Oxford: Blackwell, 1989).

Bowman, Frank, *French Romanticism: Intertextual and Interdisciplinary Readings* (Baltimore: Johns Hopkins University Press, 1990).

Boxer, C. R., *The Dutch Seaborne Empire* (Harmondsworth: Penguin, 1988).

Brantlinger, Patrick, *Rule of Darkness: British Literature and Imperialism, 1830–1914* (Ithaca: Cornell University Press, 1988).

Braudel, Fernand, *The Structures of Everyday Life: Civilization and Capitalism, 15th-18th Century*, vol. I, trans. Siân Reynolds (New York: Harper & Row, 1979).

The Perspective of the World: Civilization and Capitalism, 15th-18th Century, vol. III, trans. Siân Reynolds (New York: Harper & Row, 1986).

Briggs, Asa, *Victorian Cities* (New York: Harper & Row, 1970).

Bronowski, Jacob, *William Blake and the Age of Revolution* (New York: Harper & Row, 1965).

Brown, Marshall, "The Pre-Romantic Discovery of Consciousness," in *Studies in Romanticism* (1978).

Brown, Nathaniel, *Sexuality and Feminism in Shelley* (Cambridge, MA: Harvard University Press, 1979).

Brown, Richard, *Society and Economy in Modern Britain, 1700–1850* (London: Routledge, 1991)

Burton, Richard, *Personal Narrative of a Pilgrimage to Al-Madinah and Meccah* (New York: Dover, 1855; 1964).

Butler, Marilyn, *Romantics, Rebels and Reactionaries* (Oxford University Press, 1980).

"The Orientalism of Byron's Giaour," in Bernard Beatty and Vincent Newey, eds., *Byron and the Limits of Fiction* (New York: Barnes & Noble, 1989).

"Repressing the Past: the Case for an Open Literary History," in Majorie Levinson, ed., *Rethinking Historicism* (London: Blackwell, 1989).

"Plotting the Revolution: The Political Narratives of Romantic Poetry and Criticism," in Kenneth Johnston et al., eds., *Romantic Revolutions: Criticism and Theory* (Bloomington: Indiana University Press, 1990).

Byrd, Lynn, "Old Myths for the New Age: Byron's Sardanapalus," in Stephen

Behrendt, ed., *History and Myth* (Detroit: Wayne State University Press, 1990).

Byrd, Max, *London Transformed: Images of the City in the Eighteenth Century* (New Haven: Yale University Press, 1978).

Calder, Angus, "'The Island' Scotland, Greece and Romantic Savagery," in Angus Calder, ed., *Byron and Scotland* (Totowa, NJ: Barnes & Noble, 1989).

Carter, Paul, *The Road to Botany Bay: An Exploration of Landscape and History* (The University of Chicago Press, 1987).

Césaire, Aimé, *Discourse on Colonialism*, trans. Joan Pinkham (New York: Monthly Review Press, 1955).

Chandler, James, *Wordsworth's Second Nature: A Study of the Poetry and Politics* (University of Chicago Press, 1984).

"Representative Men, Spirits of the Age, and Other Romantic Types," in Kenneth Johnston et al., eds., *Romantic Revolutions: Criticism and Theory*, (Bloomington: Indiana University Press, 1990).

England in 1819: The Politics of Literary Culture and the Case of Romantic Historicism (University of Chicago Press, 1997).

Charlesworth, Andrew, *An Atlas of Rural Protest in Britain, 1548–1900* (Philadelphia: University of Pennsylvania Press, 1983).

Chase, Cynthia, "The Ring of Gyges and the Coat of Darkness: Reading Rousseau with Wordsworth," in Arden Reed, ed., *Romanticism and Language* (Ithaca: Cornell University Press, 1984).

"Monument and Inscription: Wordsworth's First Poetic Spirits," in Kenneth Johnston et al., eds., *Romantic Revolutions: Criticism and Theory* (Bloomington: Indiana University Press, 1990).

Cherry, Gordon, Public Policy and the Morphology of Western Cities, in Richard Lawton, ed., *The Rise and Fall of Great Cities* (London: Bellhaven, 1992).

Clark, Timothy, *Embodying Revolution: The Figure of the Poet in Shelley* (Oxford: Clarendon Press, 1989).

Cobban, Alfred, "The Revolt against the Eighteenth Century," in Harold Bloom, ed., *Romanticism and Consciousness* (New York: Norton, 1970).

Cobbett, William, *Cobbett in Ireland* (London: Lawrence and Wishart, 1984).

Coburn, Kathleen, *The Self-Conscious Imagination* (London: Oxford University Press, 1974).

Cook, Olive, *The English Country House* (New York: Thames & Hudson, 1974).

Cooke, Michael, *The Blind Man Traces the Circle: On the Patterns and Philosophy of Byron's Poetry* (Princeton University Press, 1969).

Cox, Stephen, *"The Stranger Within Thee": Concepts of the Self in Late Eighteenth-Century Literature* (Pittsburgh University Press, 1980).

Crehan, Stewart, *Blake in Context* (Dublin, NY: Gill & Macmillan, 1984).

Crompton, Louis, *Byron and Greek Love* (Berkeley: University of California Press, 1985).

Crosby, Christina, *The Ends of History: Victorians and "the Woman Question"* (London: Routledge, 1991).

Crucefix, Martyn, "Wordsworth, Superstition, and Shelley's *Alastor.*" *Essays in Criticism* (April 1983).

Cunningham, Andrew and Nicholas Jardine, *Romanticism and the Sciences* (Cambridge University Press, 1990).

Curtin, Philip, *Cross-Cultural Trade in World History* (Cambridge University Press, 1984).

Damon, S. Foster, *A Blake Dictionary: The Ideas and Symbols of William Blake* (New York: E. P. Dutton, 1971).

Damrosch, Leopold, *Symbol and Truth in Blake's Myth* (Princeton University Press, 1980).

Darwin, Charles, *Voyage of the Beagle* (Harmondsworth: Penguin, 1989).

Daunton, Martin, "London and the World," in Celina Fox, ed., *London: World City, 1800–1840* (New Haven: Yale University Press).

Davies, Hunter, *William Wordsworth: A Biography* (New York: Atheneum, 1980).

Deane, Phyllis, *The First Industrial Revolution* (Cambridge University Press, 1990).

De Bolla, Peter, *The Discourse of the Sublime: Readings in History, Aesthetics and the Subject* (London: Basil Blackwell, 1989).

De Certeau, Michel, *The Practice of Everyday Life*, trans. Steven Rendall (Berkeley: University of California Press, 1988).

Defoe, Daniel, *A Tour through the Whole Island of Great Britain* (Harmondsworth: Penguin, 1978).

de Man, Paul, "Intentional Structure of the Romantic Image," in Harold Bloom, ed., *Romanticism and Consciousness* (New York: Norton, 1970).

Blindness and Insight (Minneapolis: University of Minnesota Press, 1983).

The Rhetoric of Romanticism (New York: Columbia University Press, 1984).

Deleuze, Gilles, *Kant's Critical Philosophy*, trans. H. Tomlinson and B. Habberjam (Minneapolis: University of Minnesota Press, 1984).

Deleuze, Gilles and Félix Guattari, *Anti-Oedipus: Capitalism and Schizophrenia*, trans. R. Hurley, Mark Seem, and Helen Lane (Minneapolis: University of Minnesota Press, 1983).

A Thousand Plateaus, trans. Brian Massumi (Minneapolis: University of Minnesota Press, 1987).

De Quincey, Thomas, *Recollections of the Lakes and the Lake Poets* (Harmondsworth: Penguin, 1970).

Derrida, Jacques, *Of Grammatology*, trans. G. C. Spivak (Baltimore: Johns Hopkins University Press, 1976).

Limited Inc, trans. Samuel Weber and Jeffrey Mehlman (Evanston: Northwestern University Press, 1988).

Dupperay, Max, "A la source de la ville fantastique: 'London' de William Blake." *Etudes Anglaises*, 28:4 (1975).

Easthope, Anthony, *Wordsworth Now and Then* (Buckingham: Open University Press, 1993).

Engels, Friedrich, *The Condition of the Working Class in England* (Moscow: Progress Publishers, 1973).

Erdman, David, "Blake's Vision of Slavery." *Journal of the Warburg and Courtauld Institutes*, 15:3–4 (1952).

   Blake: Prophet Against Empire (Princeton University Press, 1969).

   "Blake: The Historical Approach," in M. H. Abrams, ed., *English Romantic Poets* (Oxford University Press, 1970).

Fabian, Johannes, *Time and the Other: How Anthropology makes its Object* (New York: Columbia University Press, 1983).

Fanon, Frantz, *The Wretched of the Earth*, trans. Constance Farrington (New York: Grove Press, 1991).

Ferber, Michael, "'London' and its Politics." *ELH*, 48 (1981).

Ferguson, Frances, "Shelley's *Mont Blanc*: What the Mountain Said," in Arden Reed, ed., *Romanticism and Language* (Ithaca: Cornell University Press, 1984).

Foster, R. F., *Modern Ireland: 1600–1972* (Harmondsworth: Penguin, 1988).

Foucault, Michel, "Of Other Spaces." *Diacritics*, 16 (1986).

Freud, Sigmund, *Civilization and its Discontents*, trans. J. Strachey (New York: Norton, 1961).

Frye, Northrop, *Fables of Identity: Studies in Poetic Mythology* (New York: Harcourt, Brace & World, 1963).

   Blake: A Collection of Critical Essays (Englewood Cliffs, NJ: Prentice-Hall, 1966).

   Fearful Symmetry: A Study of William Blake (Princeton University Press, 1969).

   "Blake's Treatment of the Archetype," in M. H. Abrams, ed., *English Romantic Poets* (Oxford University Press, 1975).

Garber, Frederick, *Self, Text and Romantic Irony* (Princeton University Press, 1988).

Gleckner, Robert, *The Piper and the Bard* (Detroit: Wayne State University Press, 1959).

   Byron and the Ruins of Paradise (Baltimore: Johns Hopkins University Press, 1967).

   "Point of View and Context in Blake's Songs," in M. H. Abrams, ed., *English Romantic Poets* (Oxford University Press, 1975).

   Blake and Spenser (Baltimore: Johns Hopkins University Press, 1985).

Goldstein, Lawrence, *Ruins and Empire: The Evolution of a Theme in Augustan and Romantic Literature* (University of Pittsburgh Press, 1977).

Gould, Steven Jay, *Ever Since Darwin: Reflections in Natural History* (New York: Norton, 1977).

   Ontogeny and Phylogeny (Cambridge, MA: Harvard University Press, 1977).

   The Panda's Thumb: More Reflections in Natural History (New York: Norton, 1980)

   The Mismeasure of Man (New York: Norton, 1981).

   Time's Arrow, Time's Cycle: Myth and Metaphor in the Discovery of Geological Time (Cambridge, MA: Harvard University Press, 1987).

Gramsci, Antonio, *Selections from the Prison Notebooks*, trans. Quintin Hoare and Geoffey Nowell-Smith (New York: International Publishers, 1971).

Selections from the Cultural Writings, trans. William Boelhower (Cambridge, MA: Harvard University Press, 1985).

Grimes, Ronald, "Time and Space in Blake's Major Prophecies," in Stuart Curran and Joseph Wittreich, eds., *Blake's Sublime Allegory* (Madison: University of Wisconsin Press, 1973).

Guha, Ranajit, "The Prose of Counter-Insurgency," in Ranajit Guha and Gayatri Spivak, eds., *Selected Subaltern Studies*, (New York: Oxford University Press, 1988).

Habermas, Jürgen, *The Philosophical Discourse of Modernity*, trans. Frederick Lawrence (Cambridge: MIT Press, 1987).

Hagstrum, Jean, "'Babylon Revisited,' or the Story of Luvah and Vala," in Stuart Curran and Joseph Wittreich, eds., *Blake's Sublime Allegory* (Madison: University of Wisconsin Press, 1973).

Hamilton, Paul, "Keats and Critique," in Marjorie Levinson, ed., *Rethinking Historicism* (London: Blackwell, 1989).

Hartman, Geoffrey, "The Romance of Nature and the Negative Way," in Harold Bloom, ed., *Romanticism and Consciousness* (New York: Norton, 1970).

"Romanticism and Anti-Self-Consciousness," in Harold Bloom, ed., *Romanticism and Consciousness* (New York: Norton, 1970).

Wordsworth's Poetry, 1787–1814 (Cambridge, MA: Harvard University Press, 1971).

"Nature and the Humanization of the Self in Wordsworth," in M. H. Abrams, ed., *English Romantic Poets* (Oxford University Press, 1975).

The Unremarkable Wordsworth (Minneapolis: University of Minnesota Press, 1987).

"'Was it for this . . . ?': Wordsworth and the Birth of the Gods," in Kenneth Johnston et al., eds., *Romantic Revolutions* (Bloomington: Indiana University Press, 1990).

Harvie, Christopher, "Scott and the Image of Scotland," in Raphael Samuel, ed., *Patriotism: The Making and Unmaking of British Identity* (London: Routledge, 1989).

Hechter, Michael, *Internal Colonialism: The Celtic Fringe in British National Development, 1536–1966* (Berkeley: University of California Press, 1975).

Heffernan, James, *The Re-Creation of Landscape: A Study of Wordsworth, Coleridge, Constable and Turner* (Hanover: University Presses of New England, 1984).

Heidegger, Martin, *The Question Concerning Technology*, trans. W. Lovitt (New York: Harper & Row, 1977).

Helsinger, Elizabeth, "Turner and the Representation of England," in W. J. T. Mitchell, ed., *Landscape and Power* (University of Chicago Press, 1994).

Rural Scenes and National Representation: Britain, 1815–1850 (Princeton University Press, 1996).

Heppner, Christopher, "*Alastor*: The Poet and the Narrator Reconsidered." *Keats-Shelley Journal* (1988).

Hertz, Neil, *The End of the Line: Essays on Psychoanalysis and the Sublime* (New York: Columbia University Press, 1977).

Hill, Christopher, *Reformation to Industrial Revolution* (Harmondsworth: Penguin, 1975).

Hobsbawm, Eric, *The Age of Revolution, 1789–1848* (New York: Mentor, 1962).

Industry and Empire (Harmondsworth: Pelican, 1969).

Hoskins, W. G., *The Making of the English Landscape* (Harmondsworth: Pelican, 1981).

Hourani, Albert, *Arabic Thought in the Liberal Age: 1798–1939* (Cambridge University Press, 1988).

A History of the Arab Peoples (New York: Warner, 1991).

Islam in European Thought (Cambridge University Press, 1991).

Huxley, Aldous, *Rotunda: A Selection from the Works of Aldous Huxley* (London: Chatto & Windus, 1932).

Hyam, Ronald, *Britain's Imperial Century* (New York: Harper & Row, 1976).

Jacobs, Carol, *Telling Time* (Baltimore: Johns Hopkins University Press, 1993).

Jacobus, Mary, "The Art of Managing Books: Romantic Prose and the Writing of the Past," in Arden Reed, ed., *Romanticism and Language* (Ithaca: Cornell University Press, 1984).

Romanticism, Writing and Sexual Difference (Oxford University Press, 1989).

James, C. L. R., *The Black Jacobins: Toussaint L'Ouverture and the San Domingo Revolution* (New York: Vintage, 1963).

Jameson, Fredric, *The Political Unconscious* (Ithaca, NY: Cornell University Press, 1981).

"Cognitive Mapping," in Cary Nelson and Lawrence Grossberg, eds., *Marxism and the Interpretation of Culture* (Urbana: University of Illinois Press, 1988).

The Ideologies of Theory, vols. I & II (Minneapolis: University of Minnesota Press, 1988).

Postmodernism; Or, the Cultural Logic of Late Capitalism (Durham: Duke University Press, 1991).

Signatures of the Visible (New York: Columbia University Press, 1995).

Johnston, Kenneth, et al., *Romantic Revolutions: Criticism and Theory* (Bloomington: Indiana University Press, 1990).

Jones, William, *The Works of Sir William Jones in Thirteen Volumes* (Delhi: Agam Prakashan, 1799).

Jump, Harriet, "'That Other Eye, Wordsworth's 1794 Revisions of *An Evening Walk*," in *The Wordsworth Circle*, 17:3 (Summer 1986).

Kabbani, Rana, *Europe's Myths of Orient* (Bloomington: Indiana University Press, 1986).

Kelley, Gary, *English Fiction of the Romantic Period* (London: Longman, 1989).

Kerr, James, *Fiction Against History: Scott as Storyteller* (Cambridge University Press, 1989).

Kiernan, Victor, *The Lords of Human Kind* (New York: Columbia University Press, 1986).

Poets, Politics and the People (London: Verso, 1989).

"Noble and Ignoble Savages," in G. S. Rousseau and Roy Porter, eds., *Exoticism in the Enlightenment* (Manchester University Press, 1990).

William Blake: His Life (New York: St. Martin's Press, 1991).

King-Hele, Desmond, *Erasmus Darwin and the Romantic Poets* (New York: St. Martin's Press, 1986).

Kipperman, Mark, "Macropolitics of Utopia: Shelley's *Hellas* in Context," in Johnathan Arac, ed., *The Macropolitics of Nineteenth Century Literature* (Philadelphia: University of Pennsylvania Press, 1991).

Kiralis, Karl, "'London' in the Light of Jerusalem." *Blake Studies*, 1:1 (Fall 1968).

Kirchhoff, Frederick, "Shelley's Alastor: The Poet Who Refuses to Write Language." *Keats-Shelley Journal* (1983).

Klancher, John, "English Romanticism and Cultural Production," in H. Aram Veeser, ed., *The New Historicism* (London: Routledge, 1989).

Knight, David, *The Age of Science* (London: Blackwell, 1986).

Lacan, Jacques, *Ecrits: A Selection*, trans. Alan Sheridan (New York: Norton, 1977).

The Four Fundamental Concepts of Psycho-Analysis, trans. J.-A. Miller (New York: Norton, 1981).

Lacoue-Labarthe Philippe, and Jean-Luc Nancy, *The Literary Absolute*, trans. P. Barnard and C. Lester (Albany: SUNY Press, 1988).

Langton John, and R. J. Morris, *Atlas of Industrializing Britain, 1780–1914* (London: Methuen, 1986).

Laslett, Peter, *The World we have lost: England Before the Industrial Age* (New York: Scribners, 1971).

Latour, Bruno, *The Pasteurization of France*, trans. Alan Sheridan and John Law (Cambridge University Press, 1988).

Leed, Eric, *The Mind of the Traveler: From Gilgamesh to Global Tourism* (New York: Basic Books, 1991).

Lefebvre, Henri, *The Production of Space*, trans. Donald Nicholson-Smith (Oxford: Blackwell, 1991).

Levere, Trevor, *Poetry Realized in Nature* (Cambridge University Press, 1981).

"Coleridge and the Sciences," in Andrew Cunningham and Nicholas Jardine, eds., *Romanticism and the Sciences* (Cambridge University Press, 1990).

Levinson, Marjorie, *Wordsworth's Great Period Poems* (Cambridge University Press, 1986).

Keats's Life of Allegory: The Origins of a Style (New York: Blackwell, 1988).

"The New Historicism: Back to the Future," in Marjorie Levinson, ed., *Rethinking Historicism* (London: Blackwell, 1989).

Rethinking Historicism: Critical Readings in Romantic History (London: Blackwell, 1989).

Linebaugh, Peter, *The London Hanged: Crime and Civil Society in the Eighteenth Century* (Cambridge University Press, 1994).

Liu, Alan, *Wordsworth: The Sense of History* (Stanford University Press, 1989).
Lovejoy, Arthur. "On the Discrimination of Romanticisms," in M. H. Abrams, ed., *English Romantic Poets* (Oxford University Press, 1975).
Lukács, Georg, *The Historical Novel,* trans. Hannah and Stanley Mitchell (Lincoln: University of Nebraska Press, 1962).
Luxemburg, Rosa, *The Accumulation of Capital* (New York: Monthly Review Press, 1972).
Lyons, John, *The Invention of the Self* (Carbondale: Southern Illinois University Press, 1978).
Mackie, J. D., *A History of Scotland* (Harmondsworth: Penguin, 1978).
Majeed, Javed, *Ungoverned Imaginings: James Mill's* The History of British India (Oxford: Clarendon Press).
Makdisi, Saree "The Empire Re-narrated: *Season of Migration to the North* and the Re-invention of the Present," in *Critical Inquiry,* 18 (Summer 1992), pp. 804–20.
    "Post-Colonial Literature in a Neo-Colonial World: Modern Arabic Culture and the End of Modernity," in *Boundary 2* (Spring 1995), pp. 85–115.
Makdisi, Saree, Cesare Casarino, and Rebecca Karl, eds., *Marxism Beyond Marxism* (London: Routledge, 1995).
Malthus, Thomas, *An Essay on the Principle of Population* (Harmondsworth: Penguin, 1976).
Manning, Peter, *Byron and his Fictions* (Detroit: Wayne State University Press, 1978).
    Reading Romantics: Texts and Contexts (Oxford University Press, 1990).
Mannsaker, Frances, "Elegancy and Wildness: Reflections of the East in the Eighteenth-Century Imagination," in G. S. Rousseau and Roy Porter, eds., *Exoticism in the Enlightenment* (Manchester: Manchester University Press, 1990).
Manwaring, G. E., and Bonamy Dobrée, *Mutiny: The Floating Republic* (London: The Cresset Library, 1987).
Marchand, Leslie, *Byron: A Portrait* (University of Chicago Press, 1970).
    ed., *Lord Byron: Selected Letters and Journals* (Cambridge, MA: Harvard University Press, 1982).
Marshall, David, *The Surprising Effects of Sympathy* (University of Chicago Press, 1988).
Marshall, Donald, "Secondary Literature: Geoffrey Hartman, Wordsworth, and the Interpretation of Modernity," in Kenneth Johnston et al., eds., *Romantic Revolutions: Criticism and Theory* (Bloomington: Indiana University Press, 1990).
Marshall, P. J., "Taming the Exotic: The British and India in the Seventeenth and Eighteenth Centuries," in G. S. Rousseau and Roy Porter, eds., *Exoticism in the Enlightenment* (Manchester University Press, 1990).
Marshall, P. J. and Glyndwr Williams, *The Great Map of Mankind: Perceptions of New Worlds in the Age of Enlightenment* (Cambridge, MA: Harvard University Press, 1982).

Marx, Karl, *Grundrisse,* trans. Martin Nicolaus (Harmondsworth: Pelican, 1973).
  Capital, vol. I, trans. Ben Fowkes (New York: Vintage Books, 1977).
Marx, Karl and Friedrich Engels, *The Communist Manifesto* (New York: International Publishers, 1983).
  The German Ideology, trans. W. Lough et al. (New York: International Publishers, 1988).
McGann, Jerome, *Fiery Dust: Byron's Poetical Development* (University of Chicago Press, 1968).
  "The Aim of Blake's Prophecies and the Uses of Blake Criticism," in Stuart Curran and Joseph Wittreich, eds., *Blake's Sublime Allegory* (Madison: University of Wisconsin Press, 1973).
  The Romantic Ideology (University of Chicago Press, 1983).
  The Beauty of Inflections (Oxford University Press, 1989).
  "The Third World of Criticism," in Marjorie Levinson, ed., *Rethinking Historicism* (London: Basil Blackwell, 1989).
Mellor, Anne K., "On Romanticism and Feminism," in Anne K. Mellor, ed., *Romanticism and Feminism* (Bloomington: Indiana University Press, 1988).
  "Possessing Nature: The Feminine in Frankenstein," in Anne K. Mellor, ed., *Romanticism and Feminism* (Bloomington: Indiana University Press, 1988).
  Romanticism and Gender (London: Routledge, 1993).
Mill, James, *The History of British India* (University of Chicago Press, 1975).
Mintz, Sidney, *Sweetness and Power: The Place of Sugar in Modern History* (Harmondsworth: Penguin, 1986).
R. J. Mitchell and M. D. R. Leys, *A History of London Life* (Harmondsworth: Penguin, 1958).
Mitchell, Timothy, *Colonising Egypt* (Berkeley: University of California Press, 1991).
Moi, Toril, *Sexual/Textual Politics* (London: Methuen, 1985).
Mojumder, Abu-Taher, *Sir William Jones, the Romantics and the Victorians* (Dacca: Begum Zakia Sultana, 1976).
  Sir William Jones and the East (Dacca: Begum Zakia Sultana, 1978).
Molesworth, Charles, "Wordsworth's 'Westminster Bridge' Sonnet: The Republican Structure of Time and Perception." *Clio,* 1:3 (1977).
Monk, Samuel, "The Sublime: Burke's Enquiry," in Harold Bloom, ed., *Romanticism and Consciousness* (New York: Norton, 1970).
Morgan, Prys, "From a Death to a View: The Hunt for the Welsh Past in the Romantic Period," in Eric Hobsbawm and Terence Ranger, eds., *The Invention of Tradition* (Cambridge University Press, 1983).
Mukherjee, Ramkrishna, *The Rise and Fall of the East India Company* (New York: Monthly Review Press, 1974).
Mukherjee, S. N., *Sir William Jones: A Study in Eighteenth-Century British Attitudes to India* (Hyderabad: Orient Longman, 1987).
Murdoch, John, "The Landscape of Labour: Transformations of the Georgic," in Kenneth Johnston et al., eds., *Romantic Revolutions* (Bloomington: Indiana University Press, 1990).

Musselwhite, David, "The trial of Warren Hastings," in Francis Barker et al., eds., *Literature, Politics and Theory* (London: Methuen, 1986).

Nesfield-Cookson, Bernard, *William Blake: Prophet of Universal Brotherhood* (London: Crucible, 1987).

Netton, Ian, "The Mysteries of Islam," in G. S. Rousseau and Roy Porter, eds., *Exoticism in the Enlightenment* (Manchester University Press, 1990).

Newey, Vincent, "Authoring the Self: Childe Harold III and IV," in Bernard Beatty and Vincent Newey, eds., *Byron and the Limits of Fiction* (New York: Barnes & Noble, 1989).

Nichols, Ashton, "Towards 'Spots of Time': 'Visionary Dreariness' in 'An Evening Walk.'" *The Wordsworth Circle*, 14:4 (Autumn 1983), pp. 233–37.

Paley, Morton, *The Continuing City: William Blake's Jerusalem* (Oxford: Clarendon Press, 1983).

"Hard Pastoral: Frost, Wordworth, and Modernist Poetics," in *Criticism*, 29:1 (Winter 87).

Parrish, Stephen, "Wordsworth as Satirist of His Age," in Kenneth Johnston and Gene Ruoff, eds., *The Age of William Wordsworth* (New Brunswick, NJ: Rutgers University Press, 1987).

Patterson, Annabel, *Pastoral and Ideology: Virgil to Valéry* (Berkeley: University of California Press, 1987).

Peckham, Morse, "On Romanticism." *Studies in Romanticism*, 9 (1970).

Perkin, Harold, *Origins of Modern English Society* (New York: Routledge, 1991).

Poovey, Mary, *The Proper Lady and the Woman Writer: Ideology as Style in the Works of Mary Wollestonecraft, Mary Shelley, and Jane Austen* (University of Chicago Press, 1984).

Uneven Developments: The Ideological Work of Gender in Mid-Victorian England (University of Chicago Press, 1988).

Pottle, Frederick, "The Eye and the Object in the Poetry of Wordsworth," in Harold Bloom, ed., *Romanticism and Consciousness* (New York: Norton, 1970).

Porter, Roy, *London: A Social History* (Cambridge, MA: Harvard University Press, 1995).

Pratt, Mary Louise, "Scratches on the Face of the Country; or, What Mr. Barrow Saw in the Land of the Bushmen," in Henry Gates Jr., ed., *"Race," Writing and Difference* (University of Chicago Press, 1986).

Prebble, John, *Culloden* (Harmondsworth: Penguin, 1961).

The Highland Clearances (Harmondsworth: Penguin, 1963).

Pucci, Suzanne, "The Discrete Charms of the Exotic: Fictions of the Harem in Eighteenth-Century France," in G. S. Rousseau and Roy Porter, eds., *Exoticism in the Enlightenment* (Manchester University Press, 1990).

Punter, David, "Blake and the Shapes of London." *Criticism*, 23:1 (Winter 1981), (1981).

Blake, Hegel, and Dialectic (Amsterdam: Rodopi, 1982).

Raine, Kathleen, *Blake and the New Age* (London: George Allen & Unwin, 1979).

Rajan, Tilottama, "The Web of Human Things: Narrative and Identity in

Alastor," in G. Kim Blank, ed., *The New Shelley: Late Twentieth Century Views* (New York: Macmillan, 1991).

Rasmussen, Steen Eiler, *London: The Unique City* (Cambridge: MIT Press, 1934).

Reed, James, *London* (London: Athlone Press, 1980).

Sir Walter Scott: Landscape and Locality (London: Athlone Press, 1980).

Reiman, Donald, *Percy Bysshe Shelley* (Boston: Twayne, 1990).

Richards, Evelleen, "'Metaphorical Mystifications': The Romantic Gestation of Nature in British Biology," in Andrew Cunningham and Nicholas Jardine, eds., *Romanticism and the Sciences* (Cambridge University Press, 1990).

Richards, Eric, "Scotland and the Uses of the Atlantic Empire," Bernard Bailyn and Philip Morgan, eds., in *Strangers Within the Realm: Cultural Margins of the First British Empire* (Chapel Hill: University of North Carolina Press, 1991).

Richardson, Alan, "Romanticism and the Colonization of the Feminine," in Anne K. Mellor, ed., *Romanticism and Feminism* (Bloomington: Indiana University Press, 1988).

"Wordsworth at the Crossroads: 'Spots of Time' in the 'Two-Part Prelude'." *The Wordsworth Circle*, 19:1 (Winter 1988), pp. 15–19.

Rieder, John, "Description of a Struggle: Shelley's Radicalism on Wordsworth's Terrain." *Boundary 2* (1985).

Rodinson, Maxime, *Europe and the Mystique of Islam*, trans. Roger Veinus (Seattle: University of Washington Press, 1991).

Ross, Marlon, "Romantic Quest and Conquest," in Anne K. Mellor, ed., *Romanticism and Feminism* (Bloomington: Indiana University Press, 1988).

"Romancing the Nation-State: The Poetics of Romantic Nationalism," in Johnathan Arac, ed., *Macropolitics of Nineteenth Century Literature* (Philadelphia: University of Pennsylvania Press, 1991).

Rudé, George, *Hanoverian London* (Berkeley: University of California Press, 1971).

Said, Edward, *Orientalism* (New York: Pantheon, 1977).

The World, the Text and the Critic (Cambridge, MA: Harvard University Press, 1982).

"An Ideology of Difference," in Henry Gates Jr., ed., *"Race," Writing and Difference* (University of Chicago Press, 1986).

Culture and Imperialism (New York: Knopf, 1993).

Saint, Andrew, "The Building Art of the First Industrial Metropolis," in Celina Fox, ed., *London: World City, 1800–1840* (New Haven: Yale University Press, 1992).

Schaffer, Simon, "Genius in Romantic Natural Philosophy," in Andrew Cunningham and Nicholas Jarine, eds., *Romanticism and the Sciences* (Cambridge University Press, 1990).

Schwab, Raymond, *The Oriental Renaissance: Europe's Rediscovery of India and the East, 1680–1880*, trans. G. Patterson-Black and V. Reinking (New York: Columbia University Press, 1984).

Sedgwick, Eve, *Between Men: English Literature and Male Homosocial Desire* (New York: Columbia University Press, 1985).

Simpson, David, *Wordsworth and the Figuring of the Real* (Atlantic Highlands, NJ: Humanities Press, 1982).

Smith, Adam, *The Wealth of Nations* (Harmondsworth: Penguin, 1982).

Smith, Neil, *Uneven Development: Nature, Capital, and the Production of Space* (London: Blackwell, 1990).

Soja, Edward, *Postmodern Geographies* (London: Verso, 1989).

Spivak, Gayatri, *In Other Worlds* (London: Routledge, 1988).

Stedman, John, *Narrative of a Five Years Expedition agains the Revolted Slaves of Surinam* (Baltimore: Johns Hopkins University Press, 1988).

Strickland, Edward, "Transfigured Night: The Visionary Inversions of Alastor." *Keats-Shelley Journal*, (1984).

Suleri, Sara, *The Rhetoric of British India* (University of Chicago Press, 1992).

Thesig, William, *The London Muse: Victorian Poetic Responses to the City* (Athens, GA: University of Georgia Press, 1982).

Thompson, E. P., *The Making of the English Working Class* (New York: Vintage, 1966).

   Whigs and Hunters: The Origin of the Black Act (New York: Pantheon, 1975).

   Customs in Common: Studies in Traditional Popular Culture (New York: New Press, 1993).

   "'London'," in Michael Phillips, ed., *Interpreting Blake* (Cambridge University Press, 1978).

Trevor-Roper, Hugh, "The Invention of Tradition: The Highland Tradition of Scotland," in Eric Hobswbawn and Terence Ranger, eds., *The Invention of Tradition* (Cambridge University Press, 1983).

Twitchell, James B., *Romantic Horizons: Aspects of the Sublime in English Poetry and Painting, 1770–1850* (Columbia: University of Missouri Press, 1983).

Van den Berg, J. H., "The Subject and His Landscape," in Harold Bloom, ed., *Romanticism and Consciousness* (New York: Norton, 1970).

Viswanathan, Gauri, *Masks of Conquest: Literary Study and British Rule in India* (New York: Columbia University Press, 1989).

Waley, Arthur, *The Opium War Through Chinese Eyes* (Stanford University Press, 1958).

Walker, Eric, "Wordsworth, Wellington and Myth," in Stephen Behrendt, ed., *History and Myth* (Detroit: Wayne State University Press, 1990).

Wallerstein, Immanuel, *Historical Capitalism* (London: Verso, 1989).

Wasserman, Earl, *Shelley: A Critical Reading* (Baltimore: Johns Hopkins University Press, 1971).

Watkins, Dan, *Social Relations in Byron's Eastern Tales* (Rutherford, NJ: Fairleigh Dickinson University Press, 1987).

Watson, Ian Bruce, *Foundation for Empire: English Private Trade in India, 1659–1760* (New Delhi: Vikas Publishing House, 1980).

Webb, Timothy, *English Romantic Hellenism* (Manchester University Press, 1982).

Weiskel, Thoms, *The Romantic Sublime: Studies in the Structure and Psychology of*

Transcendence (Baltimore: Johns Hopkins University Press, 1986).

Welburn, Andrew, *Power and Self-Consciousness in the Poetry of Shelley* (London: Macmillan, 1986).

White, R. J., ed., *Political Tracts of Wordsworth, Coleridge and Shelley* (Cambridge University Press, 1953).

Wilford, John, *The Mapmakers* (New York: Knopf, 1981).

Williams, Eric, *Capitalism and Slavery* (London: André Deutsch, 1993).

Williams, Raymond, *The Long Revolution* (New York: Columbia University Press, 1961).

Marxism and Literature (Oxford University Press, 1977).

Politics and Letters: Interviews with New Left Review (London: Verso, 1979).

The Country and the City (Oxford University Press, 1983).

Culture and Society (New York: Columbia University Press, 1983).

Wimsatt, W. K., "The Structure of Romantic Nature Imagery," in Harold Bloom, ed., *Romanticism and Consciousness* (New York: Norton, 1970).

Wlecke, Albert, *Wordsworth and the Sublime* (Berkeley: University of California Press, 1973).

Wolf, Eric, *Europe and the People Without History* (Berkeley: University of California Press, 1982).

Wood, Denis, *The Power of Maps* (New York: The Guilford Press, 1992).

Young, Robert, *Darwin's Metaphor: Nature's Place in Victorian Culture* (Cambridge University Press, 1985).

Young, R., *White Mythologies: Writing History and the West* (London: Routledge, 1990).

Index

244

CAMBRIDGE STUDIES IN ROMANTICISM

General editors
MARILYN BUTLER
University of Oxford
JAMES CHANDLER
University of Chicago